BILL REID

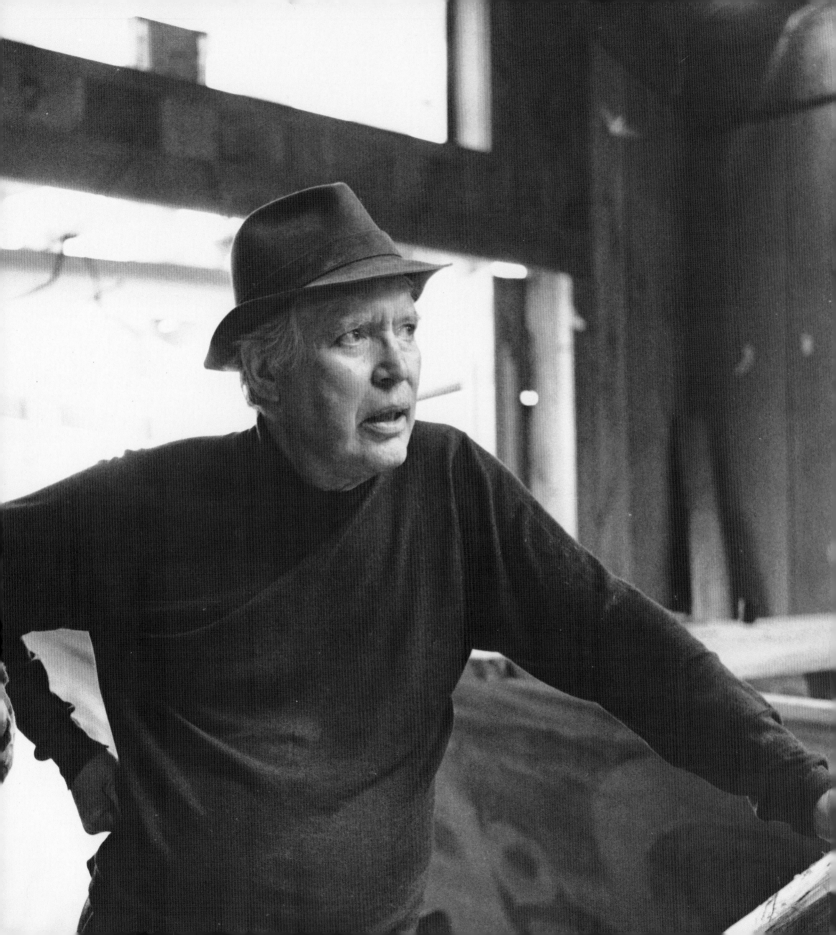

BILL REID

By Doris Shadbolt

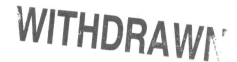
UNIVERSITY OF WASHINGTON PRESS, SEATTLE/LONDON

CANADIAN CATALOGUING IN PUBLICATION DATA

Shadbolt, Doris, 1918 –
  Bill Reid

  Includes index.
  ISBN 0-88894-503-5

  1. Reid, Bill, 1920 – 2. Sculptors –
Canada – Biography. 3. Haida Indians –
Sculpture. I. Reid, Bill, 1920 – II. Title.
NB249.R44S53 1986 730′.92′4 C86-091376-7

Published in the United States by the University of
Washington Press by arrangement with Douglas & McIntyre Ltd.,
Vancouver, British Columbia

Library of Congress Catalog Card Number 86-51122
ISBN 0-295-96427-8

PHOTOGRAPHY
Works illustrated have been photographed
by Reinhard Derreth Graphics except:
Robert Keziere pages 88 and 159
Raymond Lum pages 107, 136, 137 and 151
Bill McLemore pages 48 and 124
Paul Macapia pages 97 and 127 (bottom)
Otto Nelson page 96
George Rammell page 54

Ulli Steltzer contributed the photographs of
Bill Reid and his work pages 57 (top and bottom right),
61, 111, 114, 115, 131 and 180

PRODUCTION
Design: Reinhard Derreth Graphics Ltd.
Typesetting: Polagraphics Ltd.
Colour Separations: Cleland Kent Western Ltd.
Duotone and Line Film: Reinhard Derreth Graphics Ltd.
Printing and Binding: Hemlock Printers Ltd.
Printed and bound in Canada

CONTENTS

PREFACE

I first knew Bill Reid in the late 1950s when he was still announcing for the Canadian Broadcasting Corporation and I was working at the Vancouver Art Gallery. Among my recollections of those early days are sociable evenings spent with him, his wife and baby daughter Amanda, and other guests at his house in the Kitsilano district of Vancouver, evenings which invariably included a visit to his jewellery workshop in the basement; and the many times he phoned to let me know when the CBC was broadcasting one of the piano sonatas in a new set of Mozart recordings he knew I was interested in. In the sixties his combined living/working place on Pender Street was a couple of parking lots away from the Art Gallery where I was curator, and he would frequently stroll over to my office, always, I knew, with a treasure in some pocket — a brooch or bracelet that he was working on — which he would pull out in due course to show me. Or I would wander down during a lunch hour to see what fascinating things he had underway on his work-bench. It was a companionable place, and I was not the only friend who liked to drop in. There too I met Robert Davidson and other young carvers on whom Bill was keeping a youthfully avuncular guiding eye.

It was largely through Bill that I first began to look at and think seriously about the great art tradition to which he related and which had had no place in my own art education. When in 1967, to mark the year of Canada's Centennial, the Vancouver Art Gallery mounted The Arts of the Raven exhibition, I, as acting director, was able to state in the catalogue foreword with suitable conviction that this was an exhibition of "art, high art — not ethnology." Bill was brought into the project as a consultant, though he was much more than that, for the concept of such a show, intended to demonstrate the achievement of his ancestors in an art context, secured his enthusiastic participation in all its phases from early planning to design and installation. I wonder if he remembers a remark he made at the time. We had decided after much deliberation to include as an addendum to the collection of older traditional "masterworks" a small room of works by contemporary Indian artists, largely as a means of reviewing for ourselves just what was being done in that area. I well recall his pronunciamento when that section, which included thirteen of his own pieces, was assembled and duly appraised: "Well, I guess we might as well wrap it all up," meaning that clearly the greatness of the tradition was a thing of the past.

That was nearly twenty years ago, and in the interval he has gone on to challenge that statement through his own work, which has provided a qualitative standard against which other work must be seen, and in which he has taken on the difficult task of locating for himself modes of transformation and change so that something of the charge of the old tradition could be retained to find new form and meaning in the present. That task is not only the most vital but also the most difficult since it is the work not of the will but of the imagination and cannot be coerced or hurried.

Because of his personal stature, because of the body of work he has produced, because of his relation to the evolving culture, it is time for a book about him. For me, the challenge has been considerable. The perils of writing about a contemporary, let alone a valued, respected and living friend of long standing, are well enough known — the risks of failed objectivity, of falling into uncritical devotion, and, on the other side, the possible pain for a subject whose self-image inevitably cannot match that revealed in someone else's mirror, even in that of a friend. In addition there was the intimidating knowledge that I, an outsider, was stepping, with one foot at least, into territory where anthropological interests were heavily invested. I take comfort in the thought that while this is the first book on Reid, there will be others, for his work is not yet finished, and the whole evolving story of cultural change of which he is an important part will offer new perspectives in which to view him.

I have been encouraged and helped by many people. Discussions with Dr. Marjorie Halpin of the Museum of Anthropology at the University of British Columbia from the time I first began to think about the book have provided challenge, stimulation, and the wisdom of her experience as anthropologist. Poet Robert Bringhurst gave my manuscript a sympathetic reading and made a number of helpful suggestions for its revision. Laurinda Daniells, UBC archivist, gave generously of her time, and I would also like to thank Bill Holm for his knowledgeable and helpful reading. Edith Iglauer made available to me her original notes taken during interviews with various people in the course of researching her article on Bill for the February 1982 issue of *Saturday Night.* The staff members of the Museum of Anthropology were always helpful, and in particular I would mention Elizabeth Johnson, Curator of Collections, Audrey Shane, Librarian, Hindy Ratner, Extension Curator, Anne-Marie Fenger, Programme Assistant and Karen Duffek, Research Associate. I am more grateful than I can say for Bill's co-operativeness and patience and for that of his wife Martine. My editor, Marilyn Sacks, gave valuable help in clarifying and tightening my manuscript which I gratefully acknowledge. I should like to thank the owners of Bill's pieces — who have usually become his friends — for parting with the objects which have become precious to them so that they could be photographed. The generosity of Ulli Steltzer in permitting several of her photographs to appear in this book is much appreciated. Lastly, I acknowledge my indebtedness to my husband who is always my first reader, and whose steadying encouragement and perceptive artist's eye were always there when needed.

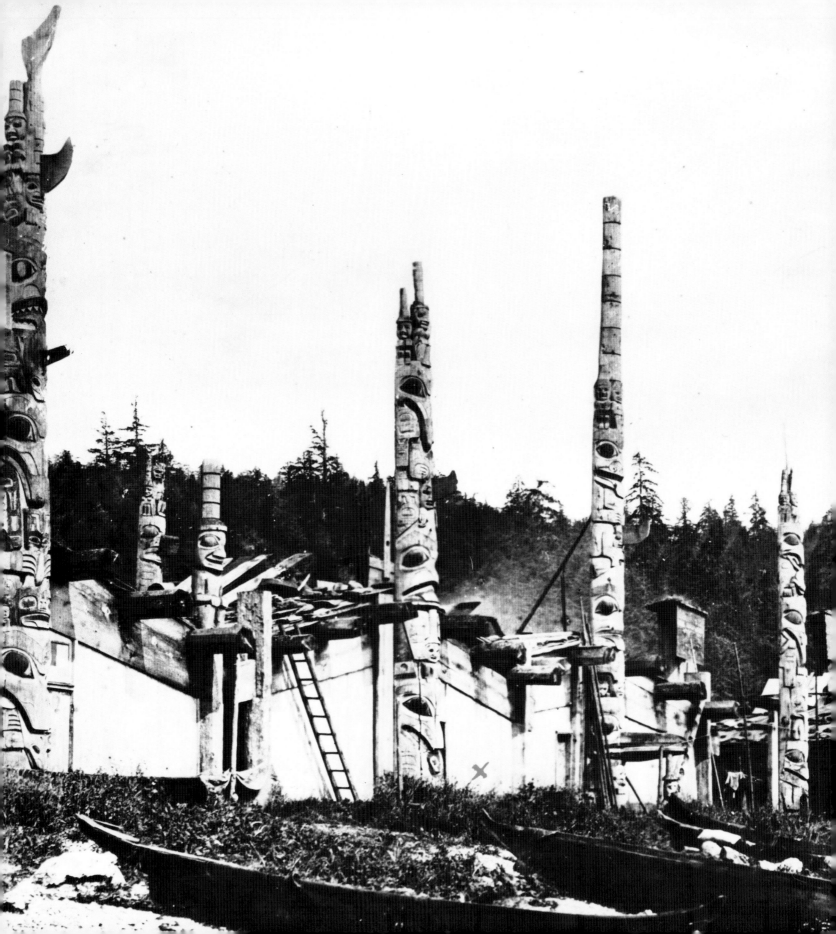

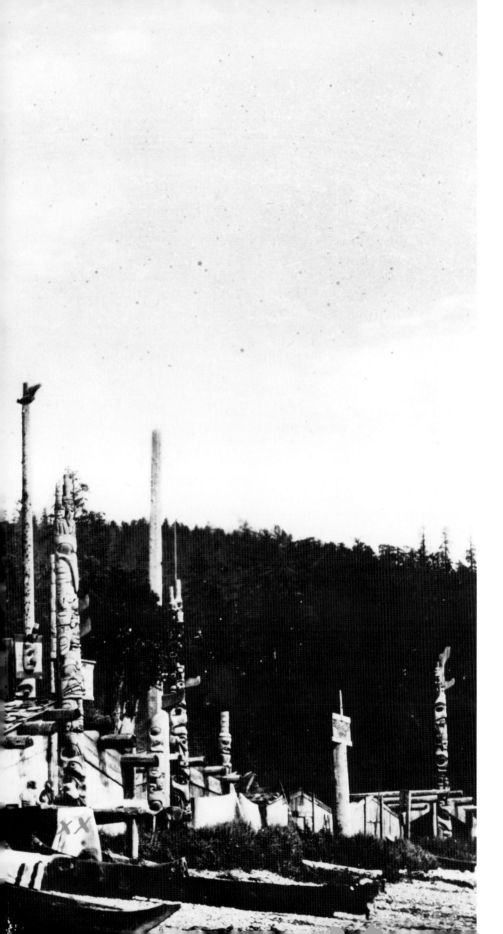

INTRODUCTION

The traditional culture of the Indian peoples of this country's northwest coast, developed to its high point over several thousand years, is today admired and studied around the world for its distinctness and its richness. Its deterioration in response to outside pressures and determinants began with the arrival of the first European visitors in the eighteenth century. For a while the new wealth foreigners brought along with their trade in the form of tools and materials caused the native culture to grow and flourish, and stimulated it into even greater self-identification; but inevitably, hidden within that vitality the infection had begun. Like the speeded-up conclusion of a film that has run out of time, the eighty-five-year life-span of Charles Edenshaw, from 1839 to 1920, makes an accelerated presentation of the transition from the old mode, in which changes could be resisted or came at a pace that could be absorbed, to a time of penetration by white people and their ways so pervasive as to raise the very question of cultural survival.

Village of Skidegate, 1857
Photograph: Provincial Archives of
British Columbia (Newcombe)

9

Charles Edenshaw was the last great Haida carver permitted by history to work to the needs of an integrated traditional Haida society. Even though seriously ravaged in his day, that society was still able to reflect the great accomplishment of his people. Yet it could be said that by the time his life was finished, using the words of his great-nephew Bill Reid, "the great [cultural] feast was over." The progressive intrusion of outsiders into traditionally held lands and the superimposition of white man's social practices, legal structures and religious beliefs onto those of Indians by agents of government and missionaries had effectively ended the old ways of life in native communities and eroded the belief systems to which they related. The bond with the natural world had lost its tightness, and the life of ceremony, ritual, dance and song was stripped of its purpose in the new emerging pattern. The great houses in which that life had centred and the masks, poles and ritual objects had outlived their time as meaningful elements in the material and spiritual culture, just as the need to hand on the knowledge and skills necessary to their making disappeared. It could indeed be observed that the great feast was over, leaving only a few crumbs as reminders of the richness that once was.

William R. (Bill) Reid, born in 1920, a Canadian of Haida blood relationship on his mother's side, must be seen from several perspectives. The first places him against a background of that long story of his mother's and great-uncle's people from whose shadowy reaches he draws his inspiration and where the conceptual and formal roots for his art are to be found. He relearned the old skills and techniques which had been long consolidated but which, by the time he came along, were virtually lost. Working devotedly through many years, he was able to master the form into which his Indian ancestors had enfolded their understanding of the nature of the world and their shared wisdom about its ordering. He has done this with such authority and serious-ness, and has become such a strong presence in the community of those with any interest in native culture, as to elicit Claude Lévi-Strauss's statement that "our debt to Bill Reid, an incomparable artist, is that he has tended and revived a flame that was so close to dying. That is not all; for Bill Reid by his example and by his teachings has given rise to a prodigious flowering, the results of which the Indian designers, sculptors and goldsmiths of British Columbia offer today to our wondering eyes."[1]

So he must also be seen in relation to an emerging present in which natives of the northwest coast are today reclaiming the identity and self-deter-minism they had lost and creating a new reality for themselves in the modern world. While drawing strength from their great past, their aware-ness is of a present that is alive and taking shape, however painfully, in preparation for a future that will be. The resumption within the past thirty or so years of the making of native art — an event in which Reid is recognized by Lévi-Strauss and others to have played a leading role — preceded and seemed to be independent of the broader social, political and spritual reawakening. However, it is becoming clear that the impulses underlying the resurgence of the art cannot be neatly isolated from those underlying other expressions of native vitality; they are part of the same cultural fabric in the process of regenerating itself. Reid is woven into that larger fabric too, for in recalling their great artistic past to Indian people — and to the world at large — and adding to that his own distinguished achievement, he has contributed to the store of native pride and confidence which was at one time nearly depleted. To younger Indian artists who have followed him he is a venerable figure — an artist who showed them how the old art might be translated into new forms and materials and related to a new purpose, and from whose success they might take encouragement.

While Reid has often laughingly referred to his "leaning on his ancestors," he must also at times have felt his ancestors leaning on him. He is commonly labelled "a Haida artist," an identification whose inference is to link him with the old stylistic tradition rather than merely to suggest his racial origin. But while he happens to have an Indian ancestral connection through which he has found a continuing source for and enrichment of his art, he is also a contemporary in the broad community of artists at large. Although he chose for himself a tradition on which to base his work that was different from those prevailing in western art, he has elected to go through the same search as must any other thinking artist in our time to locate himself in relation to his sources, and to find his own centre. For him this has been a long and slow pursuit. He was late in starting and innocent of what today would be thought of as artistic ambition, and for a time he was unaware of the real nature of the search into which he was being drawn. There may be those who would prefer to have seen him locked into the past as an admirable anachronism, someone who, in an age marked by the absence of cohesive myths and a corresponding emphasis on individualism, had continued — in the words in which he has often referred to his working activities in the past — to "play the game of the nineteenth-century devotee with much dedication." Anyone familiar with the range and development of his work and with his latest pieces, however, knows that he has achieved a degree of individuality of statement and expression that would have been inconceivable — and of course irrelevant — to his artist ancestors. He therefore asks to be taken as a person on his own, engaged in the making of art, not in the making of *Indian* art.

It is the attempt of this book to bring some understanding of Bill Reid's art in its slow unfolding, in relation both to its grounding in Haida tradition and to his evolving inner self.

1 *Bill Reid: A Retrospective Exhibition* (Vancouver, B.C.:
   Vancouver Art Gallery, 1974), n.p.

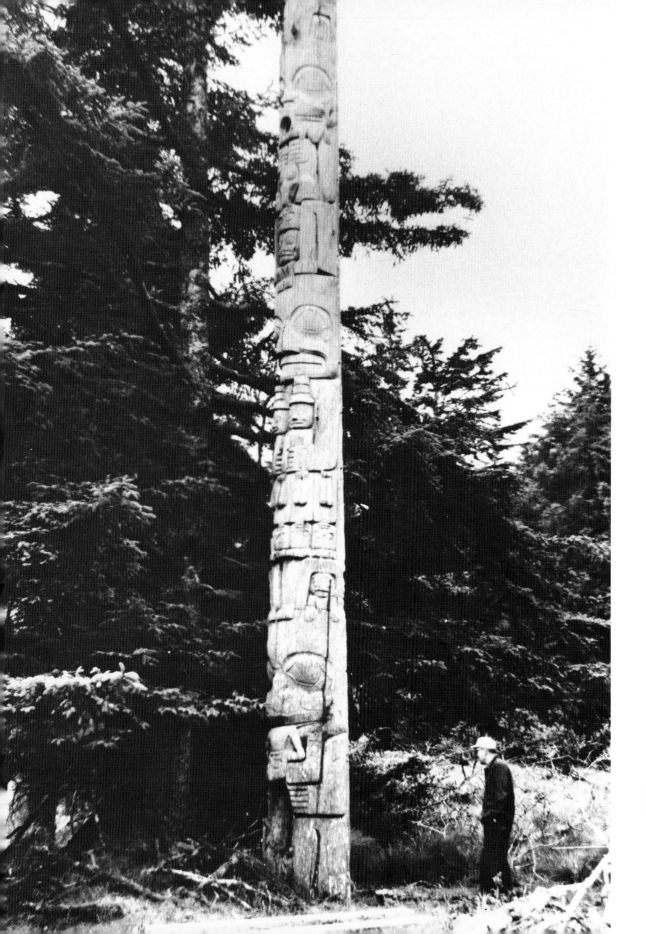

Bill at Ninstints 1957
Photograph:
U.B.C. Museum
of Anthropology

BECOMING HAIDA

*In this chapter, and throughout the book unless otherwise noted, quotations by Bill Reid are from conversations with the author.

Although laid out with no greater appearance of destiny than one would have any reason to expect, the pieces in Reid's background all come together in his evolving present. His father, William Ronald Reid, born an American citizen in the Detroit area of Michigan and later to become a naturalized Canadian, was of German and Scottish parentage. Something of an adventurer, he left home at the age of sixteen and began an itinerant career that took him to various parts of the United States and Canada working as "an end of steel man,"* that is, someone who followed in the wake of railroad-building. He was running a hotel in Smithers in northern British Columbia when he met and married Sophie Gladstone. There is a saying that great men tend to have strong mothers and weaker fathers. Sophie was that strong mother to Bill just as William seems to have been a less dominant father, perhaps only because he was frequently absent.

Bill's mother was Haida, one of the six children of Charles and Josephine Ellsworth Gladstone, anglicized names which they, like all Canadian natives, had been given by non-native authorities as part of a widespread program of deculturalizing the aboriginal population. His grandmother was a native of Tanu on South Moresby in the Queen Charlotte group of islands, one of the villages that George MacDonald has "reconstituted" in his book *Haida Monumental Art.*[1] She belonged by birth to the Raven side of her people's clan groupings (as opposed to the Eagle side) and her family crest was the Wolf. Tanu was abandoned before the turn of the century and today exists as a collection of ghostly shapes, sunken and settled, shrouded in irridescent green moss, reminders of the rectangular forms of the once great Haida houses. Not much is known of Josephine's first husband, a man considerably older than herself, with whom an "arranged" marriage had been worked out according to the Haidas' complex lines of matrilineal descent. She was among the survivors who moved to Skidegate when a smallpox epidemic in 1886 almost wiped out the little community of Church Creek across from Cumshewa. Church Creek was already a position of retreat for villagers from Tanu and Cumshewa in the gradual movement of depleted and demoralized populations from the southern parts of the Charlottes northward to join the people in Masset or Skidegate, the only remaining occupied Island villages by the end of the century. And there in Skidegate, now a widow, she married Bill's grandfather. According to traditional tribal structure, he was the "right" husband for a person of her rank and social position as well as being a fine man. Through him Bill can claim the relationship of great-nephew to the famed carver Charles Edenshaw, whose sister was Charles Gladstone's mother and Bill's great-grandmother.

Charles Gladstone was originally from Naikun on the extreme northeastern tip of Graham Island, but he spent the first six years of his life in Victoria. When the liaison there between his unidentified aristocratic English father and his Haida mother broke up, he was taken into the home of his uncle Charles Edenshaw in Masset. This "adoption" confirmed a pattern central to Haida society in which the uncle-nephew bond — since a young man's inheritance was through his mother's brother — had real importance. It was a relationship that made Edenshaw seem closer to Bill, even though they never met. By the last decade of the nineteenth century, Charlie Edenshaw (named after Scotland's Bonnie Prince Charlie) was known to anthropologists with northwest coast Indian interests as an authority on Haida life and as an artist who carved pieces both for museums, usually in wood, and for the commercial market, usually in the slate for which he is so well known. Edenshaw was a bridging artist whose career began while the traditional culture was still relatively intact and continued into its conspicuous breakdown. Franz Boas's book *Primitive Art*[2] includes important information and drawings the ethnologist received from the carver. Edenshaw was also informant to John R. Swanton when he was in the Queen Charlotte Islands in 1900–01, and made for him some house and pole models and drawings.

Proximity to his talented uncle did not make Charles Gladstone a great artist, but after he retired from fishing and boat-building, he acquired sufficient carving and engraving skills to be discussed by Marius Barbeau in his book *Haida Carvers in Argillite*.[3] These skills impressed Bill when, in his early twenties, they first met. Bill remembers his grandfather as "a big, wonderful fellow, extremely handsome, a nice and gentle man," and his earlier superb boat-building ability also won Bill's respect. Unfortunately he never met his grandmother, who predeceased her husband by some twenty years but whom Bill's mother spoke of as "a saint." According to Bill, his mother described her as an intelligent woman who spoke wonderful English, the only person in the world superior to her father. However, Bill suspects this evaluation was all part of his mother's tidying up a past she did not wish to remember too clearly.

However fictionalized in their daughter's memory, these were the parents of Sophie Gladstone and her five sisters and brothers. Although born in 1895 in Port Essington, a west coast cannery town where her father was a carpenter at the time, she spent her early childhood in a Skidegate that was very different from the modern reserve village of Skidegate Mission, where Bill's daughter Amanda and her children — Mrs. Reid's great-grandchildren — live today. A decisive break came in Sophie's childhood when, around the age of ten, she was sent as a year-round student to the Anglican residential school at Coqualeetza, near Chilliwack, about one hundred kilometres east of Vancouver. Reid believes his grandmother had by then accepted the fact

Bill's mother as a young
woman, Skidegate

Bill with his grandfather,
Charles Gladstone,
in Skidegate

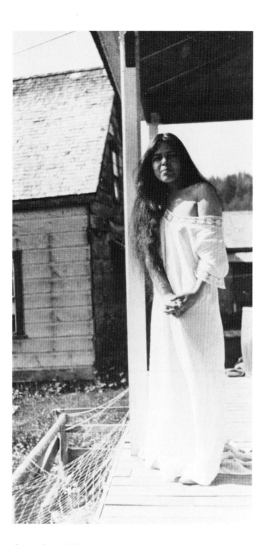
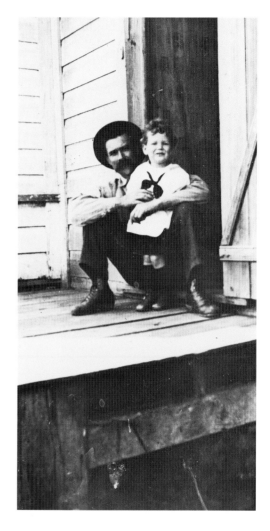

that the old ways were over and believed the best thing for the children was
to get them out of the villages and educated. At the school, Sophie learned
to speak the excellent English in which she took pride, and to sew expertly,
two skills that would enable her to move and function in the dominant
society in which she now found herself. That society was separated from the
life and expectations of those living in a village reserve by such a wall of
inequalities, misunderstandings, prejudices and legislation as to be impen-
etrable by all but the sturdiest and most resolute of its inhabitants. Ambition
and the urge to self-determination, of which Sophie had her share, meant
moving through that wall — meant suppressing, or at least muffling, one's
origins while taking on the values and habits of the white culture during
a time of helpless demoralization for natives, when it was difficult to take
pride in being Indian. Perhaps her "invention of her own persona" began at
that residential school in the populated southern part of the province.

15

Now her life took a clear divergence from that of her siblings and village life in an unaccountably lost five-year period of her teens, spent in Mt. Vernon, Washington. Bill thinks she may have been employed as a maid with a family, or worked in the hospital there, but presumably she had some occupation which further developed her progress towards anglicization. She later managed to ''forget'' that she had ever lived in a native village.

How, or even whether, she received a teacher's certificate is not known, but she was teaching school in New Hazelton, a cluster of houses encompassing a white community and a reserve in the Skeena River area, when she met and married Bill's father. He had been operating a hotel in the nearby town of Smithers since the 1914–18 war, and shortly thereafter moved his business farther north to Hyder, on the Alaska–British Columbia border where a river splits the town into American and Canadian components. On the American side was Mr. Reid's Alaskan Hotel. In Hyder, B.C., a village built mostly over the mud flats, the Reids had the only house on dry land.

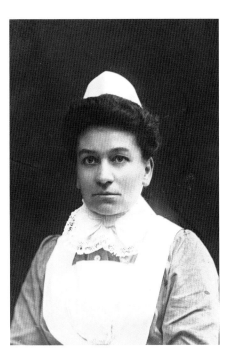

Bill was born 12 January 1920 in Victoria, B.C., during the first of several moves his mother made between that city and Hyder. His sister Peggy, now the retired Dr. Margaret Kennedy (formerly chief psychologist at Hackney Hospital in London, England), was born in Hyder the following year. His mother and the two children then returned to Victoria where they remained for six years and where for one year Bill attended Alice Carr's one-room private school on St. Andrew's Street. He has vivid recollections of Alice as a ''fierce disciplinarian,'' striding up and down in front of the high desks, rapping on the knuckles those pupils' hands which strayed over the lines on their drawing cards. He also remembers Alice's more famous sister, the painter Emily, who was at that time living not far away in her ''House of All Sorts,'' coming into the classroom from time to time. Some years later, when Alice's teaching days were over and the sisters were living together, that schoolroom was to become Emily's last studio.

It was during this period in Victoria, too, that another person was added to the Reid household who was to become virtually a third parent and a great influence. Bill's mother, in her constant search for respectability and European identity, decided that she needed a combination maid, house-keeper, nannie and nurse-mother to help with the household and children. Mrs. Brown — ''Ga Ga'' to the young children — had her own extraordinary story. The child of French parents killed in the Franco-Prussian war, she was raised by relatives who worked her mercilessly on their farm until, in response to British recruiting teams who had been sent to France in search of midwives, she escaped to London. There she learned English and, no doubt in reaction against her harsh French experience which included rape by a French country priest, became an ardent Anglophile and Church of England supporter. Leah Alphonsine Delcuisse subsequently came to Canada as

Mrs. Brown (Ga Ga),
the Reid's housekeeper and
"nanny" in her nursing days

Family Portrait: Bill as a baby
with his mother and father

Bill as a small child on a visit
to his father in Hyder

a practical nurse, working for a time in Cranmore, Alberta, before being sent to Skidegate as the village nurse. There she met her husband, an Englishman by the name of Brown, who had come to the Queen Charlottes in a land settlement program designed to put British soldiers on land throughout the Empire. Sometime after her husband's early death, Mrs. Brown met Sophie and began what was to be a lifetime relationship with the Reid family. In her old age, when her support role turned into one of dependency, she went to stay with Peggy until her death. Bill remembers Mrs. Brown as an important presence, and one whose love-hate relationship with his mother and open dislike of his father were constant elements in the household atmosphere. A strong personality, alternately cruel and soppily sentimental, she was the mainstay of the household while his mother became increasingly occupied with earning a living for the family. She was the one who was "always there." It was she who took the children on cultural outings including visits to the Provincial Museum in Victoria.

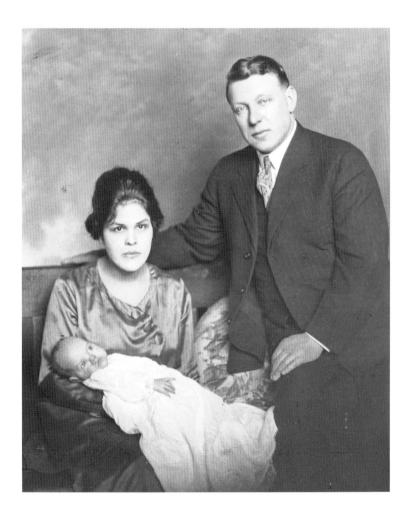

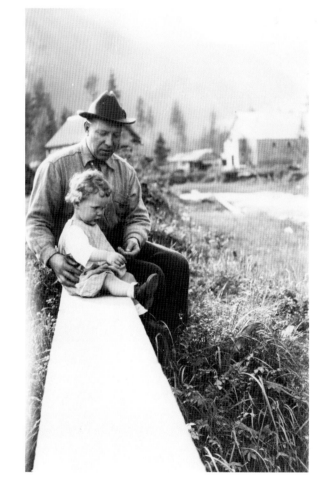

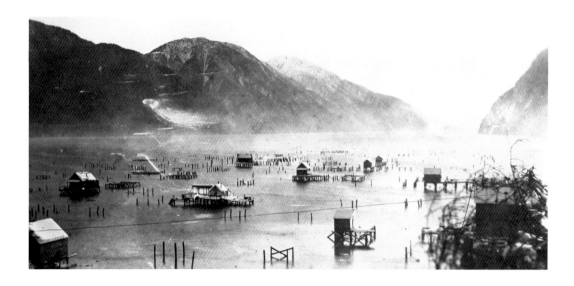

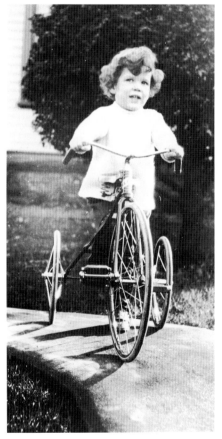

In 1926 it was back to the north. Prohibition and anti-gambling legislation had forced William Reid to move his business across the border to the Canadian side, but since the Canadian school was two difficult miles distant in Stewart, Bill at first attended Hyder's one-room American school. This was the beginning of a terrible period of growing up. In Victoria he had been taught to be "a nice little boy"; his mother dressed him in short pants, sailor suits, and — the ultimate sissification — kid gloves. He was large for his age and soft; in fact, he recalls resembling, in his own mind, the fat child of a friend who had the soft plumpness of "jello." Hyder was then a rough frontier mining town. His father's hotel business was really the business of selling beer, and just below the house where the Reids lived, among the stilted structures that straddled the mud flats, was the domain of the "ladies of the night." At the school, which was taught by an uninspired fresh graduate of Normal School, he was ready game for the rough, scrapping wolverines who were his classmates. At Alice Carr's genteel kindergarden he had had no experience of violence; children were not supposed to fight back.

Bill recalls his father as a macho, blustering person who considered himself a great outdoorsman. As evidence there was his good .22 rifle (which Bill was never allowed to touch) and fishing gear for the local waters teeming with fish. Yet Bill remembers going fishing only once. Having left home at the age of sixteen and a bachelor until he was forty, his father lacked a sense of family life. To him this glove-wearing son "who couldn't hold his own with kids half his size" was a disappointment. His dominant refrain, repeated by Mrs. Brown, was that Bill was "ugly, stupid, doomed to be a failure, doomed to be a bum." His father had "all the bigotry of a nineteenth-century red-necked American." Today Bill recalls more positive aspects of his father: the fact that he never mentioned his wife's native background and was always

Bill in Victoria on his tricycle

A view of Hyder, B.C.

Bill in sailor suit with his
mother and sister Peggy

Mr. and Mrs. Reid with
Bill and Peggy, Hyder

kind to her relatives when they visited or came to work at summer jobs in the
local mine or in his hotel; the beautiful and productive northern garden he
maintained. And as his own present success softens the memory of earlier
failures, he is touched by the thought of his father's failed life. His father's
ambition was modest, he says today, "just $50,000 to buy a farm in the Fraser
Valley and raise pigs." "Losers," Bill adds, "are an interesting bunch of
people," clearly implying that he is someone who speaks from early experience, half in admiration of a father who was a gambler and had been in
every state and province, making lots of money then losing it. He remembers his father's partner too, "black Jack McDonough who made and lost
fortunes, who also was always waiting for the big win." When the Depression came, his father gave up in defeat — according to Bill he "just lay down
and died." Sometimes Bill feels that his image of his father as an ogre may
be exaggerated, yet there is no question that he disliked the man and
suffered intensely during this unhappy time. School was an unproductive
ordeal (he averaged C grades) and since he hated going home to the constant
fighting and bickering, he faced punishment for his frequent lateness.

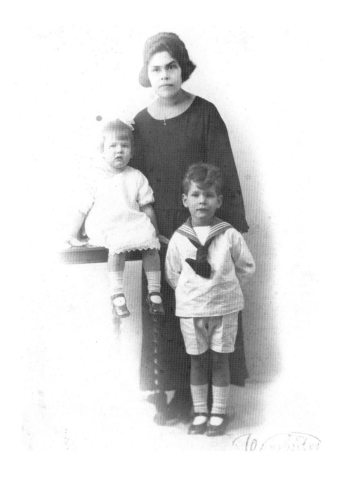

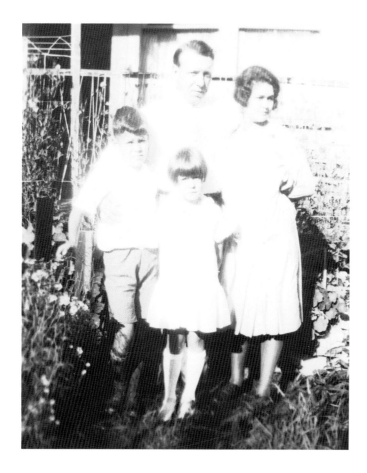

His mother spent most of her time in her workshop making clothes, but her presence in the family was strong. She had a great respect for things cultural, not through knowledge of them but only as symbolic of the world she aspired to. Although there were no tangible cultural evidences in the house — no books, music, art or stimulating conversation — papers and magazines were read at night. Everything Sophie did herself she did well, and she left little doubt that the children were expected to be "flaming successes." Bill's good memories of childhood are mostly connected with natural surroundings, though he also remembers pleasurably a friendship he and Peggy shared with an American brother and sister from Washington State whose family sent them north in the summers to stay with relatives. They were somewhat more civilized than the tough Hyder kids, and the four of them spent their holidays digging caves and tunnels in the piles of sawdust at the uncle's sawmill. After completing grade 6 Bill was transferred to the Canadian school in Stewart which was thought to be a sufficiently better school to merit the long walk to it, and there he finally made some friends and began to adjust a little to life in a mining town.

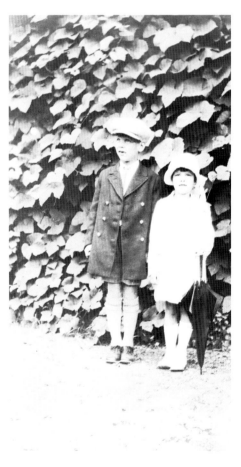
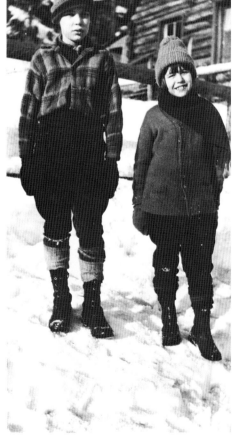

Bill and Peggy as
children in Victoria

Bill and Peggy,
Hyder in the winter

Bill holding his young
brother Robert, Hyder

Until the Depression, Bill's father had provided well for his family. Then in 1932 the failure of the American bank that held his notes caused him to close the hotel, ending the family's stay in the north. When Bill was thirteen Mrs. Reid took him, Peggy, a new son, Robert, born in 1928 (today the owner of an art advertising company in Toronto) and the ever-present Mrs. Brown once again to Victoria. There she set up a dressmaking business since she was now virtually the sole support of her family, a role she managed with reasonable success over the coming years. Bill, still convinced that he was ugly, worthless and talentless, was never again to see his father, though he kept up a desultory correspondence with him until his death in Stewart in 1942.

His mother's gift of dignity and pleasing formality seemed to find its proper setting in Victoria, whose English ambience, social values and life style she easily assimilated. She demanded a certain quality of behaviour and performance of her family — manners should be minded, thoughts should be well spoken, things should be well made — and here she set the tone by her own attitude and work. She was a superb artisan, loved fashion and clothes, had her own sense of style, and was able to sew and design for fashionable families in the city including the wife of the Lieutenant Governor. Unquestionably her eldest son's central passion for making things, and for making them well, comes from her, though he claims he was not precocious in this regard, and in fact was clumsy and inept in manual training classes in Victoria. He began making things with his hands around the age of twelve or thirteen. Out of boredom in school he would carve sticks of blackboard chalk, showing an ability to do fine work and a fascination with things miniature: a tiny tea-set coated with nail polish has survived to represent these early efforts. He remembers making a ten-inch wooden model of a Viking boat, working from a little drawing, and an Arab dhow.

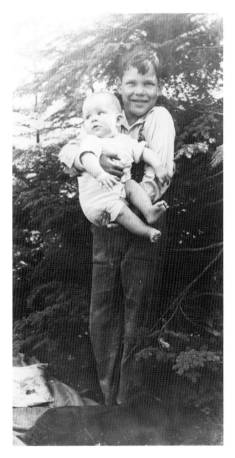

There were visits to Victoria from the aunts and uncles, Sophie's sisters and brothers: Eleanor, the youngest girl, a graduate of Columbia Business College in New Westminster who was employed by a Vancouver hardware firm; Irene, who exhibited sewing skills like her sister Sophie; Percy, the youngest, who earned his way through the University of British Columbia to a master's degree in economics, the only member of the family and the first west coast native to so distinguish himself; and Ernie and Bill who were boat-builders and fishermen. The strong feeling for extended family, of which his childhood experiences had given him a taste, continued, though he never thought of his relatives as being native; for one thing, only the younger aunt was recognizably "Indian" in appearance, the other being blue-eyed, small featured and red-haired, and Uncle Bill could have been taken for a Swede. His mother rejected this family community for the native connection it was, and was far from enchanted when later on Bill developed an interest in his Indian heritage — "digging up those old bones which she had spent her life trying to bury." Even in her old age, and long after he had demonstrated his unique talents, she would give no more than grudging acknowledgement of his evident success while showing little warmth or enthusiasm for the accomplishment that had earned it.

Victoria now became for Bill more than a geographical location. In grade 8 at South Park Elementary School he remembers the visits of a substitute teacher, Jack Shadbolt, then in his early twenties, who read poems and stories to his class and got them "drawing Kandinskys." When he entered Victoria High School, he encountered a number of remarkable teachers whose impact he has not forgotten. Ira Dilworth, who was later to become the west coast regional director of the Canadian Broadcasting Corporation, was then school principal. A romantic idealist and a man of cultivated literary and musical tastes, Dilworth dominated the school, introducing such programs as music appreciation in which records were played on a wind-up gramophone. These gave Bill a taste for classical music, adding to his existing fondness for jazz and the songs of Gershwin and other Broadway musical composers. There was a tough, stimulating English teacher who improvised poems in Greek; a fine mathematics teacher (Lewis Clark) who became known for his photographic flower books; and a chemistry lab which provided the equipment Bill and his closest friend (later to become a chemist for Shell Oil) stole in order to build their own small lab in a household closet where among other things they experimented with glass-blowing. There was no particular emphasis on art training, and the one available course was an option he had no interest in taking.

In Hyder reading had been his escape, and the modest but surprisingly good local library permitted him to acquire the reading habit, particularly of romantic adventure stories and "sentimental stuff." In school there he encountered Tennyson, whose poetry, as for others of Reid's generation, provided standard material for memorization. He dipped into the "Idylls of the King," acquainted himself with Kipling's *Kim* and the *Just So Stories*, read Edgar Rice Burroughs, to say nothing of the *Boy's Own Annuals.* In Victoria his reading habit found fresh stimulation and improved opportunity; reading a book a day, he worked his way through the Carnegie Library, devouring such contemporary playwrights, poets and novelists as Thornton Wilder, William Saroyan, Maxwell Anderson and Stephen Vincent Benét, whose prologue to "John Brown's Body" he still considers a great work.

Surprisingly, he remembers the Depression as a stimulating period, for there were many interesting adults around who had time on their hands and were willing to talk to a responsive teenager. One of them was Tom Wylie, then a mostly unemployed young husband and father, with whom Bill developed a decisive friendship. Wylie later studied anthropology at UBC, became the first curator of Vancouver's Maritime Museum, and was for a time a museum

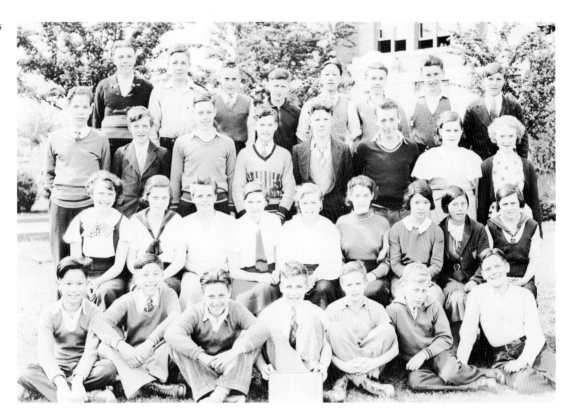

Victoria High School class with Bill second row from top, extreme left, 1934

worker in Africa. It was Tom who introduced him to James Branch Cabell's 1919 novel *Jurgen,* an allegorical fable set in medieval times, whose hero, after a prolonged and skeptical pilgrimage which takes him to places and among personages that are sometimes legendary and often wildly fictional, returns to his prosaic life. This book's gloss of romanticism appealed powerfully to Bill at the time, and its questioning of the nature of illusion, disillusion and reality he still finds interesting.

Through Margo Sanderson, the daughter of a warm and vivacious French woman who taught her native language at Victoria College, he encountered the work of Vachel Lindsay, just one of the American poets of the thirties with whom he is impressively familiar. Margo, whose favourite poem was Lindsay's "Chinese Nightingale," yearned without fulfilment to be an actress, which perhaps aligned her with the theme of the "beautiful loser." Some years later Leonard Cohen was to give name and lyrical enlargement to that theme, and in so doing endeared himself to Bill. The attraction to expressions of aspiration, romantic energy and dramatic power, especially when tinged with the shadow of darkness — the impossible romantic dream and the dark premonition — developing out of his own childhood loneliness and alienation, and given form in his adolescent reading and listening, remains true for him today even though his tastes are more sophisticated.

23

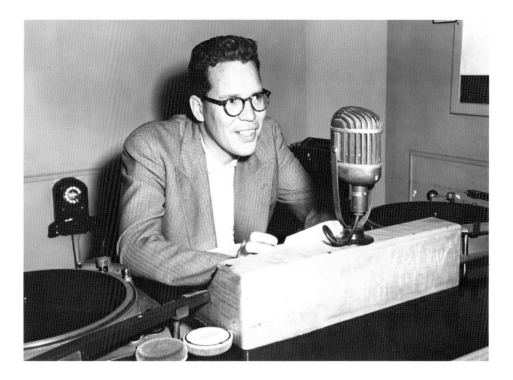

During that time of economic and social dissatisfaction, it was again through Tom Wylie and others, including Bruce Mickleborough, a brilliant contemporary who was capable even in early youth of living out his political and social convictions, that Bill became aware of socialist, communist and anarchist theories and writing. His formal education ended in 1936–37 with a single year of the two that Victoria College then offered. There, in a general arts program, he was fortunate enough to encounter Dr. Jeannette Cann, an outstanding teacher through whom he was introduced to twentieth-century English literature in a more formal way, and to the work of such modern artists as Cézanne, Van Gogh, Picasso and others. To have pursued a university education, he would have had to take a second year at Victoria and then gone on to Vancouver, but he had neither the financial means nor the motivation.

"In those days you could pretty well walk into a radio station, sit down and start announcing," Bill says, and that is what he did when he left home at the age of twenty. He had, then as now, a superb command of the English language and an excellent speaking voice, and after a year's unpaid announcing for CFCT in Victoria he went on to a paid position in Kelowna, B.C., selling soap ads over the air. So began sixteen years in broadcasting which would take him to a number of commercial stations in eastern Canada, including Kirkland Lake in northern Ontario and Rouyn in Quebec, before he joined the Canadian Broadcasting Corporation in 1948. He stayed with the Corpor-

ation, working first in Toronto, mainly with the radio news department, and
then in Vancouver until he left it in 1958. Bill still has anxiety dreams from
his broadcasting days: fifteen minutes of radio time remaining and no script
prepared; records to be played and the turntable broken down. Sixteen
"wasted years," as he now thinks of them, though the experience, which
forced him to speak in public and to take other social action to which he
was little inclined, was helpful in overcoming a painful shyness and a with-
drawing nature. He had earlier been rejected for military service because of
myopic vision, but finally in 1944 he was inducted into the army, though his
military career "consisted entirely in starting training programs which were
discontinued because various sectors of the warfronts became inactive."
Finally at the end of 1945 he was discharged, having been no farther from
home than Calgary.

Reid recalls the beautiful September afternoon in 1948 when he and his
first wife Mabel ("Binkie"), a girl of Dutch extraction, were living in Toronto.
They were walking down the street when a notice in front of the recently
opened Ryerson Institute of Technology caught his eye. He looked over the
list of courses, thinking that he might take one in jewellery engraving. There
was no such course, but one in platinum and diamond setting (the only time
it was ever offered), intrigued him though that aspect of the craft held no
special interest for him at the time. The Institute was close to the CBC offices
where he had just begun employment, and his night working schedule
permitted him to attend full days. He promptly registered and, during the
two years he spent there, received a fairly thorough indoctrination in the
techniques and processes of European jewellery-making. Fortunately, the
narrowly traditional teaching was counterbalanced by Bill's own interest,
stimulated largely through his avid reading of the magazine *Arts & Archi-
tecture,* in the spurt of fine contemporary industrial design coming out of
Scandinavia and the United States in the late forties and early fifties, such as
that of Charles Eames. For a time he envisioned a future as a contemporary
jeweller like Margaret Depatta, an American craftswoman then well known
in jewellery circles.

He is apt to attribute the artistic course his life has taken after a rather late
start to this fortuitous stroll past a sign, but the wheels of his history had
been set in motion long before that. An important fact to realize in considering Reid's development is that unlike other contemporary native artists,
all younger than he, such as Robert Davidson, Joe David or Beau Dick, who
grew up in their villages or whose ties with their ancestry remained close
and strong, who emerged into a sharper social and political climate, and who
knew with the unchallengeable sense of inner knowledge that "they were
Indian," Reid was in his early teens before he "even became conscious of the
fact that I was anything other than an average Caucasian North American."

"My mother had learned the major lesson taught the native peoples of our hemisphere during the first half of this century, that it was somehow sinful and debased to be, in white terms, an Indian, and [she] certainly saw no reason to pass any pride in that part of their heritage on to her children."[4] For him there had to be at some point a conscious decision to reach out and grab that thin, fraying line of connection, for by this time he was equipped, in all the obvious ways, to ignore it. His sister and brother who grew up under the same conditions he had moved into careers and got on with their lives as part of the larger society with no apparent need either to deny or declare their maternal ancestry. For Bill his quest probably began with the natural curiosity of most teenagers to know where they come from. In his case, since he had no knowledge of his father's relatives, those of his mother became the objects of his attention, whether she welcomed the implications of such attention or not.

In traditional Haida society where each village was its own community, and each extended household a smaller one within it, the matter of lineage was one of central importance: who had rank, who was descended from whom, through what connections, with identities confirmed by the giving of this or that name and the possession of crests. Over centuries lineage had become one of the control patterns that kept a society constantly threatened with chaos orderly and together. Even after it lost its vital structural and utilitarian function and its strictness, this framework of society persisted, and the question of blood relationships continued to be an engrossing preoccupation, carrying on the sense of community; that which once had the force to express itself in necessary, set, public ritual became a matter of family and personal relationships. Solomon Wilson, a friend of Bill's who lived his early years in a traditional native house, told him how the evenings were spent, a social practice which was carried on until quite recently. Every night the elders would sit around and talk, the children having been cautioned to keep quiet. There was only one topic of conversation — genealogy. In connection with this game of "how are you related to me" as it came to be played in beer parlours, Bill tells of Jimmie Siwid who finally withdrew from one such session saying, "I have better things to do — let's just settle that everybody is related to everybody else."

Reid derives energy from the people around him, and there is obviously a part of him that longs for the warmth and security of the extended family community, though at this late date he is too much the critical observer to put himself inside any lingering tribal consciousness. So his awakening awareness had to do with family, for he was as yet unacquainted in any conscious way with the whole body of Haida culture or art — the art that would in fact be the door through which he would make his entry into the culture's history.

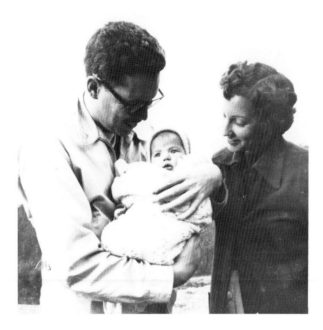

Bill, Binkie (his first wife)
and Amanda as a baby,
Vancouver c. 1950

His familiarity with silver and gold bracelets bearing Haida designs, however, dates back as far as he can remember to those worn by his aunts on their visits to Hyder and Stewart. Bill believes Charles Edenshaw to have made the first bracelets and to have been "the inventor of the tradition," and from him others took it up. The most important of these for Bill was a brother-in-law of Bill's grandmother Josephine, John Cross. He had been trained as a tattoo artist, for it was the frequent custom of Haidas to have their crests tattooed on their bodies. There was also Tom Moody, as well as Bill's grandfather. The Kwakiutl people, too, turned out many copies of Edenshaw's work, and bracelets became a commonplace. Although there is a photograph to prove that he was once taken to Skidegate as a baby, it was not until 1943 at the age of twenty-three that Bill finally boarded a co-op seiner boat, with Clem Moody as skipper, and as engineer Raymond Cross, the father of Raymond, Bill's adopted son of some twelve years later, and went to the Queen Charlotte Islands on a trip of self-discovery. He would visit those Islands, which have become his interior landscape of feeling and conscience, innumerable times in the years to come, and he is still drawn to them like a magnet. There at last in Skidegate he would meet his grandfather, whom Charlie Edenshaw had taken in as a youth and from whom he had borrowed the habit of making engraved bracelets and carving argillite. Bill was to see and handle Edenshaw's tools, inherited by his own grandfather and carried on his back the eighty miles from Masset to Skidegate. He remembers those tools, all engraving tools, some with Edenshaw's own ingeniously made handles of bone or ivory, and all having the personal quality that a skilled user somehow imparts to his implements.

27

Charles Gladstone, a white-skinned, fair-haired man with Haida features, spoke virtually no English and his grandson certainly spoke no Haida, so verbal communication was limited, but the two developed an empathetic bond which he had never experienced with his father. Through him Bill came to know a number of the older men and women for whom the old tradition as it had been lived was still alive in memory, and whose bearing and presence bespoke their pride in being who they were. Henry Young, who had given information to Marius Barbeau, the Dominion ethnologist at the National Museum in Ottawa, and was his grandfather's best friend, was among these new friends.

A sense of affinity with the ancestors, a recognition of common experience across the years, a belief in their essential honesty and sensitivity, and a respect for their accomplished and responsible art — for it was art in the service of the community — began then and was to remain with him, deepening until it has become the firm core of his life. Sitting on a moss-covered, mist-drenched stump amidst the ruins of Tanu some thirty years later, he would confess that in turning to his ancestors, in reclaiming his heritage for himself, he was, far from merely expressing an enthusiasm for things Indian, looking for an identity which he had not found in modern western society with its lack of real traditions and its mistrust of intuition. He would share the apprehension implicit in a psychiatrist's statement that "if no instinct tells man what he *has* to do, and no tradition tells him what he *ought* to do, soon he will not know what he *wants* to do."

The timing of Ryerson's course in jewellery-making in Toronto may have been fortuitous, but Reid's quick response was no accident, nor was it mere chance that the first object he wished to make after finishing his training was a Haida bracelet. In Toronto he also introduced himself to the great totem pole, one of several inserted in the stairwell of the Royal Ontario Museum where its full extent is accessible for study. This pole's presence there must have seemed particularly significant since it came from Tanu where it would have been part of his grandmother's everyday experience as a child.[5]

Reid spent a lot of time with that pole, gradually beginning to see its characteristic forms and their interrelationships. "Things began to come together in that pole," he says, things he had sensed in his grandfather's village and things he had by now begun to read about in writings by Bruce Inverarity, Franz Boas and others. After a year and a half apprenticing in Toronto with the Platinum Art Company, he and Binkie returned to Vancouver where their daughter Amanda was born in 1950 and where he set up a basement workshop for his jewellery-making, selling pieces to friends of friends as well as through Bessie Fitzgerald's Victoria Quest Shop which specialized in Canadian craft. He remembers selling unique sterling cufflinks for ten or fifteen dollars a pair. However, he continued to work for the CBC until 1958, chiefly

28

announcing but also writing and broadcasting the occasional talk, one of the early and memorable pieces being a eulogy to his grandfather who died in 1954. The half-finished Haida bracelet found on his grandfather's workbench, perhaps the last traditionally made bracelet in existence, Bill undertook to complete in time for the funeral. Significantly too it was at his grandfather's funeral at Skidegate that he first encountered the work of Charles Edenshaw. At that time he saw only two gold bracelets, but "the world was not the same after that," for he found in Edenshaw the quintessential statement of Haida artistic form, that style in which "each object becomes a frozen universe, filled with latent energy."[6] During the 1950s Edenshaw became central to Reid's patient and thorough studies; borrowing and copying from him as necessary, he gradually acquired the theoretical understanding of the style and the ability to express that understanding in his own increasingly ambitious and masterly jewellery pieces.

Informed interest in the Indian heritage of the west coast had manifested itself belatedly, sporadically and usually ineffectively in the early years of this century. By the 1940s and fifties, while Bill was still in the East, the climate of awareness on the Canadian west coast was gradually changing. The centres of that change were the University of British Columbia and the British Columbia Provincial Museum in Victoria. In his annual report for 1947–48, UBC president Norman McKenzie referred to the initiation of plans for constructing a Totem Park on campus and to the collection of some twenty poles which had already been donated or purchased, giving particular recognition to Professor Hunter Lewis of the English Department for his role in the enterprise. The year 1947 was significant in bringing anthropologists Drs. Harry and Audrey Hawthorn to the university, Harry as founder and first head of the Department of Anthropology, and Audrey, who became the original guiding force behind the Museum of Anthropology which in 1949 began its existence in the basement of the UBC library. They, along with Wilson Duff, then at the Museum in Victoria, were soon passionately engaged in west coast Indian studies, building museum collections, collecting and publishing information, and drawing on the knowledge and skills of native people. They were also leaders in eliciting support and organizing the action that took place in the fifties to save some of the poles which had been rotting in northern villages since their abandonment.

If Duff and Harry Hawthorn are to be given credit for having triggered the resurgence of serious west coast native art activity of the past thirty-five years, then Mungo Martin, a Kwakiutl carver from Fort Rupert, was the first substantial artist to be reactivated, so to speak, through non-Indian initiative and to enter a relationship with the anthropological community in which that community became both client and patron. An experienced carver who had worked with Willie Seaweed (now well known through Bill Holm's work on him), Martin had turned to commercial fishing, once the ban on potlatching had had its destructive effect and he was no longer able to support himself as an artist. In the late forties Harry Hawthorn invited this carver, already about seventy, to Vancouver to restore a group of old poles that had been brought to the campus from various deserted village sites. This task was virtually beyond the possibility of accomplishment, by Martin or anyone else, but the assignment gave him the opportunity to carve full time, first on the campus of UBC and later at the Provincial Museum. In Victoria he and his family carved among other things the totems in the well-known park adjacent to the Parliament Buildings, and his descendants today have a successful Indian art business in that city.

Reid met Martin in 1957 when Wilson Duff invited him to spend his two-week vacation from CBC in Victoria working with the older carver on a pole (which is now at the Peace Arch on the Canadian-American border at Blaine, Washington). Reid welcomed this first opportunity to work on a large scale with an experienced carver, but it could hardly be said that he received instruction from Martin, as is sometimes claimed. As Bill reports it, when Wilson introduced him as a Haida, which was understood to mean that he could be relied on, Mungo simply said "carve there," pointing to the head of a little "watchman" figure about a third of the way up the pole. This was Reid's introduction to monumental wood carving, something which, as he happily discovered, came to him quite naturally. He was also introduced to a tool he values highly — the lipped adze, an adaptation of the ship's carpenter's adze, which Mungo's son David invented. More valuable than anything specifically learned in the exchange was the association with a carver and a man who had grown up within the tradition, and who was determined to keep the old ways from being forgotten. Mungo was for Bill a wonderful person, one whose greatness was projected as a matter of inner conviction. He was a beguiling raconteur in the great Indian tradition of storytellers, and his stories were invariably punctuated by songs. Mungo became very fond of Amanda and made her a doll and cradle, the first in a series of gift exchanges which Bill finally had to halt, knowing he would be unable to keep up with a spiralling "potlatch" situation. (The habit of gift-giving today persists in the native villages as an echo of the potlatch, once a ceremony vital and integral to the society just as the old rank and lineage structures still have echoes in the importance attached to community and family.)

Reid had been part of the Provincial Museum's teams that had gone north to salvage poles from abandoned village sites on the Queen Charlotte Islands: in 1955 to Tanu and Skedans, with an exploratory trip to Ninstints on Anthony Island, a location very difficult of access; and then in 1957, a second trip to Anthony Island. Those trips were dramatically moving experiences, and the latter one was filmed by the CBC for Bill's scripting and narration.

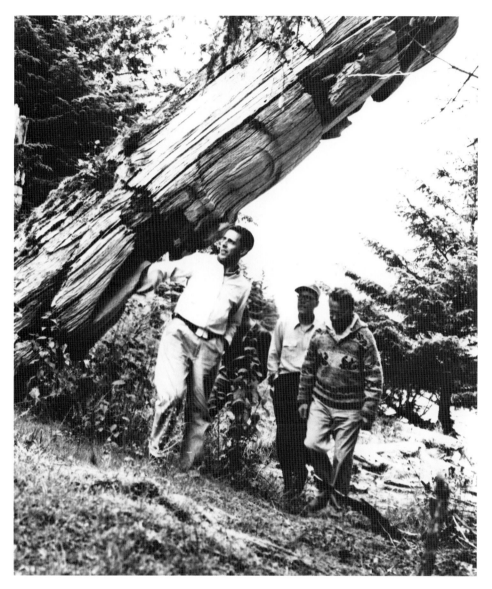

In 1958, in what Bill considers an extraordinary act of faith, for he had had
only ten days of experience with Mungo Martin on a large pole, Dr. Hawthorn
invited him to take on a major project — the restoration of some old poles in
its collection, among them some in whose rescue he had assisted. The invitation offered vital encouragement, and he immediately handed in his resig-
nation to the CBC. Those old poles are now safely housed in the Museum of
Anthropology, a splendid building on the UBC campus designed by Arthur
Erickson and completed in 1976, but they never received the restoration by
Reid that had been envisioned for them, for their advanced stage of deterioration made that task impossible.

31

It was decided instead to construct a portion of a Haida village on campus, with Reid in charge as designer and director and with talented Kwakiutl carver Doug Cranmer as his assistant. Between 1958 and 1962 he and Cranmer completed two traditional house structures and seven attendant poles and other massive wood carvings — an extraordinary accomplishment. He remembers as an idyllic experience the stretched-out time spent working in the carving shed under tall trees on the edge of the campus in what then seemed to be open country; except for the occasional tourist dropping by to see what was going on, the serenity was uninterrupted. This was his first large-scale public undertaking, and the first of now many requiring the collaboration of other workers, particularly, when he can arrange it, that of younger natives to whom he can pass on some of his knowledge and his skills. The park was opened in 1963, and though the poles and structures have since been moved to the site of the new Museum of Anthropology, overlooking the waters of the Strait of Georgia, the carving shed is still there under the trees where Bill or other carvers are often to be found busy with more recent projects.

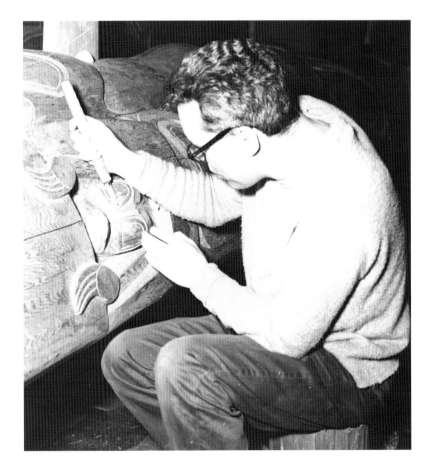

Reid in the university carving shed
at work on a pole for Totem Park,
University of British Columbia 1959–61
Photograph: U.B.C. Museum
of Anthropology

Double Mortuary and other Poles
and House carved by Reid and
Doug Cranmer between 1958 and 1962
Originally in the University's "Totem Park,"
today they stand on the grounds outside
the Museum of Anthropology, University
of British Columbia, Vancouver

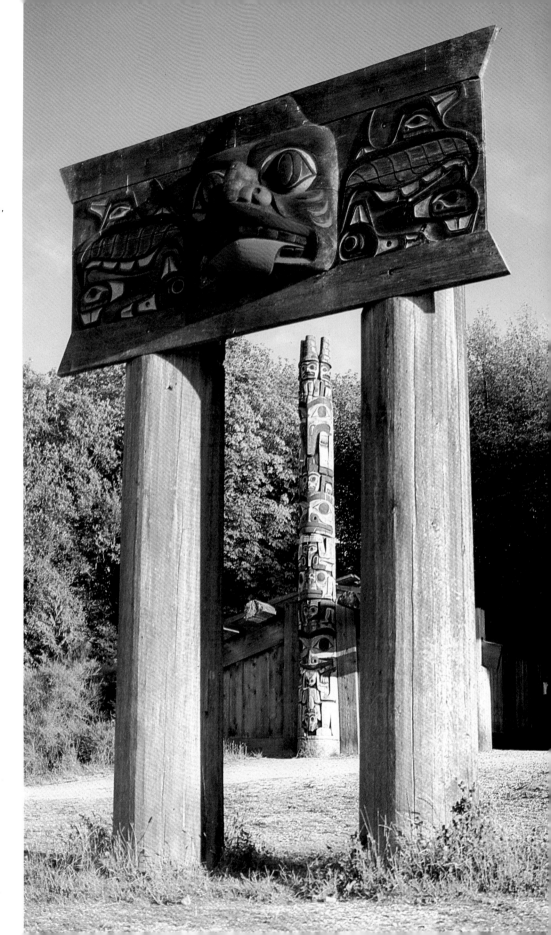

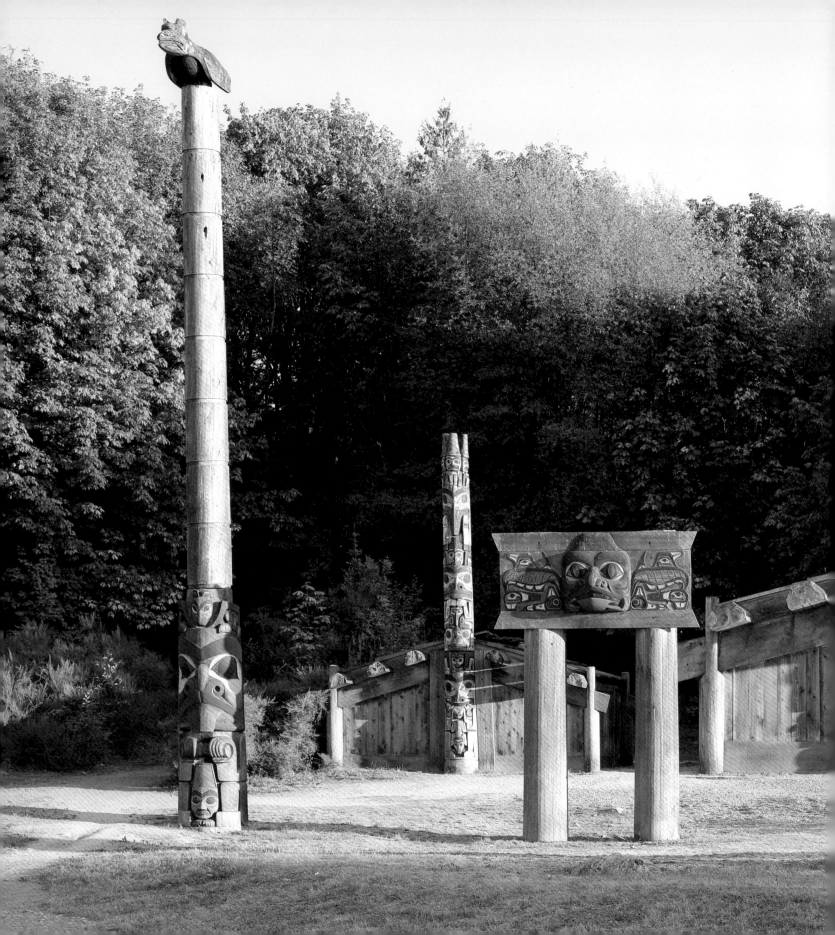

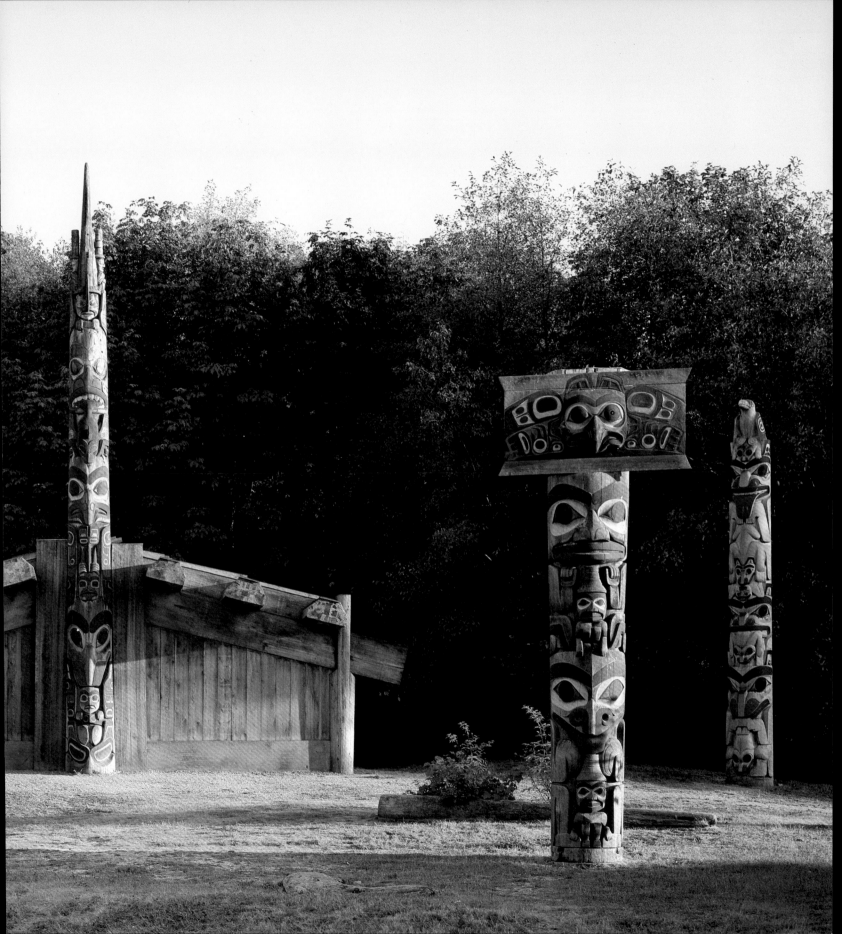

During these years his personal life was less than idyllic. His marriage to Binkie ended in divorce in 1959, and there was a second marriage of shorter duration, ending in 1962, to Ella Gunn, a social worker. Adoptions were common occurrences in the social patterns of traditional society, and it was an early manifestation of his Haida empathy when he and Binkie adopted a son, Raymond, in 1955, the child of Haida parents whose troubled village lives made it difficult for them to take care of him adequately. Raymond's own life was to follow anything but a smooth pattern, and its tragic ending in apparent suicide was but one experience that has added to Bill's growing concern over the years for the fate of the village natives — people suspended in a consciousness that has no time frame. The frequent depression to which he was given in his younger days was at least in part his share of the larger pain suffered by the people beside whom, through his work, he now walked, even though he could not identify with them. Over the years of demoralization and humiliation, they had been rendered helpless to express that pain in anger or effective dialogue or action. Fortunately Bill, who until recently has seen himself more outside than inside the problem, has been able to give his concern positive expression — on public platforms, in his writing, as a consultant to responsible authorities and in specific action.

After the completion of the Haida Village project, in the spring of 1963 Reid set up his own jewellery business in the rambling second floor of a temporary building on Pender Street in downtown Vancouver. There in a combined living/working situation he had two or three jewellery benches, each with some interesting pieces always in progress. The Pender Street studio became a convenient drop-in place for a growing circle of friends and acquaintances who were attracted not only to the fine work he was doing but also to his substantial personality which even in its reserve was strongly projected. There were also two adjoining rooms where at his invitation young natives newly arrived in the city from one of the villages had the opportunity to work within range of his experienced eye. One of these was Robert Davidson, the great-grandson of Charles Edenshaw and a generation younger than Bill. For a time in the mid-sixties Robert lived and worked with Bill on Pender Street, and their close association continues. Today Davidson is an artist as well known and respected as his senior peer. In acknowledging his early debt, he confirms that one always learns in Bill's presence whether the teaching is intentional or not. Reid tends to make little of what others see as his truly large role in helping aspiring young artists. He states that, as with any good apprentice, it was unnecessary to teach Robert anything; it was required "merely to tell him what was possible." In 1968, when the 'Ksan project was started in Hazelton as a federal government program for the training of young native artists in the production of high quality artifacts, Reid arranged for Davidson to take his place as one of the chief instructors when another commitment precluded his own participation.

36

Hinged Silver Bracelet
Bear design c. 1964
2.2 cm wide

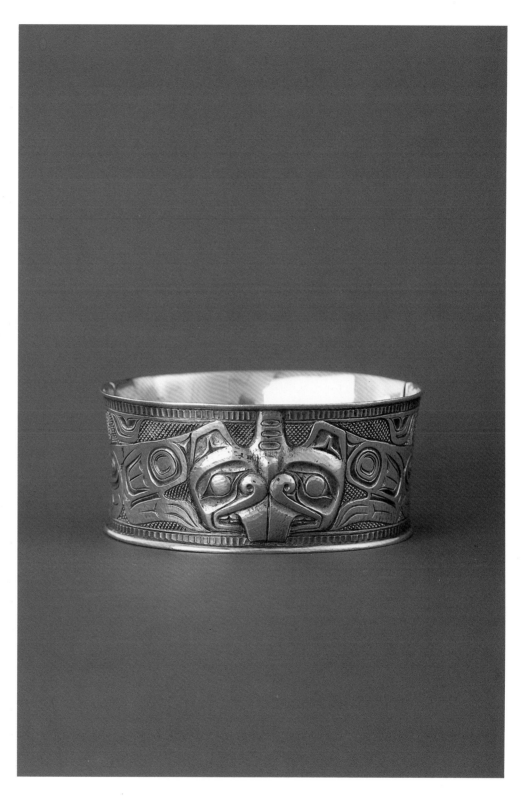

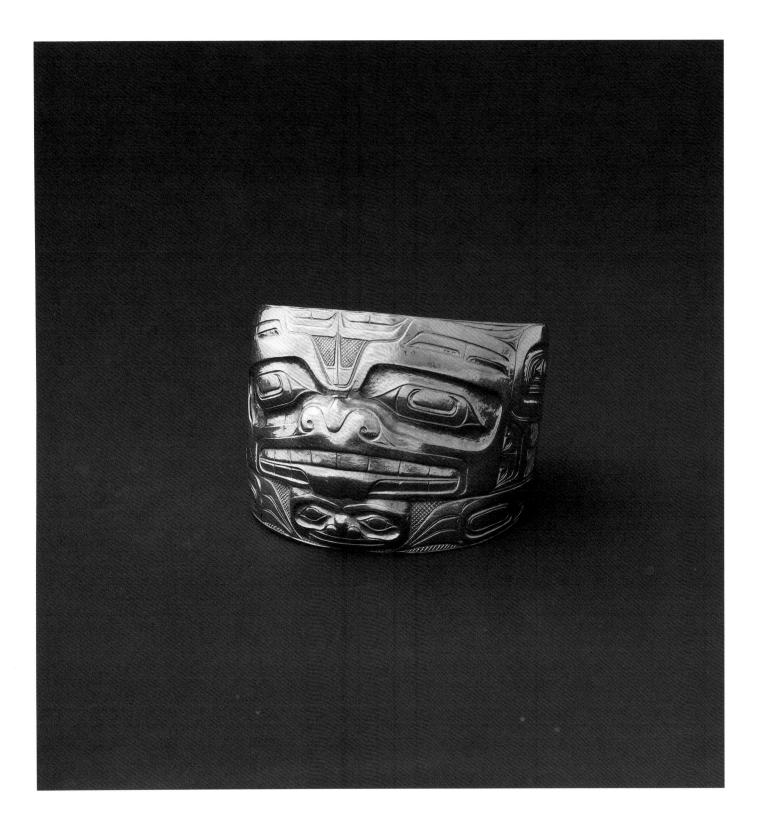

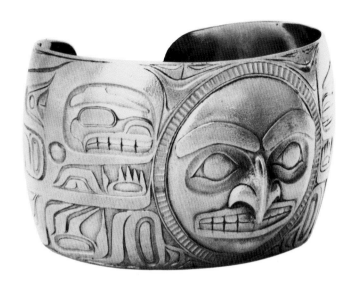

Gold Bracelet
Bear and Human 1965
5.3 cm wide

Gold Bracelet
Thunderbird design 1972
4.1 cm wide

Gold Brooch
after a bone shaman's charm
originally collected by Paul Kane
and now in the collection of the
Royal Ontario Museum, Toronto 1964.
2.9 cm long, 7.1 cm wide

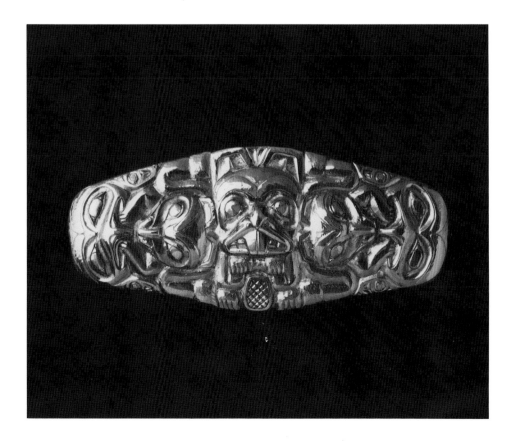

In the mid-sixties he did a series of black-and-white illustrations for Christie Harris's *Raven's Cry*,[7] a book of solid enough research to win the approval of Wilson Duff. Intended for a youthful readership, it is a somewhat sentimental fictionalized account of the Edenshaw family's journey through acculturation. The story is brought into the present with a section on Reid as the great-nephew of Charles Edenshaw, a nephew already seen in the book as the artistic successor of his famous relative. The drawings have the look of engravings, reading as white on black and using crosshatching and other hard-line patterning to achieve graded tones between white and black. Actually, the effect was achieved by using an old photostat camera which produced a paper negative of his drawn image which he could then rework directly. In a revealing self-view at the time, Reid in the book's last illustration pictures himself in the lower foreground at work on a pole, the tools of the traditional carver which he so much reveres laid out ceremonially across the bottom of the page. Lined up behind him loom the gigantic silent ghosts of his ancestors — "Uncle Charlie" directly centre at his back. These presences hold the secrets to his own growing rootedness and are therefore benign; but they are also disturbing because he has suffered the ambivalence of drawing his real support from one culture, to which he has a legitimate claim, though having been nurtured in another. Behind the ancestors stands a row of their great carved poles. This illustration is a telling summation of his self-image some twenty years ago, but it also reveals an artistic problem which he was facing for the first time and to which the illustrations have not found the answer: the creation of an imagery and a mode of representation that would, within the required illustrative framework, successfully bridge the gap between a mythical and iconically known and presented past and a historic present that is experienced in "real life" terms. That problem did not exist for a splendid set of oak doors he carved around the same time wherein some thirty-odd sea and bird creatures, conceived as the products of nature uncomplicated by Haida ancestry, swim or float in the recessed lake and river system that meanders over the doors' surface.

By this time Reid was becoming known in scholarly and journalistic circles as an unusual person, someone who had a root by blood in the Haida culture, but also a critical distance from it; someone knowledgeable, thoughtful, responsible, who could write and speak precise, poetic and eloquent English, qualities his experience in broadcasting had revealed and developed. In the mid-sixties, along with Wilson Duff — then with the Department of Anthropology at the University of British Columbia — and Bill Holm of Seattle — curator of Northwest Coast Indian Art at the Thomas Burke Memorial Washington State Museum — he was invited to work as a consultant for the Vancouver Art Gallery's major exhibition, Arts of the Raven, celebrating the Canadian Centennial.

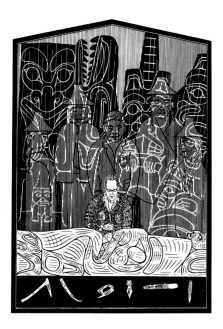

Pair of Oak Doors
Marine Motif 1964
2.2 m wide, 63.1 cm high,
6.5 cm deep

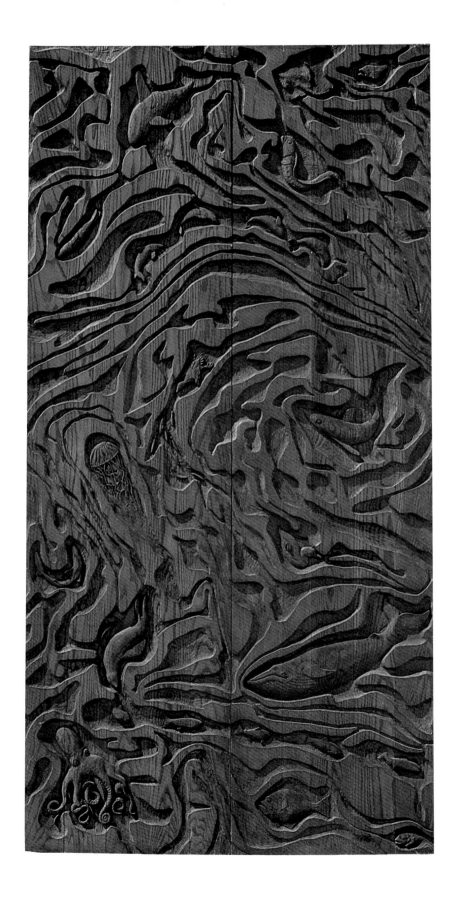

This exhibition undertook to gather outstanding works of northwest coast Indian art from leading museums and private collections of North America and place them in an art context. The project was close to Reid's heart and he threw himself into it with enthusiasm, doing research, assisting in the selection process, designing a splendid poster and banner based on the famed Tlingit partition screen in the Denver Art Museum, contributing an essay to the catalogue and helping with the installation. Allowing the stature and uniqueness of his ancestors' art to reveal itself in a twentieth-century public setting, in an art rather than an anthropological context, was for him an important way of doing them honour.

The first in the line of spectacular gold boxes he would produce, one with a three-dimensional eagle on its cover, was exhibited in the Canadian Pavilion at Montreal's Expo 67. Much of his early jewellery had been in sterling silver, but he had learned by this time that only by working in the more valued gold could he command the prices that would begin to bring him a reasonable return for his work. A Canada Council senior grant in 1968 enabled him to go to London where he further honed his goldsmithing techniques, using the facilities of the Central School of Design. There, perhaps prompted by the physical distance he had put between himself and his Haida roots, he produced an ambitious gold and diamond necklace of contemporary design. A technical tour de force, it consists of a lower course of small gold pyramids, superimposed by a network of fine gold wire sections set with small diamonds at the joints and larger ones scattered among the intersections. Together the two form a flexible circle fitting the neck, and a central detachable section can function separately as a brooch. Although the piece has no visible connection with the Haida tradition, Reid points out that the notion of dual presences occupying the same space at the same time, a notion his ancestors had no problem in presenting in their art, was one that had also intrigued him for some time. He gave it a contemporary expression in this necklace with its two components — the wire "theme" and the pyramid "theme" — which are theoretically capable of separation. He would make several other contemporary pieces in the next year or so, a direction which had long attracted him but which he was not to pursue. For one thing, to be successful in a non-Indian jewellery market, he felt he would have needed an establishment — a place in which to exhibit and a collection to show — and he had no capital. Probably more important, he doubts he "would have been happy making pretty baubles for pretty people," whereas jewellery with Haida designs at least had a connection with the later phase of the tradition (in the form of the bracelets) through which he in turn was connected.

Reid at his jeweller's bench in the
Pender Street workshop working on
a miniature ivory totem pole, c. 1963

Bill Reid and Robert Davidson
(wearing head-dresses and blankets)
with Audrey Hawthorn (left) and
Mayor Drapeau at
''Man and his World,''
Montreal 1970
Photograph: U.B.C. Extension
Department

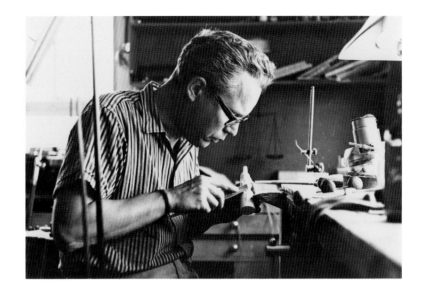

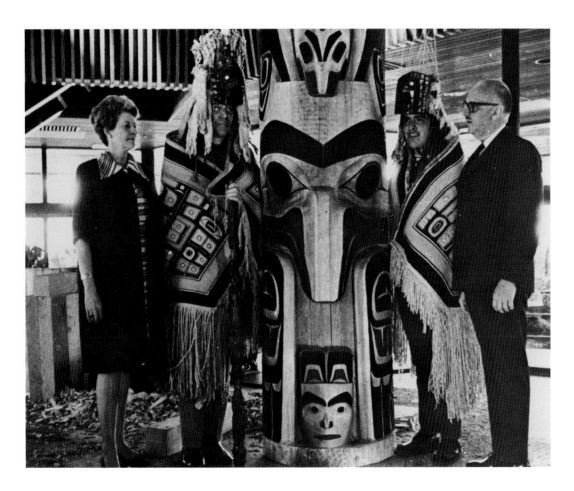

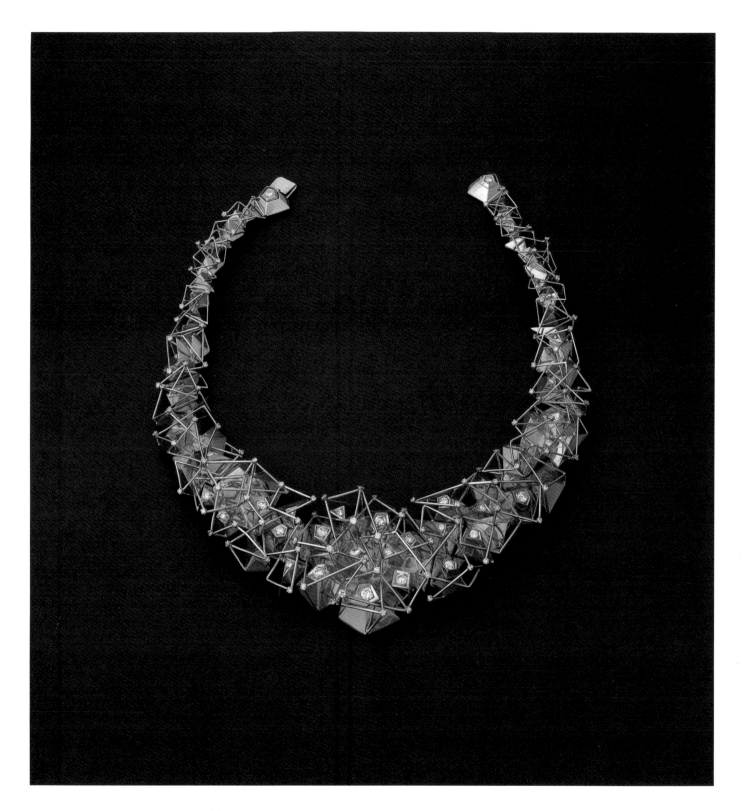

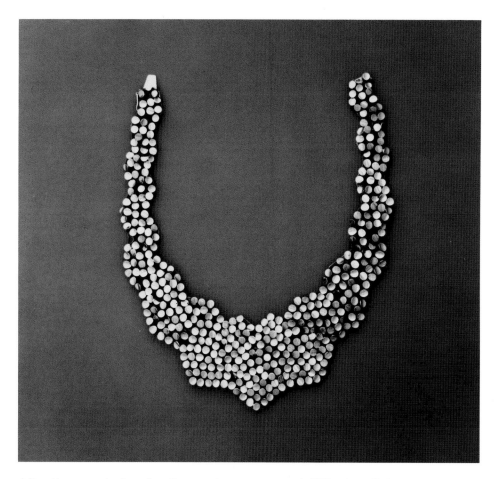

Gold and Diamond Necklace 1969
Detachable centre section can be worn
separately as a brooch
18 cm diameter

Silver and White Gold Necklace 1972
13 cm diameter

After the year in London the west coast seemed difficult to fit into again; he had no place to go to, no family he was now close to; he was tired of Vancouver, and half-tired of "the Indian thing." He moved to Montreal, thinking of it as a buffer midway between Vancouver and Europe, and set up a workshop. During the next three very productive years there he made several of the outstanding pieces of his career, for curiously the distance separating the west coast from Montreal seemed to clarify and intensify his Indian inspiration. Among these were the tiny boxwood carving illustrating the Haida myth in which the Raven discovers mankind in a giant clamshell, the progenitor of the large-scale sculpture which now occupies a special position in the Museum of Anthropology at UBC in Vancouver; a gold-lidded container surmounted by a whale in the round which in its turn has spawned the large bronze work for the Vancouver Aquarium; and, most technically ambitious of all, his small precious metal vessels, the gold-footed casket surmounted by a three-dimensional group of the Bear Mother suckling her twin cubs which was subsequently purchased by the National Museum of Canada.

45

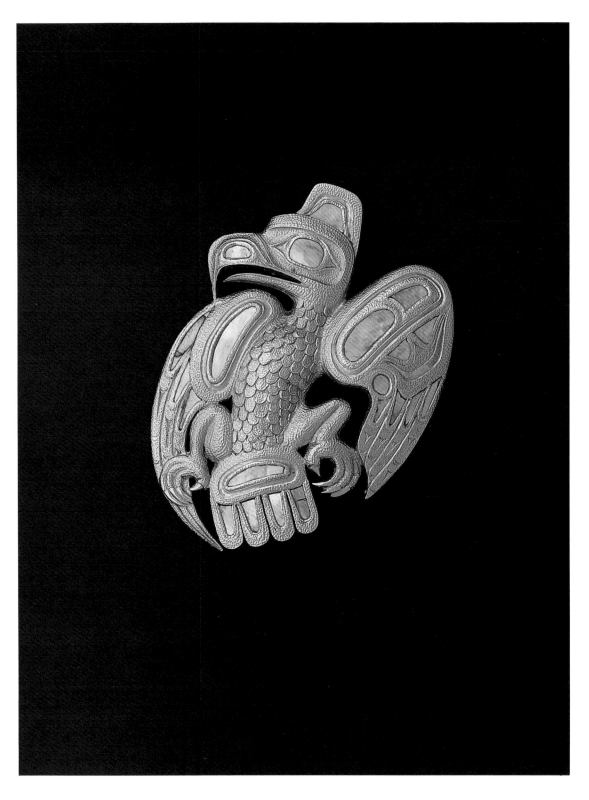

Gold Brooch with Abalone inlay
Eagle design 1970
6.5 cm long, 4.7 cm wide

Gold Brooch with Abalone inlay
Hawk design 1971
Oval, 5.8 cm long, 5.4 cm wide

Gold Earrings with Abalone inlay
Killer Whale design 1972
2.8 cm long

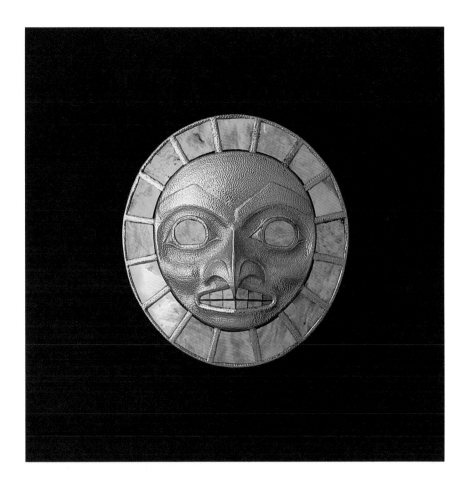

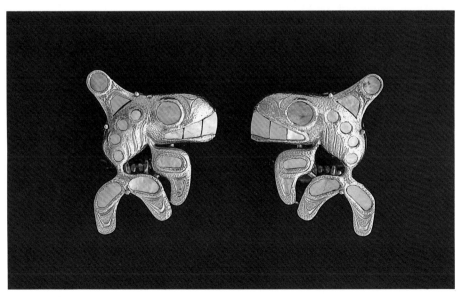

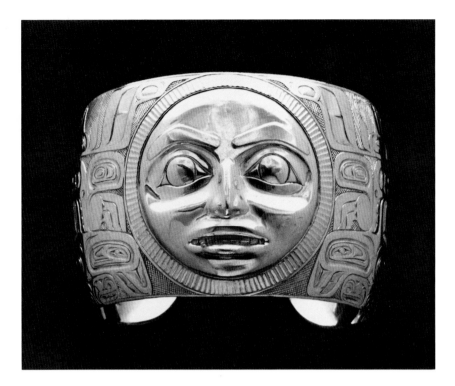

In Montreal too, after an aborted first beginning, he finally produced the text for a book of Adelaide de Menil's photographs of the old crumbling poles slowly returning to the earth from which they originally sprang. He had been approached to undertake such an assignment in the late sixties when he met Miss de Menil and the anthropologist Ted Carpenter on the west coast, but then, about to go to England, he was not particularly interested in what he understood was to be a coffee-table book. However, the offer repeated when he was penniless in Montreal proved to be more attractive. Reid, who writes frequently with passionate lyricism and always with apparent ease and simplicity, often seems to need a crisis situation to get started. He recalls a week or ten days "locked up in a flea-bag hotel in New York" where he was expected to produce a manuscript. After writing a few paragraphs but really getting nowhere, he gave up and returned to Montreal. Finally, while an exhibition of the photographs to appear in the book was being prepared for the Amon Carter Museum in Fort Worth, Texas, Reid received another telephone call from Carpenter. The situation had apparently reached a point of sufficient desperation to release the flow of words, and Reid wrote the whole text in about two hours, dictating it over the telephone. It appeared as the book *Out of the Silence*, published in 1971. Responding to the powerful poetic impact of Reid's solemn bardic prose, Bill Holm was moved to say of the text, "Who but a shaman could write the four words — Oh the cedar tree — and make me cry."

Gold Bracelet
Design refers to the
Nanasimget story 1974
4.2 cm wide

Why did Bill leave Montreal, a city he really liked and where by this time his adopted son had joined him, to return to Vancouver in 1972? There was the prospect of the large Raven sculpture, a project whose materialization at that time appeared imminent, and no doubt there was the tug of the west coast which in so many ways, tangible and intangible, provided him and his work with the ambience of support it could have in no other place. He would produce no further ambitious work of contemporary design, none that in some way did not draw on the old traditional art, once he left Montreal.

For a time he shared working space as well as the mutual admiration and friendship that began years before, and still continues, with Toni Cavelti, a Vancouver jewellery-designer-craftsman of Swiss origin. Cavelti's experience in the international field of fine metal-working gives weight to his opinion that Reid may be compared with any of the European masters of gold- or silversmithing, starting with Cellini and Fabergé and continuing to the present. Sometimes Bill thinks he might have been happy working in some kind of partnership with Toni, whose "top flight" mechanical ability and merchandising methods he admires enormously. Successful merchandising involves a talent which Reid admits to not possessing, but surprisingly he also says, even today with all the evidence to the contrary, that "starting late, he never had confidence in his ability as a maker," and when he once jokingly asked Toni for a job, the latter's reply "any time" pleased him greatly.

It was again Ted Carpenter who invited Reid's participation, this time along with that of Bill Holm, in a book published in conjunction with a northwest coast Indian art exhibition at Rice University, Houston, in 1975. Called *Form and Freedom,* it is a beautiful and unusual book in the form of an illustrated dialogue. In it Reid and Holm present to each other masks, pipes, boxes, shamanic charms and other objects, one after another, bringing their separate but parallel experience and sensibility to bear in an illuminating informal discussion. On the whole Reid derives most satisfaction from those projects which maximize his role as fully involved "maker." Two earlier commissions for large works, the Haida village at UBC and the cedar screen for the Provincial Museum in Victoria, had satisfied that condition even though the former drew him into companionable working with other carvers.

He had been troubled for some years by spinal problems and in 1973 it was discovered that he had Parkinson's disease. Looking at his production since that time it would scarcely appear that his increasingly frail health has had any limiting effect. The shaking of hands and arms characteristic of Parkinson's can be controlled temporarily by exerting the muscles involved, and Reid these days is rarely to be seen in repose without something in his hands against which to exert pressure — a tool handle, a wooden spoon or a set of elegant salad servers — on which he is quietly carving away.

49

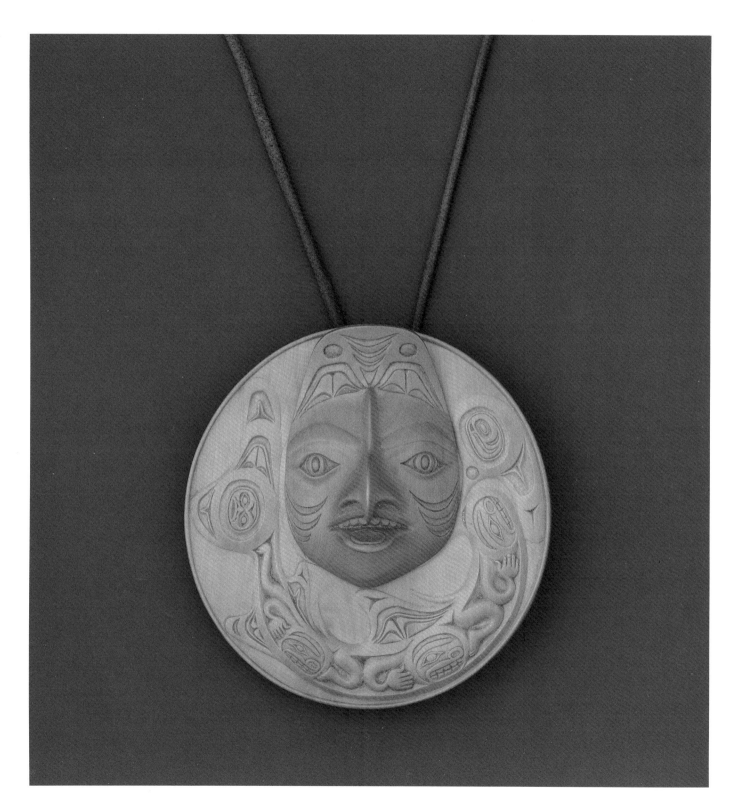

He has continued to make jewellery, though in less profusion than in the early years, preferring to concentrate on major pieces such as the astonishing transformation gold pendant of the Dogfish and the Dogfish Woman with its flexible chain made of intricately shaped sections. Its prototype was a version he made in 1980 for his present wife Martine in boxwood, a material he has come to love for its fine grain and density which can take the most detailed and intricate carving. The head of the Dogfish Woman in the centre is a separate section which flips up (and can be removed to be worn separately), revealing underneath her mythical alter-ego.

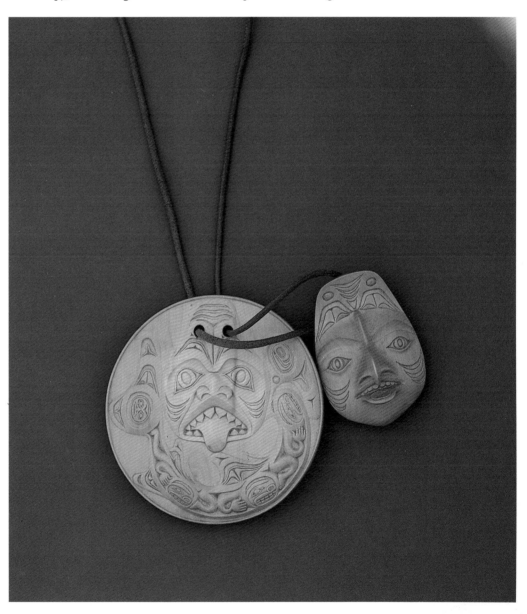

Boxwood ''Transformation''
Pendant with detachable ''mask''
Dogfish Woman design 1982
8 cm diameter;
mask head: 5.5 cm long

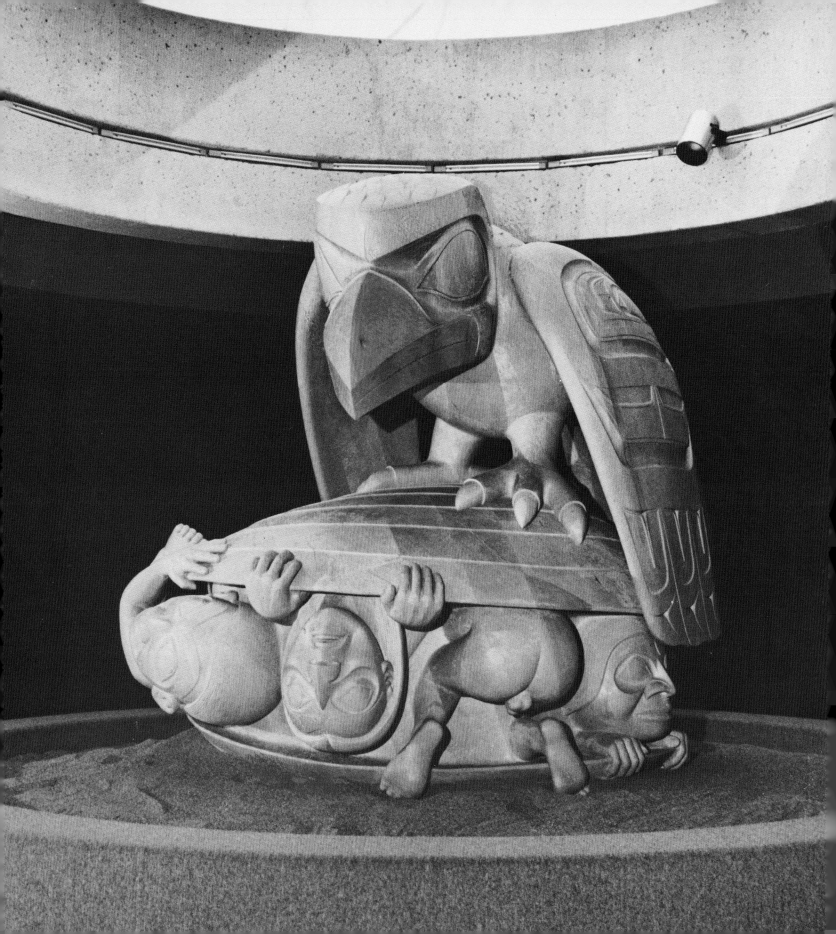

The larger commissions that have been coming his way in recent years have had, both by their nature and because of his diminished strength and resistance, to become joint efforts under his control though he still does as much of the direct work as he can. Walter Koerner, a retired Vancouver industrialist, had long been interested in the west coast Indian heritage; he had partially funded the 1958 trip to the Charlottes to rescue decaying poles, and his collection of native work is now at the Museum of Anthropology at UBC. An early patron and one of the most ardent collectors of Reid's finest gold pieces, he had seen the small boxwood Raven carving in Montreal and leapt at Reid's suggestion that a larger version might be possible. He promptly conceived the notion that Arthur Erickson should design a special space for such a work in the new Museum of Anthropology, by that time in the planning stages. Although Reid returned to the coast in 1973 with that task in mind, it was not to be accomplished for another ten years. The 3.05-metre cube of cedar he requested was almost impossible to obtain and when located and transported proved to be too flawed for use. Finally a solution was found; a series of kiln-dried sections were laminated to form a block of the required size. Since by this time he had become involved in carving a pole for Skidegate, Reid hired Vancouver sculptor George Norris who for two years worked at the preliminary stages, first making an intermediate scale model in clay, which he cast in plaster, and from that proceeding to rough in the large sculpture in wood. A number of native carvers also worked on the project, including Reggie Davidson (a brother of Robert) and Jimmie Hart, both descendants of Charles Edenshaw — a fact which pleased Bill — and Gary Edenshaw of no relation to the famous carver. George Rammell, a prodigious and ingenious worker and a sculptor in his own right, was called in during the later stages to work on the emerging little humans, and towards the end Bill himself did some of the finishing carving. Koerner's role both in subsidizing the work and seeing it through all its difficulties to the finish was vital.

The Raven and the First Men, seen by the thousands of visitors to the Museum, is today the single work by which Reid is most widely known. Then there have been the two outdoor commissions, the Killer Whale, which rises from its own pool outside the Vancouver Aquarium in Vancouver's Stanley Park, and the Mythic Messengers, commissioned by Teleglobe Canada for its building in Burnaby, B.C., a municipality adjoining Vancouver. Both of these bronze works were ventures not only in design but also into technical areas where Reid had not embarked before, that is, large-scale casting requiring the preparation of scale models, the making of sectional moulds, the actual casting at a foundry capable of handling such large works, and finally the finishing. Reid likes to think that his Haida ancestors, who showed themselves so adaptable to new techniques and materials, would be entirely sympathetic to the extension of his practice beyond the traditional wood.

Cedar Sculpture
The Raven and the First Men
Completed 1983
University of British Columbia,
Museum of Anthropology

On most of his large work of the past ten years, whatever helpers have come and gone, he has had the invaluable assistance of George Rammell, who is gifted with the technical ingenuity and engineering skills Reid so admires. The 5.5-metre canoe and its prototype model, commissioned by the Museum of Anthropology and the Expo 86 Corporation, was a project that demanded Reid's most intimate participation. Working once again in his beloved cedar, he was fulfilling a long-held dream.

One large work, however, was not commissioned — the totem pole, raised with ceremony in June of 1978, that he made for his mother's village of Skidegate. It was designed for a position in front of the new Band Council Administration building which is constructed in the traditional Haida style. There above the pebbly beach around which the modest houses of the present village cluster, it stands looking out to sea. Bill remembers that his grandfather's little one-room workshop occupied that very location. A few yards away is the leaning and rotted pole, the sole remaining one of the long row which used to stand between the houses and the sea.

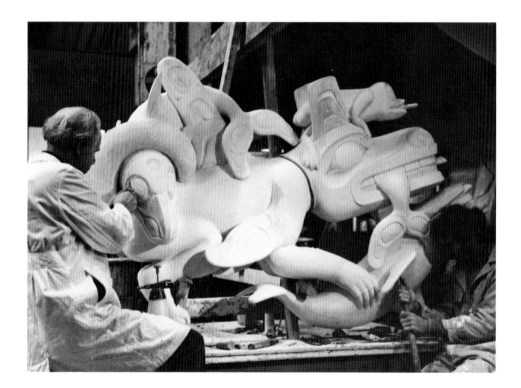

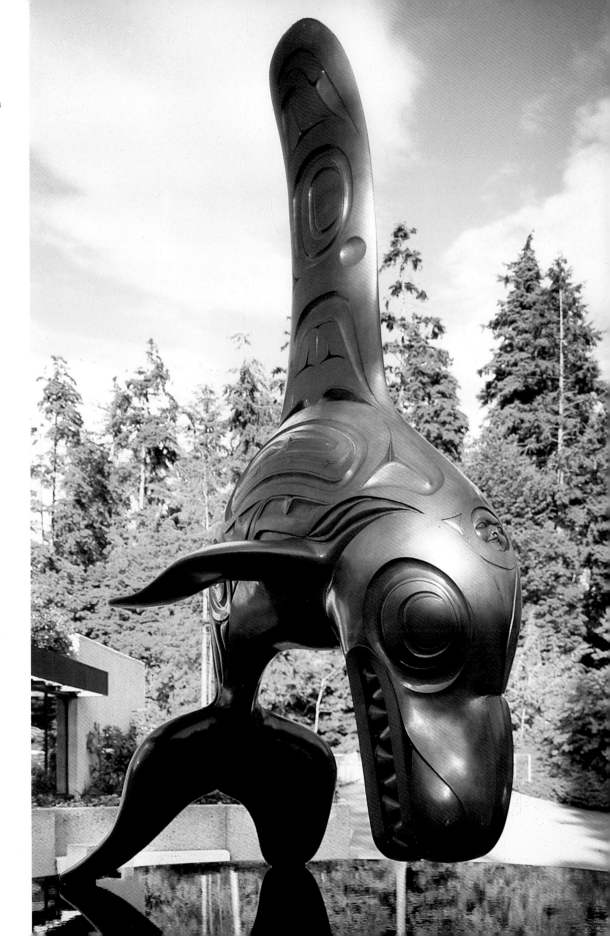

Reid and George Rammell at work on the plaster model for a section of *Mythic Messengers* in Reid's studio on Granville Island, Vancouver

Killer Whale
Bronze, completed 1984
5.5 m high
Vancouver Public Aquarium, Stanley Park, Vancouver

Always a little troubled to think he was making a living by "flogging the bones of his ancestors," he wanted to repay some of his debt to them and to provide some tangible recognition of his gratitude. Besides, he felt the village should not be without a pole. Although he would have liked to donate his skills and services, he felt that the pole would have more meaning for the villagers if the community indicated some commitment to it by contributing to expenses. But the making of voluntary cash subscriptions was not built into the community consciousness, and in the end the grant money he would have preferred to avoid was resorted to. He designed the pole and carved it together with Gary Edenshaw, and with some assistance from Robert Davidson, Gerry Marks and Joe David. Living in a trailer not too far from the pole's destined location, he improvised a temporary workshed shelter with a plastic covering and began the task which would take about nine months, spread over two years, to complete.

Not much interest was shown by the residents of Skidegate during the making of the pole, but the community rallied to arrange a great celebration for the pole-raising day. There was a dinner served to 1500 guests, both native and non-native, and a great deal of appreciative speech-making. Temporarily at least Bill could feel that he was *living* a part of his heritage, not just contacting it through his art. That day has been celebrated now for each of the succeeding seven years as a "Skidegate pole-raising day," a community occasion the likes of which had not happened in a long time. Perhaps, Bill muses, his pole has brought the village "back into time."

The carving of the pole for Skidegate is associated with a happy change in Bill's personal life. Studies in northwest coast anthropology had brought Martine de Widerspoch-Thor, a French student of Claude Lévi-Strauss, to Vancouver from Paris in the mid-1970s. As a candidate for a doctorate in anthropology at UBC she had spent a year and a half among the Kwakiutl at Fort Rupert, Alert Bay, Campbell River and other centres on northern Vancouver Island. She had studied Kwakwala, the language of the Kwakiutl people, acquiring some understanding of it and a limited ability to speak it, but when she met Bill through Wilson Duff, English was still a tongue in which she had trouble communicating. She spent most of the summer with him in the Charlottes when he began work on the pole, a summer they both remember as idyllic. They have been together ever since, and were married in 1981, a liaison obviously wonderfully satisfying to Bill, and incidentally pleasing to his mother, whose taste for social and intellectual sophistication and elegance were fully gratified in Martine. Mrs. Reid died in a nursing hospital in Vancouver in the spring of 1985 at the age of 90. The oldest child of the family, who had shown her determination and strength of character at an early age, was obviously the most tenacious, having outlived all her brothers and sisters.

Reid in the work shed at Skidegate
in 1978 working on the pole

Sophie Reid, Bill's mother
as an older woman

Bill and Martine in 1978 in Skidegate
at the time of the pole-raising

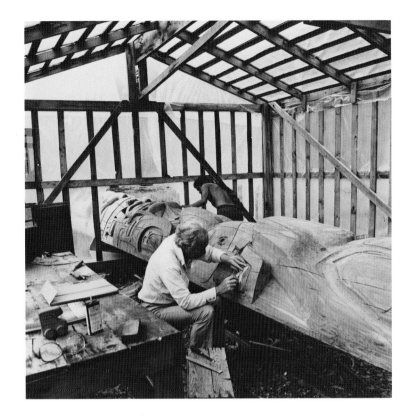

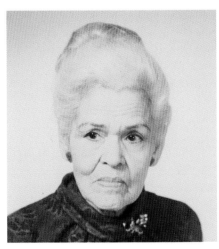

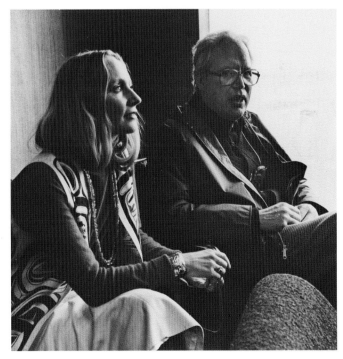

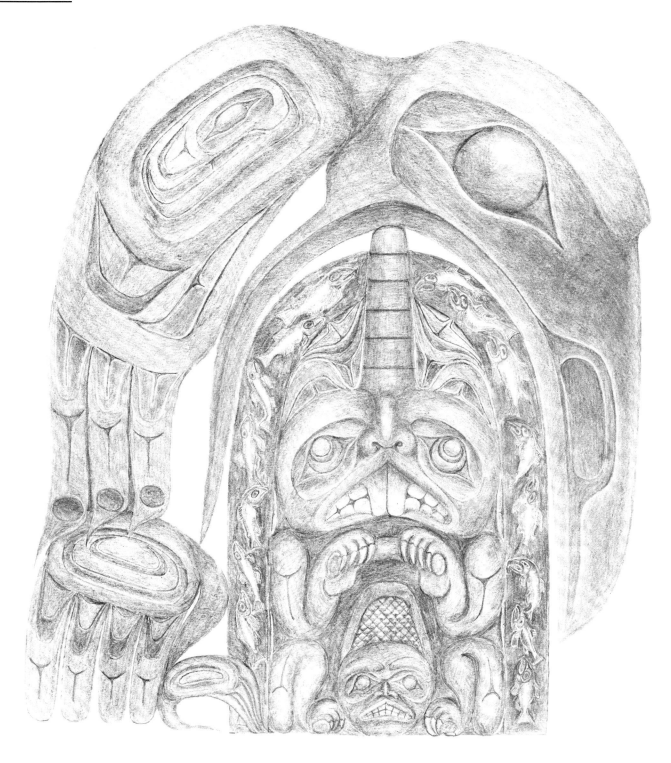

The idea for the book *The Raven Steals the Light,* published in 1984, grew out of the set of drawings that Reid had done as chapter headings for George MacDonald's 1983 book on Haida villages, *Haida Monumental Art.* These he decided to supplement with ten additional drawings to constitute a more substantial group for exhibition in Vancouver. He called on his favoured mythic characters and allowed them to settle into narrative configurations appropriate to the stories he had lived with so long — the Bear Mother and her husband, the Raven and the First Men, the Raven with a Broken Beak, Nanasimget and his Wife, and so on up to ten subjects. He had already written an engagingly told story of The Raven and the First Humans in connection with his large sculpture at the Museum of Anthropology, which had been published in their Museum Notes; now he went on to provide stories to accompany several other drawings in the exhibition. A publication based on this combination seemed the logical next step, but when production deadlines loomed Reid was preoccupied with other projects, and four drawings remained without their stories. He wrote an eloquent apologia to replace the missing tenth and last story in the book, that on the Dogfish Woman, while poet and designer Robert Bringhurst, editor of the project, ended up writing the three others.

Reid first heard some of the old stories from his father's great friend Henry Young, whom he first met when Young was in his eighties and he was a twenty-year-old youth, and it was to him that Reid dedicated the book. Reid points out that Young would have had to learn the stories word by word, for there was a very conservative tradition in the preservation of myth among the Haida, even though variation was bound to creep in over time. The stories in this book, he wants it made clear, are not entirely based on the conventional sources: he simply "took the bones from those sources, then fleshed them out and made them more lively." These stories therefore are to be taken as his interpretation, and he is hopeful that what he has done with them is not inconsistent with the long process of change they had already undergone. On a recent trip to Skidegate he visited Henry Young's daughter and was relieved to find that she was not displeased with his retellings. Still, when he hears that his versions are turning up as scholarly sources in students' term papers, he is naturally a little nonplussed. The myths are in fact written in a simple storyteller's oral style that calls for them to be read aloud, and they have a wit and a narrative structure that makes them appealing to modern ears. The tonalities and ancient resonances of the stories of Young and Mungo Martin, which Bill heard as a young man, still ring in his ears; and they and his enduring passion for ballads, sung or recited, and for lyrical poetry are all layered and fused in these tales.

Tributes and awards have come Reid's way in recent years: honorary degrees from five Canadian universities, the Molson award, the Diplôme d'honneur from the Canadian Conference of the Arts, the Saidye Bronfman Award for Excellence in the Crafts, enconiums from such distinguished persons as the world-famed French anthropologist Claude Lévi-Strauss, the declaration of his sixty-fifth birthday by the mayor of Vancouver as Bill Reid Day. The list of honours continues to grow.

Today in his mid-sixties, a strong man with a progressively enfeebling disease, illness is a large part of his existence. "My life is shared with Dr. Parkinson these days," he will say after a bad spell, "and unfortunately he decided to pay me a visit last night," calling on his unexhausted well of humour to help him through. And so he carries on with incredible courage and spirit, when his health permits travel flying off to give a paper in New York or San Francisco or Toronto, or going "one last time" to his beloved Queen Charlottes, and always in between back at work in his shop on Granville Island — designing, carving, drawing, polishing. To his many friends and acquaintances he is still the urbane and sophisticated man, quietly witty, often melancholy, an avid listener to classical music, highly literary and much given to apt quotation, frequently of poetry. He is not a talkative person, but in conversation he always projects intelligence.

He has a quality of mind and presence that make people see him as *special,* as being destined and wise, and they rightly attribute his tendency to gentle pronunciamento to the outward manifestation of a mind that is constantly engaged in its own dialogue on problems of human concern. In his bad moments, when the medication on which he is dependent seems to be losing its power, he schemes with a friend, planning with dark mock-heroic glee how his body should be returned to feed the sea creatures at Tow Hill on the northwestern arm of Graham Island where the Raven started all that "funny business" aeons ago. This is not morbid indulgence. It is the just and poetic recognition of a man who has travelled the longest of all routes, the one in search of himself — including in his case his cultural location — and who, having known the world, has found his home. He has made his peace with the past; returning from a trip to the Charlottes last summer he announced that "the ghosts have left Tanu." Today the contradictions are gone; he is proud that part of him is Indian and reacts as one, and that that part is not in conflict with his Canadian, North American or global being. Bill Reid has truly "walked forward into the past."

Reid May 1986, with Billy Stevens on left and nearly finished canoe in background.

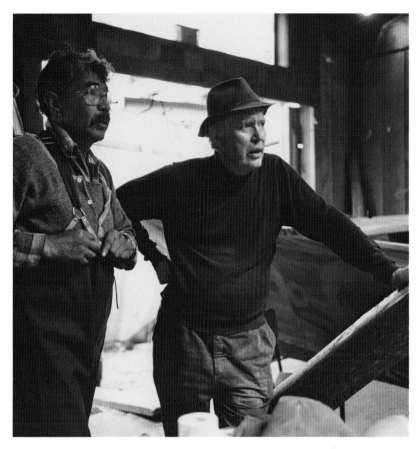

1 *Haida Monumental Art: Villages of the Queen Charlotte Islands* (Vancouver, B.C.: University of British Columbia Press, 1983), pp. 87–100.

2 New York: Dover Publications, 1955, pp. 71, 158, 159, 193, 201, 212, 275.

3 Ottawa: National Museum of Canada, Bulletin 139 (Anthropological Series no. 38), 1957.

4 *Bill Reid: A Retrospective Exhibition.* (Vancouver, B.C.: Vancouver Art Gallery, 1974), n.p.

5 Bill still has in mind the writing of a children's story about the creatures on that pole. In response to the Raven's bell-like call — special among that bird's repertoire of sound — they decide to go back to the Charlottes and see what is going on there. They make their way across the country — birds by air, sea creatures by various waterways, earth creatures overland — to Tanu, only to find the people and most traces of them gone. What they see of the settled parts of the Islands does not please them either, so they decide to return to the Museum for another hundred years. When the museum opens next morning, they are back in their usual places on the pole.

6 *Arts of the Raven: Masterworks by the Northwest Coast Indian* (Vancouver, B.C.: Vancouver Art Gallery, 1967), n.p.

7 Toronto: McClelland & Stewart, 1966.

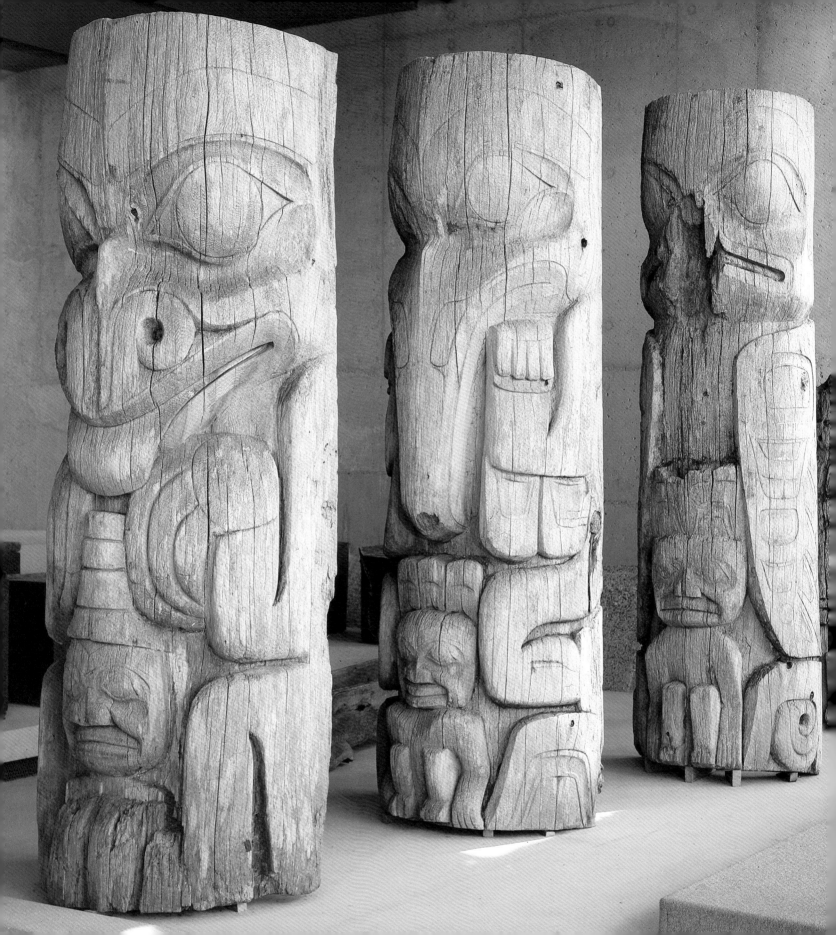

LOOKING BACKWARD

Bill Reid is a bridge figure, that is, someone who must be seen against a background (where, in his case, virtually no middle ground exists) of the past, and of a future just starting to be sketched in. We cannot understand him if we do not make the attempt to grasp in our present terms, as he has had to do, that artistic past to which he has anchored his future. We too must first look backward.

We can never know fully what the vast array of objects we now call art meant to their prehistoric Indian makers and users, but that does not prevent us from picking up messages from them across the missing years with our own sensibility, culturally conditioned as it must be. The messages are bound to be grossly incomplete, and we will interpret them in terms of our own attitudes and experience, but their impact on us cannot be denied. And should they turn out to have meaning for us, then perhaps we have tapped a current strong enough to have retained its vitality, despite the altered terrain through which it has had to make its way.

There are, to be sure, many difficulties. We have to contend with the aura of sentiment and association in which our own need has enveloped the whole Indian past: a compound of many things including guilt for the insensitive suppression of native culture, and an aching nostalgia for the almost unimaginable times to which these objects belong, when men had broken neither their deep bond with the natural world nor with that of the spirits. The art seduces with its patina of age — figuratively, like many things from the past, and literally in its weathered wood, muted forms, faded paint, eroded textures. Then there is the vast accumulation of information about both the culture and the art it produced, fascinating in its detail and bewildering in its abundance and the complexity it reveals. On it we rely for any extension of our response into the fabric of the old life, and for resonance, but it can as often deflect our vision from its object as art as it can illuminate. Still, we should be able to penetrate the thickness of surrounding erudition and romantic aura and, while denying neither, yet holding all our information at the ready, make direct contact with the art — that is to say, approach it as an experiencer of art, not as anthropologist or art historian.

Section of a Haida House Frontal Pole from the Village of Tanu, Queen Charlotte Islands. Mid-nineteenth century. Pole at left, Bears and Human with ringed hat University of British Columbia, Museum of Anthropology [A 50000 d]

63

The art under discussion was produced by people inhabiting a vast area of the west coast of North America stretching from the Gulf of Alaska to the southern tip of Vancouver Island, but numbering, it is estimated, no more than 100,000 to 150,000 at the time of their greatest cultural vitality in the mid-nineteenth century. We have to imagine the "great invention" of this art as taking place over some unmeasured stretch of the past, for by the time it became known to the outside world there was a central pattern in existence, ready made as it were, whose variations spin off from a clearly identified core of sensibility and configuration. We can assume a multitude of small changes and developments by which this paradigm came about, but our first general impression is of an established, stable and continuing mode which the individual Indian artist, who lived and breathed the cultural air in which the art came into existence, had no need to reinvent, only to restate — to reaffirm in his own act of art. We see more continuity than change, more similarity than difference. Still, while the seven major linguistic groups who together make up the larger Indian culture of this area do have many cultural and artistic features in common, the northern tribal grouping — the Haida of the Queen Charlotte Islands, the Tlingit of the Gulf of Alaska region, the Tsimshian of the Nass and Skeena rivers area and the Bella Bella (or northern Kwakiutl) who lived in an area south of the Tsimshian — constitute a special subdivision. Each of these groups spoke different languages, and all developed stylistic and expressive characteristics in their art. But compared to the more southerly tribes — the southern Kwakiutl, the West Coast (Nootka) and the Salish — the northern tribes form a coherent group, sharing common characteristics rather than revealing distinct differences. In fact, experts are often unable to identify the particular origin of old northern pieces which have no documentation, even though their northernness is not in dispute. Frequently scholars have only stylistic details or mannerisms to guide them, such as the treatment of an eyelid or the profile of a nose. It is primarily in the context of the northern art that Reid, himself of Haida connection, is to be seen, and in the discussion which follows and throughout the book, unless otherwise stated, the reference to northwest coast Indian art is primarily to that of the northern peoples.

The art has its own variety — variety in scale (from the great houses, canoes or poles to the shaman's tiny charm); variety in material (the all-important wood, but also metal, stone, horn, ivory and wool); variety of function (ceremonial and ritual pieces, such as totem poles and masks and those which combined ceremonial and practical function, such as chests and blankets). Two main types of form are immediately distinguishable: three-dimensional sculptural forms, as in house posts or totem poles; and, as in the case of painted house screens or relief-carved and painted boxes or chests, what is generally referred to as "flat design." The term *design* is used here not to suggest an expressionless solution to a given problem or mere filling of a

64

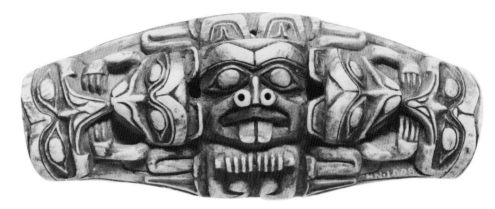

given space but to refer to imagery which, for purposes of discussion, can be separated from the form to which it adheres.

Still, despite this great variety, the body of northerly west coast Indian objects bears the indelible imprint of a particular people in a particular place. And in general those objects deliver the same overall expressive impact. That impact derives from two main aspects of the art: there is the world proposed by the formal concept, a world so contained, so controlled, so immobile, so arrested and austere, so taut with repressed energy; and there is the omnipresence of a throng of compounded interlocking creatures, all eyes, all mouths full of tongues and great rows of teeth, who constitute a seething, pressing presence within that first world. Together they form a third aspect: they assert a dichotomy — the forces that contain, the spirit that would break out — an underlying theme of contained opposition which is reiterated on various levels, in any number of ways, throughout the art.

THE CONTAINING FORMAL WORLD

To recall the animal paintings of the Lascaux caves with their quality of visual immediacy is to be reminded that not all primal people create a formalized art — many do, but not all. The coastal Indians' art, particularly that of the northerly people, is so formalized as to appear to have been based on a set of rules and conventions formulated in some unknown past and thereafter serving as a collective model from which surface changes could be made while leaving the inner form matrix intact. Formalization within the creative process in itself announces the priority of the cognitive ordering mind over the spontaneous, intuitive or emotive mind, which is more apt to express itself in open movement or gesture. Formalization, in Indian art as elsewhere, does not, of course, reflect an absence of those human qualities of spontaneity or personal freedom in artists as individuals, but relates rather to the particular role their society gave them to fulfill, and to the fact that, as artists, they were working out of their experience as members of a closely bound cultural group and not as individuals expressing personal emotions and sensibilities.

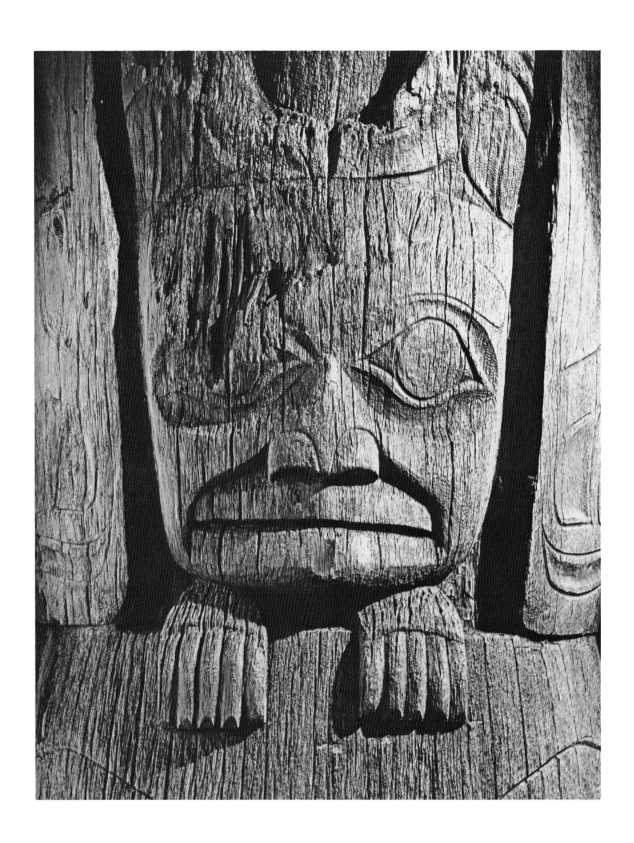

We see at once that it is a highly formalized art, one that is ordered and controlled, and based on some concept of reality other than that of the external temporal world of our everyday vision. That formality moreover is of a consistent, pervasive character, one qualifying the major character of the overall form within which the effective oppositions and tensions can be set up. The central paradigm has to do with qualities of *containment, confinement, enclosure, stability*, which in turn embrace particular characteristics such as symmetry, frontality, a preoccupation with surface rather than depth.

The traditional society required a surprisingly large number of its objects for ceremonial and ritual purposes (art objects as we think of them) to be literally containers: the splendid wooden chests, lidded and unlidded; ceremonial food vessels, from large wooden feast dishes to bowls of wood or horn for holding oil; spoons with elaborately carved handles; the huge rectangular communal houses which were given names and which, in a metaphysical way scarcely comprehensible in a modern society's understanding of houses, "contained" the people and the ceremonies that bound them together. There are the woven Chilkat blankets, made not to be spread out flat in a museum case but to enclose, to "contain" the wearer like a different skin, just as in the myths the salmon can don his human skin when he leaves his watery domain. There are the all-powerful masks which in covering the head or face confer on the wearer another identity. There is that wonderful mobile container, the dugout canoe. Even the shaman's rattle frequently takes the form of a container. These containers, which functioned in a practical and symbolic way, are for us also expressive forms in themselves as *forms* embodying the idea of holding — whether offering openly, or protecting or confining tightly — a thing which both guards and gives shape and identity to its contents.

That the containing form seems to have had some deeply interiorized meaning for the society, and not simply an expressive meaning for us, is suggested not only by its frequent ceremonial use but also by its special status as an object to which elaborate artistic effort was devoted through the addition of imagery carved, beaten, painted or woven into, onto or out of the underlying form. But designs in coastal Indian art do not exist in a vacuum, that is, apart from the containers whose elemental containing-meaning they echo, and to which they add other, more specific meanings having to do with mythic belief. For instance, the animal-creature-spirit encoded into the carved or painted front, back and perhaps sides of a wooden chest can be seen by our western eyes long conditioned to two-dimensional pictorial experience as very handsome separate panels. They are in fact often displayed in museums so that only the front panel can be seen. But to do so is to separate them from their prior meaning, in which the animal-creature referred to and represented is also container; it is also the skin, another form of container welded to and become that which is the box.

Detail of Haida Totem Pole
University of British Columbia
Museum of Anthropology
(A50002)

The idea of container is deeply woven into the fabric of the culture beyond the field of art, a fact affirmed by ethnologist William Sturtevant who points out that there is a single Tlingit word to convey the meanings of "box, coffin, bivalve, shell, womb, outside, opposite moiety — in short, container — [which] identifies a key central concept around which Tlingit life and thought can be seen to have been organized. The notion is essential to the Raven myth that explains the creation of the present order of the world, it is crucial to the life career of individual Tlingits, it elucidates the structure of Tlingit social groups, and it typifies the artificial objects with which and in which the Tlingit lived."[1]

But the container can also be seen as an appropriate form metaphor applicable to the character of objects even when they are not containers in a literal or functional sense. They belong to the same expressive family; they are "self-contained." The giant cedar tree with protruding branches lopped off becomes relatively compact, a compactness which the carver of the totem or house pole finds suited to his purposes. The straight pole's visual tendency to shoot upward without pause into space is countered by the carver's mode of composition by stacking forms one on top of another, creating horizontal breaks. But the core of the pole is not touched, literally and conceptually; its density, its weight remain unchallenged. The carving is not deep in relation to the diameter of the pole but wraps around it like a thick blanket or skin; beaks, tongues, snouts, tails, legs, paws tuck back in against bodies so as not to break the skin's meaning as that which encloses, clearly demarcating that which is outside from that which is held. Among the Kwakiutl, those theatrical people to the south of the Haida, the forces of restraint and control are not so dominant, and the confining skin is often stretched to the limit or broken by great protruberant heads, wings or beaks. The typical Haida mask prefers a shell of shallow curvature minimally opened up by the features, whereas the Kwakiutl are known for their dramatic transformation masks, or those, for example, of the 'Dsonoqua in which convexities and concavities push and pull at the container "skin" from either side while opened eyes and mouth pierce great holes in it.

The device, most apparent in the two-dimensional designs on boxes or painted skins, of "splitting" animal forms down the centre and spreading the halves out laterally on either side, has been variously interpreted. But surely, among other possible meanings, it can be viewed as a way of making a cloak of the creature, so that it can be "wrapped around," and can serve its containing-enclosing purpose without sacrifice of its frontality. While still in the area of flat design, *framing* might be a more appropriate way of stating the containing principle — determining the area within which the design can work, setting boundaries which the design must reflect and respect.

The horizontal *symmetry* which characterizes so much of the coastal Indian's art (as anyone familiar with the art has observed), the dividing of a composition into answering halves about an implied or clearly stated central axis, can be seen as another way of containment using an internal structure, the axis, rather than the enclosing frame as the device. It is not an invariable rule, and the two halves of a whole are not necessarily always the exact reverse copy of each other. Reid takes pleasure in pointing out the variations in design on the ends of a box, for instance, which at first appear identical but on closer examination — requiring a viewer to move from one end of the box to the other — turn out to incorporate quirky surprises, indications, he is convinced, of the maker's sense of humour, or at least of his individuality. The presence of symmetry as a directing idea nonetheless is strong. Symmetry, it is worth noting, is not used in this art as it is for instance in Byzantine art, to assist in the assigning of status to central and lesser characters; ranking, so vital in the social structure of the Indians, has little reflection in their art. The totem pole serves to declare the position of its owner, but that is a meaning conferred on it by custom and the social structure, and is not revealed in the work itself.

Frontality is another conspicuous component in the formal set. The heads and bodies of creatures on boxes and chests face outward, confronting the observer (though detached parts, like wings or abstracted motifs appear in profile). Poles and house posts in general present forms facing frontally, and backs usually are not carved. The creatures who inhabit these objects obey the dictum: the bear, beaver, wolf or raven turn neither right nor left, nor do they twist about on their inner axis. Within each object and within each creature there exists a gravity-bound, undisturbed core of matter and spirit beyond the reach of time and change. Small shamanic objects like charms sometimes challenge this principle. Does this relate to the fact that the shaman operates in his own realm of spirit power, outside the common constraints?

These formative notions of containing, enclosing, framing, symmetry, frontality together constitute a family, a central set of qualities, which gives powerful expressive tone to the art, qualifying the particular notes that are struck within its framework. They project values of stability as against change, timelessness rather than the moment, corporeity and weight instead of that which is insubstantial and prone to restless movement. They speak of definition, identification — not vagueness, openness, anonymity — a world beyond the small nudges of particular time and place. Such persistently central qualities in the art carry their own message and must represent a cultural imperative, a dictum delivered by a society that required of artists that they represent that message, for it is too strong to suggest merely a set of stylistic habits mechanically repeated. The artist, like other individuals bound together in a tightly integrated society, had no impulse to question its underlying assumptions. It was not in his power (or interest) to step outside those assumptions or to challenge the essential character of the basic model posited by those formal dictates. That this did not deny the artist the possibility of leaving his individual imprint on his work is quite evident, but while the culture remained intact, basic conceptual innovation was pretty well precluded.

Support for this view can be found in the character of the slate (argillite) carving which was introduced into the artistic repertoire after the first quarter of the nineteenth century and which demonstrates some departures from the classic set of the old style. For the most part the objects made in this soft stone were intended not for ceremonial use by Indian people but for exchange with white people, and the intrusion into the culture from outside was now sufficiently felt to be reflected in the art. Not only did new subject matter appear — men with hats and pointed noses and sometimes inset white faces, and their animals and equipment — and was treated with a new degree of naturalism, but there were also new forms — unsmokeable "panel pipes," musical instruments, free-standing figures of white people, miniature "model" totem poles — all small and portable objects which had detached themselves functionally from the culture and become for the first time art in the modern sense. The shallow plate or platter appears as a form for the first time, as though the full-containing of the traditional deep bowl or feast dish was losing its symbolic meaning. At another level of significance, seen very clearly in the panel pipes, is the break in the fundamental formal set of the pieces: unsymmetrical forms, free of containers, presented in profile in a lateral or narrative, rather than frontal, composition. A shift in the culture and a shift in the art form; the old time warp has been disrupted in the new medium.

LIFE WITHIN THE "CONTAINER"

The preceding discussion, approached from the point of view of art, has suggested that the ancient traditional artist worked within basic forms that symbolically represent principles of containment and control. It is what goes on within those basic forms, or frames, acting within and against their authoritarian structures, that creates the life which gives the northern art its particular character.

Wilson Duff, many of whose investigative trial balloons were still afloat at his early death, was interested in cracking the mystery of the *ovoid,* that basic form motif of northwest coast Indian art which is neither circular nor rectangular but combines elements of both. It is most conspicuous in two-dimensional design on flat surfaces, but is also central to three-dimensional sculptural form where its origin in animal forms — heads, eye-sockets, ears,

70

mouths, fists — is more clearly suggested. Peter Macnair, curator of ethnology at the British Columbia Provincial Museum, describes the ovoid as having "steep sides which expand outwards slightly as they flow upward from rounded bottom corners, a gently upward-curving top and usually a slightly concave bottom."[2] The ovoid is, in fact, a simple abstract leitmotif that recurs with infinite variation in proportion, curvature or angle of expansion.

Whatever cultural secrets future anthropologists will find to have been encoded in the ovoid, surely among other meanings is the possibility — no, the certainty, since it is immanent in the form itself — that it is at once the container and the forces energizing it that would break out. The ovoid obeys the primal dicta of symmetry, frontality and containing, but at the same time it is a sprung rhomboid, compressed and held in tension by its swelling sides, whose rounded corners and curving top and bottom form a perimeter of running energy which the Indian artist exploited to the full. This moving perimeter band swells and narrows as it flows, heavier at the top, thinner on the bottom, rounding the corners easily or more abruptly; it is, one might say, bound into its dual function as maker of the containing shape and as carrier of the linear energy. Duff also remarked that the true circle, while almost always implicit in Haida art, is almost never explicit.[3] But then it might be pointed out that the circle is poised, inert and gravity free; it is perfectly contained but has no earthy inner tension and thus was not best suited to this art's purposes.

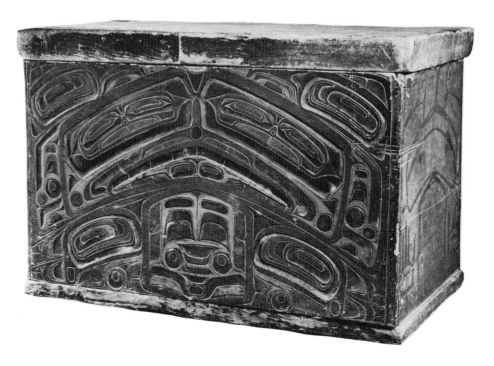

Painted and carved Wooden Chest
Private Collection

The ubiquitous ovoid usually echoes the shape and feel of the larger container which frames it, as in chests and bowls, or Chilkat blankets, or house front designs and screens, and there is no shape, line or form within the composition that is not sympathetic to it, for it contains the essential genetic substance. As though spawned by it are secondary and tertiary forms, and that remarkable system of fluent bands and lines that state the ovoid and subsidiary shapes, moving throughout the whole like an interconnective vascular system, charging the entire design complex with its surge of life without ever violating the overall context of holding and restraint. A formal dialogue is created which takes over the areas on which that system is set in motion. The great works have the integral quality of indivisible wholes: the basic form of the object with the design it bears, and each major or minor line, shape or flourish welded together within the design matrix. The condition of integrity in this art is such as to suggest a state prior to differentiation — or one at least in which differentiation has not advanced very far. Not only do the creatures share the same space (or absence of it), similar attitudes and some characteristics but the forms too have their capacity to resist simple categorization. A curving "line," say, has its own slow sweep, but it also marks the edge of a broad bandlike form, perhaps a brow, to which it belongs, while at the same time it is inseparable from the reverse shape it contours on its other side. There are no holes, no rents, in the fabric of this design when it has been well made.

Reid, in *Islands at the Edge,* pays tribute to the style of his ancestors: "the heraldic art which they developed stands alone among the arts of the world in its concept of the formline, one of the most intellectually refined and aesthetically powerful systems of expression, a feat of the imagination that truly deserves to be called unique."[4] He, as everyone now does, employs Bill Holm's term *formline,*[5] using it to designate the whole elaborate system of shapes, broad and thin curving bands and lines, by means of which the Indian artist filled and animated his given space. It would be hard to think of a more comprehensive term even though to the uninitiated the word *line* does not evoke the broad flat curving and tapering forms that are so distinctive in the style. Nor does it include the notion of containment which the ovoid carries as part of its message — the necessary partner/opponent in the stylistic and expressive equation. Reid likes to speculate on the style's evolution, finding its genesis in the carcass of a dogfish, or in the plan view of a Haida canoe. Or he makes a series of diagrammatic drawings, starting with a broad, straight line with tapered ends and working through a series of curved line-forms and U-shapes until closure and the ovoid are attained. Perhaps a stronger argument exists for seeing the evolution in reverse order, commencing with the ovoid, the paradigmatic form in which so much of the culture is symbolized and sublimed, a form which one imagines having been shaped with great pressure in some early aesthetic forge. And from this core the formline system develops its life-giving elaborations.

Whatever the evolutionary story, herein indeed lies the essence of the overall expressive impact of northern coastal art: the controlling, restraining, containing imperative in tension with the forces that would break out. This might seem a truism, as applicable to life as it is to most art, but in fact it is rarely obvious in the daily confusion of life and not necessarily conspicuous in art. In Indian art, particularly that of the northern people, and perhaps strongest of all in the Haida, it is stated with the force and clarity of truth — that which is. The two sides of the duality are presented as felt qualities, not as ideas. And the balance stated is very clear: the controlling elements are ascendant; order and stability are maintained.

This central dialectic is in the area of the two-dimensional art developed and elaborated as a pre-eminently formal statement, especially in painted compositions, however intricate, where the technique, without the curbing effect of relief carving or engraving, permits a greater ease of execution and a more decorative tendency. Moreover, the Indian artist, whose requirement was for iconic, timeless and symbolic imagery, had no need to develop a depth mode of representation that would place his creatures in space or even suggest a spatial existence. Flat design therefore was confirmed in its potential for abstraction while the sculptural forms, automatically existing in three dimensions and having some measure of volume, have, at least in our perception of them, a heightened sense of creature presence. Nonetheless, despite that stronger sense of presence, the dialectical proposition finds its effective formal expression in the three-dimensional art too. For instance, in the totem pole the confining frame against which energy is exerted is the tubular "skin" of the pole. This skin squeezes animals into its own rigid stance and compels forms that would obtrude (like beaks, paws or tongues) to channel their thrust up or down, or to swell outward against its rounded circumference. There are exceptions to this, as in everything else. There are poles with projecting dorsal fins, killer-whale tails or bird beaks. But in Haida examples, such protuberances tend to be thin or planular, and to declare their character as structural additions to the pole rather than organic growths out of it. A particularly strong respect for the containing principle is in fact characteristic of Haida artistic expression with its concomitant habit of cramming creatures and forms densely within their frame or skin, and the consequent communication of restrained energy — all, of course, still within the context of elegant and precise formulation that is also typically Haida.

The formline system of expression is surely, as Reid claims, one of the "most refined and powerful" in the world. And yet thought of as a whole, this is an art in which the compelling sense of psychological presence, of creatures mutely imprisoned in their timeless matrix, is an equally compelling component in its overall impact.

73

THE SPIRITS WITHIN

There is "a magic place where the dreams of childhood hold a rendezvous, where century-old tree trunks sing and speak, where indefinable objects watch out for the visitor, with the anxious stare of human faces, where animals of superhuman gentleness join their little paws like hands in prayer for the privilege of building the palace of the beaver for the chosen one, of guiding him to the realm of the seals, or of teaching him, with a mystic kiss, the language of the frog or the kingfisher."[6] Those are the evocative words of Claude Lévi-Strauss in 1943 after a visit to the section of the American Museum of Natural History in New York which houses its collection of Pacific northwest coast material.

Visitors not having as much experience with expressions of primal cultures might find less gentleness than he did, and more awesomeness, more strangeness, in that spirit world which the art projects. For spirit world it suggests itself to be, that crowd of creatures — not human, though with humanlike heads and faces, and standing or sitting in humanlike stances. We may distinguish a bird or a four-footed creature, but rarely do individuals clearly identify themselves to us as this or that particular animal; instead they seem to be a compound of somewhat generalized parts. There is a preponderance of eyes, bulging, staring, sometimes two pairs in one set of eye-sockets, and a multitude of small circular forms which turn out not to have been intended as eyes but read as eyes nonetheless, adding to the sense of watching and silent waiting. There are great prominent mouths with wide rows of teeth, often with tongues extended. Heads are large — frequently as large as bodies — and sometimes while paws grab and hold, their mouths swallow smaller creatures. Bodies in fact almost disappear in this revised anatomy. These creatures pile on top of one another on poles, spoon or staff handles, or take up positions on the fronts of chests. Almost always they confront us, head on, challenging with their presence while remaining restrained within their confining forms.

The traditional artist often pushed the conventionalizing process very far along the way towards abstraction in the surface design forms of the art. But even in a work like Reid's beloved "black box" (so named by him when he discovered it, neglected and grimy, in a New York museum's storeroom), a box whose highly abstracted and elegant painted design is considered by both Reid and Duff to be a masterpiece, the evocative power of the creature-ness which underlies the conventionalization still asserts itself.

The Indian saw himself as a part, not the centre, of a vast cosmic system. The universe he envisioned, a layered and intricate formal structure, reflected his dependence on his natural environment — the animals and plants of sea and land and the forces of elemental nature — and his belief in the super-natural powers that invested it. Although his rigidly ordered culture separated

Base Section of a Haida Frontal Pole
from the Village of Ninstints
Queen Charlotte Islands.
Mid-nineteenth century
University of British Columbia,
Museum of Anthropology [A 50013]

him from the creatures of earth, sea and sky, they had their being similar to his within the system. At one time they had been able, with the easy donning or removing of a skin, to slip into another creature's identity and live and breathe in other of the world's realms. Humans indeed were animals who had shed their particular skins as salmon, raven, bear, wolf or whatever. This view gave direction and spiritual tone to daily life; it underlay the myths and stories whose origins belonged to some unknown past time though their truths and lessons still applied to the present; it was reiterated in the myriad major and minor rituals and ceremonies which affirmed it, and it was enfolded deeply into the art. These myths, ceremonies and art served as constant affirmation of the belief system that gave the people their identity, and acted to keep it intact.

Anthropology and ethnology fill in the details of the cultural context within which early art resonates and from which it cannot be wrenched without losing its original full relevance. But even on its own, the art is strong enough to tell us what it is about, at least at certain levels of experience. The art stems from the Indians' sense of oneness with the animals on whom they depended for food and with whom they shared the basic conditions of phenomenal being: hunger (and the body's knowledge of mouths, teeth, tongues, swallowing); fear and anxiety (and the need to be "all eyes and ears"); the elemental state of existing in a sensate corpus (one that sits or stands in archetypal posture, one, so to speak, *that is*, prior to movement or taking action, that knows its hands and feet). We know the art is about these things through our own experience as living creatures aware of our own bodily sensations and needs, and as sentient beings needing also to be in touch and communication with other beings and the environment. We know this through the expressive messages of the creatures presented *as creatures* — rigid, taut, glaring, devouring and so on — and through the form in which they are cast — facing front, squeezed in, knees up, paws tucked in and so on — the anatomical expression of the set of formal constraints. Naturally we feel this empathy most strongly with those animals, such as the bear, the wolf, the beaver, whose bodies most closely resemble our own and which in the art are given humanlike postures. They also have a prominent place in the art, being the class from which many (though by no means all) of the crest animals were chosen.

These messages of course do not always come through clearly to us, particularly when we are dealing with the work of a lesser artist from the anonymous past. The distinguished artist always made the containing principle work to his advantage. He used it to create compression from within the container so that the meaning and force of both components of the opposition could be felt. They had, as Reid says, "the impulse to push things as far as possible,"[7] so as to express "the precariousness of the society

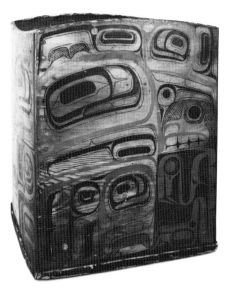

Wood Tlingit Box
Seal design
45 cm high
The American Museum
of Natural History

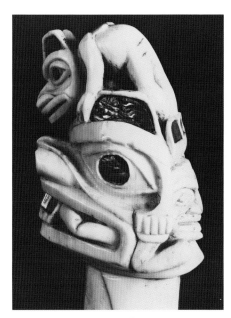

Dagger Handle, origin unknown
Bears and Man
Ivory with Abalone inlay
9.5 cm high
Private Collection

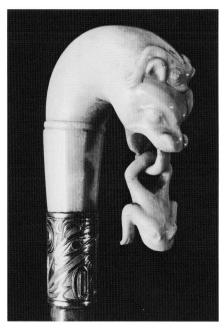

Charles Edenshaw Walking Stick
Ivory head with silver engraved collar
British Columbia Provincial Museum,
Victoria

that had been tightly structured over a long period and had developed to a point where all its parts had to fit together perfectly to function as it did."[8] That translates as: eyes that push out to the maximum from their sockets, straining the surface skin that holds them, staring with unseeing omniscience into an unknowable beyond; paws that hold limbs contrary to their inclination to extend, tight against the body; ears extended in full dimension — a crush of animal forms and parts, ensphered and interlocking, and inseparable from each other or an environing background.

This evoking of primary sensations of our bodily existence in attitudes expressive of tension and anxiety is strong in the sculptural work such as the poles. The evocation rarely extends into highly articulated body states (which might diminish their prototypical character); for instance, paws and feet remain fist- or clublike. In surface design, as discussed previously, where the reference to animals and creatures is often less explicit, more stylized and abstracted, and without the support of tactile three-dimensional form, the felt "life" or tension is more a matter of formal composition, with all its interrelationships of shape and line systems, not just filling but pushing against and forcing the container to exercise its will.

The game of giving creatures their identity, which is sometimes well concealed in the deeply encoded forms of the art, goes back a long way. Wilson Duff cites a 1907 monograph by the eminent ethnologist John Swanton on the Chilkat blanket. "Under each illustration there is an interpretation by Emmons [another early authority] which says that it depicts a particular thing, perhaps a whale diving. Then there is another interpretation by Boas who steps in as editor and says 'no, it represents a bear sitting up on his haunches.' Sometimes there is even a third interpretation by Swanton, who is also an expert, giving a third thing that it might depict."[9] Decoding the design of a Chilkat blanket, perhaps the most abstracted of all the Indian forms, presents obvious difficulties, but we might also cite Bill Holm, engaged in an attempt to identify the creature referred to on a wooden bent-corner bowl, in *Form and Freedom*. "I'm going to play the most dangerous game in Northwest Coast Art — interpretation. No one has ever successfully done it. Early anthropologists tried and tried to get interpretations from the artists themselves, but got widely differing interpretations from everybody."[10] After lengthy and fascinating speculation as to the possible reading of the design forms and details on the four sides of the bowl, he "opts for calling it a whale." To anthropologists the identification of creatures is something that cannot be neglected; it is part of the vast work of observation and information-building out of which their cultural insights will emerge. It was vital to the native Indian for whom the animal might have had value as a crest relating him, or his neighbour, to the all-important matter of lineage and rank; and certainly the creatures would have had meaning within the myths and stories which were part of his living heritage.

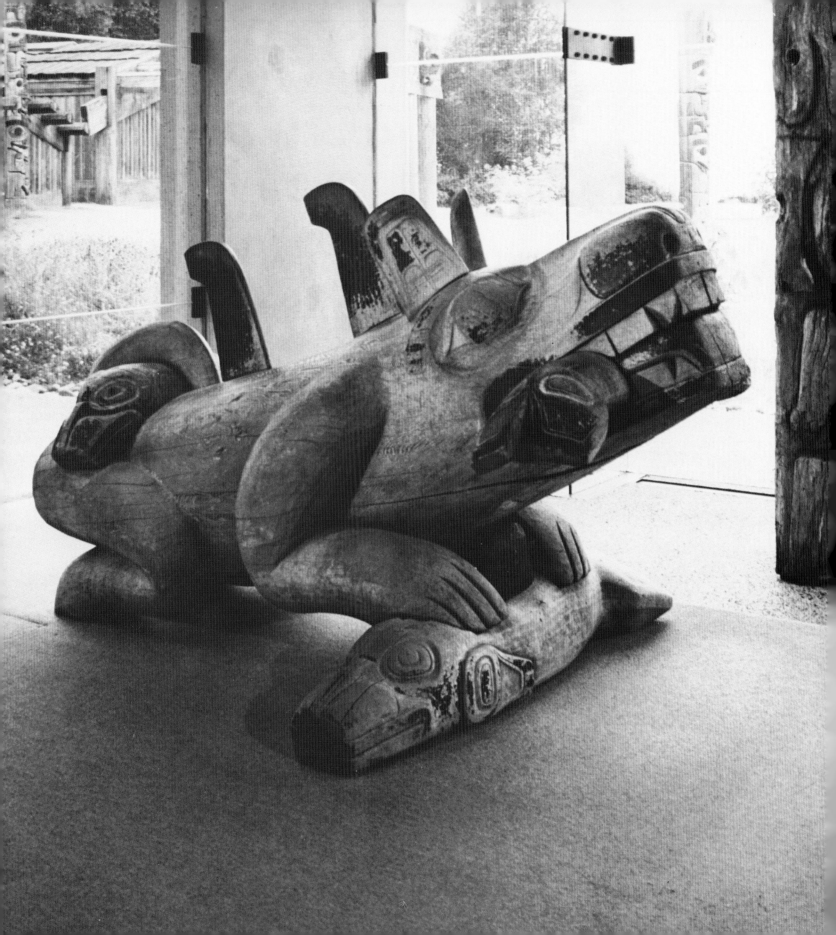

From the point of view of experiencing the art in today's terms, the matter of identification is not of central consequence. Such knowledge provides an enriched background against which we can experience the work, but identification is not a key which will magically open up the art in all its import or substitute for that import. There exist guides to the identifying features employed in the conventions of the art: broad set of teeth, paws holding stick, crosshatched tail for the beaver; long, slightly curved beak for the raven, shorter curved beak for the eagle, strongly curved beak turning back into the mouth for the hawk or some other creature, and so on. One admires the sharp observation that underlies the conventions. The early formulators of the conventions knew the creatures they were stylizing from direct prolonged experience, and grasped their salient characteristics. And if we are to catch some glimmer of the integrity the art had within the culture, and of the way it interconnected with the ceremonial life and the mythology, it is important to have some familiarity with the chief characters in the ambient drama and the kinds of roles they were accustomed to play — again, the raven, wolf, beaver, killer whale, sea-wolf as well as mythical creatures like the Tschumos (a fearsome seamonster which sometimes took the form of a seabear but was capable of a number of other configurations). But as far as the visual art itself is concerned, once a creature was incorporated into an object, it lost its dramatic aura or expressiveness and became encapsulated in its iconic, timeless state of being. That expressive aura or dramatic or narrative meaning exists only by virtue of knowledge outside the object, and it can be captured and added on only by reference to the mythology and belief system. From this point of view it is a semiotic art we are dealing with.

The dramatic or narrative interaction of "figures" with each other or in implied interaction with the environment is very limited until the early nineteenth century when, once again, the introduction of carving in slate reflects a clear loosening of the cultural hold on the art. Until then it is largely limited to acts connected with mouths and eating — one creature with another appearing from or disappearing into its mouth, tongues extending in long arcs from one mouth to another, and often a small creature, perhaps human, held right-side up or upsidedown in the paws of a bear or other animal. Anthropologists have invented illuminating cultural answers to some of these iconographic puzzles. For example in *Feasting with Cannibals* by Stanley Walens,[11] the frog, who had life-bringing and death-bringing meanings, extends his tongue as a "bridge of vital force" to the mouth of the human lying on his back on the top of the shaman's rattle. But many such intriguing moments in the iconography will remain for us as just other layers in the wonder-filled mystery of northwest coast Indian art. We find little watchful humanoid faces inserted in animal ears or eyes, or in joints, perhaps with hands pushing through as though a creature is about to climb out — and sometimes they *have* climbed out. In their way they speak to us

Cedar Sea Wolf carved by
Bill Reid 1960
2.7 m long, 1.35 m high
University of British Columbia
Museum of Anthropology

79

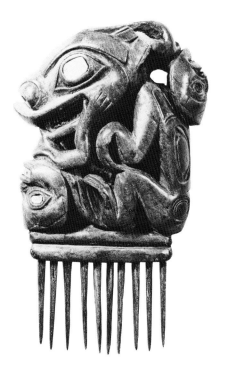

Tlingit Comb
Bear and Humans. Wood, abalone
16.5 cm long. The American Museum
of Natural History

of a man-animal relationship that today could only exist in our dreams or in a lingering primordial memory. Reid likes to think of them as little jokes indulged in by the ancient artists. A frog disappearing head first into the mouth of a human-faced, double-sided rattle to emerge from the mouth on the reverse side evokes in us strong visceral sensations, as does much of the oral imagery so prominent in the art. Walens gives us a background context which throws light on this prominence in the art when he states as a fundamental assumption of the culture: "the universe [for the Indians] is a place where some beings are eaten by other beings and where it is the role of some beings to die so that other beings may feed on them and live. Theirs is a world where the act of eating becomes the single metaphor by which the rest of their lives is interpreted."[12] Walens is speaking specifically of the Kwakiutl people, but after we have responded to the prominence of mouths, teeth, tongues and swallowings in the art of the northern people as well, we feel a burst of recognition in his statement that suggests it has broader co-cultural application. It comes to us like a truth that gives cultural dimension and anchorage to the experience we have had of the art. And yet, however our knowledge of the historical and cultural past is enlarged, the little faces and the frog being swallowed remain intact in their magic. They *do,* they *can* live in our dreams. Even were there cultural explanations for all such puzzles, other layers of mystery and wonder would fortunately remain, including the miracle of collective imagination in which such imagery was born.

We do indeed admire the sophistication and developed refinement of this art of the past; we marvel at the existence of a formal system of such intricacy. But what finally comes through to us with such impact is the result of its collective creators' relentless preoccupation with fundamental realities and with nothing else: with life and death, and with the way the world keeps together and continues. Naturally these realities are dealt with in the terms generated by their culture, but they are realities common to the human mind, and through the transforming medium of art we are able to understand them and share their revelations. The Indian art of the northwest coast takes us to a shadowy area of primordial memory where differences give way to oneness. The deep level of its imagery, and the equivalent messages carried in its formulation, remind us of an oceanic realm that still lies buried someplace within our being, where from time to time our imagination can make contact with it — a realm where creatures have not yet been isolated from their natural backgrounds, where the distinction between humans and animals or between the sexes does not yet exist, where life and death are not so far apart, and where minutes and hours have not been invented. In a modern world that precludes our feeling "one with the universe," such a reminder is probably salutary.

80

1 *Boxes and Bowls: Decorated Containers by Nineteenth Century Haida, Bella Bella, and Tsimshian Indian Artists* (Washington, D.C.: Smithsonian Institution Press, 1974), p. 12.

2 *The Legacy: Tradition and Innovation in Northwest Coast Indian Art* (Vancouver/Toronto: Douglas & McIntyre, 1984; Seattle: University of Washington Press, 1984), p. 29.

3 "Two things which are almost never explicit but almost always implicit in Haida art are sex and the true circle." From the introduction to a book on Charles Edenshaw, unpublished papers of Wilson Duff, University of British Columbia Museum of Anthropology Archives.

4 Part I. The Legacy of Change, "These Shining Islands" (Vancouver/Toronto: Douglas & McIntyre, 1984; Seattle: University of Washington Press, 1984), p. 28.

5 Elaborated in *Northwest Coast Indian Art: An Analysis of Form* (Seattle: University of Washington Press, 1965; Vancouver/Toronto: Douglas & McIntyre, 1965).

6 *The Way of the Masks* (Vancouver/Toronto: Douglas & McIntyre, 1982; Seattle: University of Washington Press, 1982), p. 3.

7 *Form and Freedom* (Houston, Texas: Institute of the Arts, Rice University, 1975), p. 32. Also published as *Indian Art of the Northwest Coast: A Dialogue on Craftsmanship and Aesthetics.*

8 Ibid., p. 35.

9 In Douglas N. Abbott, ed., *The World Is as Sharp as a Knife: Meaning in Northwest Coast Art* (Victoria: British Columbia Provincial Museum, 1976), p. 211. The interpretations of Boas, Swanton and Emmons were those given them by Indian informants rather than being their own.

10 *Form and Freedom*, p. 10

11 Princeton, N.J.: Princeton University Press, 1981, p. 14.

12 Ibid., p. 12.

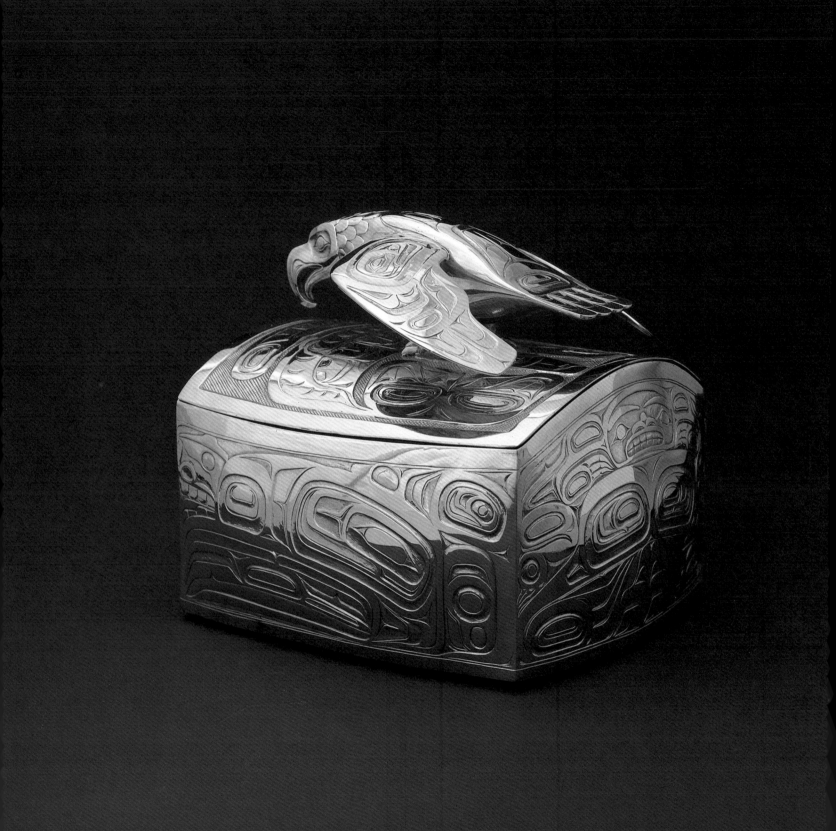

DEEP CARVING

Among the rotting fragments that still remain of the old village of Skedans, reminding us of the life that once was there, is an undistinguished housepost leaning into the tall grasses which almost conceal it. Although shaped for its structural purpose, it is unadorned by the carving that marks its more conspicuous companions in decay, the adjacent mortuary poles. Nonetheless, Bill Reid chooses to draw attention to this modest post, pointing out that its concave back, though hidden in the original house, has been carefully finished and its edges rounded, an example of the conscientious workmanship belonging to the "elder days of Art." He looks around to see who has caught the reference to one of his favourite quotations, Longfellow's "In the elder days of Art, / Builders wrought with greatest care, / Each minute and unseen part; / For the Gods see everywhere." References to the "well made" run like an undertone in Reid's speech and writing. "I try to make a well-made object; that is all that anyone can do." He will look critically at one of his earlier pieces and say: "Well, it's not a bad bracelet (or ring or whatever), but I sure wish it were better made."[1] He has written that "once we discard our ethnocentric, hierarchical ideas of how the world works, we will find that one basic quality unites all the works of mankind that speak to us in human, recognizable voices across the barrier of time, culture and space: the simple quality of being well made." He suggests that the ability to recognize a well-made object is a basic qualification for a museum director or curator, and that the skill and motivation to make such objects would alleviate the problems of many of the younger generation.

Reid tells of his first encounter with the work of Charles Edenshaw (1839–1920), who was to become his touchstone during his early exploration of Haida form. He had known of Edenshaw only as the carver-uncle with whom his grandfather lived as a boy. When Reid was in Skidegate for his grandfather's funeral, George Brown, who was his grandfather's friend and carving companion, told him he should go down into the village to see a Mrs. Tulip who had two bracelets made by Charlie Edenshaw that were *really deeply carved.* Reid went and saw the bracelets and after that, he says, "the world was not really the same."

He goes on to say that "deeply carved," a phrase that has its equivalent in the Haida *naagwiǥagwii ḵ'idaa*[2] really just means "well made." The remark is presented casually but seriously, for he is making an equation in which both components may be seen to have central significance in the context of northwest coast Indian art, and certainly in Reid's own work and attitude. What is commonly thought of as well-making, that is, careful and conspicuously skilled workmanship, has tended to be considered irrelevant to much recent art, certainly to that which values the spontaneous and the expressionist approaches. It is, at any rate, not too often seen as a value in itself.

But consider a situation (so unlike our own today) in which the artist is not expected, or needed, to be an innovator or truth-seeker; in which a stable, relatively unchanging society requires of its artists that, among more specific assignments, they confirm and assure the continuity of that particular order of stability, an order shared and accepted by everyone because *that is how things are known to be.* In such a situation where the artist as individual does not assume the burden of the *why* to make or the *what* to make, the well-making might assume central importance. Well-making affirms respect for and belief in the meanings and purposes invested in the art at society's imperative; it speaks of man's control of his material environment and of his ability to shape the mental and spiritual forces that animate his work and life. It represents the civilized alternative to chaos. A tradition of well-making in Haida art is firmly in place by the time our familiarity with the art commences. Such qualities as attention to detail and finish and fine construction speak of care and skill; but more telling is the complex and already evolved formal style which could not have been achieved had accomplished artistry not long been a criterion. Given a well-developed style within which to work, given specific functions to fulfill, given by the culture he shared the fundamental content for his art, given a limited choice of materials, the northern Indian artist's creativity in an important sense lay in doing well what he was given to do. His individuality was bound to be expressed in special touches, variations, mannerisms or style, but his quality as a good artist was a matter of "deep-carving."

Gold Box
Bear design on box and three-dimensional cast Eagle on lid 1967
10.2 cm high, 11 cm wide,
13.3 cm long

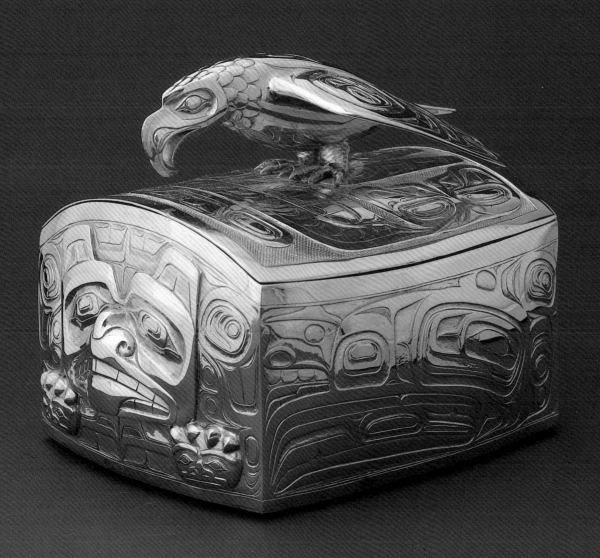

What quality or qualities can we, twentieth-century non-Indians, and presumably nineteenth-century Haida carvers as well, identify in the well-made piece? On the first level, of course, will be included good craftsmanship — that visible result of familiarity with and easy control over tools and material in a context of care and attention. The Indian artist, however, was not dealing only with tools and materials; he was dealing with images that carried vital meanings and with forms that, however conventionalized they had become over the centuries, were also charged with those meanings. The true artist, as distinguished from a competent repeater of the given formula, consciously or unconsciously *felt* the forms he created — the hollows and protuberances, the shapes and lines, their interrelationships within a whole — as carriers of that charge, whether experienced as low or high-voltage. As with any artist any place any time who works in tangible material, this is an understanding that involves the whole person: the body — the eye/hand connection — as well as the cognitive and affective mind.

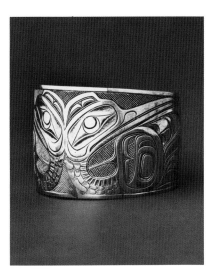

Silver Bracelet by Charles Edenshaw
with "hooked" closing
"Split" Raven design 4 cm wide
University of British Columbia,
Museum of Anthropology [A 8093]

Although not identified as such, it is largely this aspect of well-making that Bill Reid and Bill Holm are talking about in *Form and Freedom,* a discussion of the strengths and relative merits of various pieces selected from an exhibition of Northwest Coast Indian art, organized by the Institute for the Arts at Rice University in Houston, Texas. And in his now classic *Northwest Coast Indian Art* of 1965, Bill Holm presents in juxtaposition a silver bracelet by Charles Edenshaw, and another copied by an unnamed contemporary Indian artist from a drawing of the Edenshaw bracelet. Edenshaw, who of course had the advantage of growing up in the tradition and sharing its collective assumptions, shows in the arc and return of every curve, in the swelling and restraint of every ovoid, that he understands the principle of *energy firmly contained* which underlies Haida art; and that he has not forgotten the bracelet's primary meaning of arm-encircling, enclosing, which the engraved design must somehow share. The copier clearly had not inherited or acquired the sensitivity to understand those principles, and as a result his design, sitting unconvincingly on the surface of the silver, lacks the restrained tension of the best Haida art. It is not "deeply carved" in the literal sense of biting more deeply into the material and thus heightening the sculptural quality of low-relief, creating an in-depth tension in addition to that of surface design. Nor is it deeply carved in the metaphoric sense that the design must carry the charge that invests the images with their life as form and hence their meaning, empowering them, in short, to be carved deeply into our consciousness.

Doing things well represents a central morality for Reid — speaking, dressing, cooking, making objects, handling equipment. The more superbly and elegantly they are done, and the more clearly they manifest the human care and skill that has gone into their doing, the farther back they push the

Silver Bracelet
Tschumos design after
Charles Edenshaw c. 1958
5 cm at widest. Clasp with hinge
University of British Columbia,
Museum of Anthropology
[Reid A 1500]

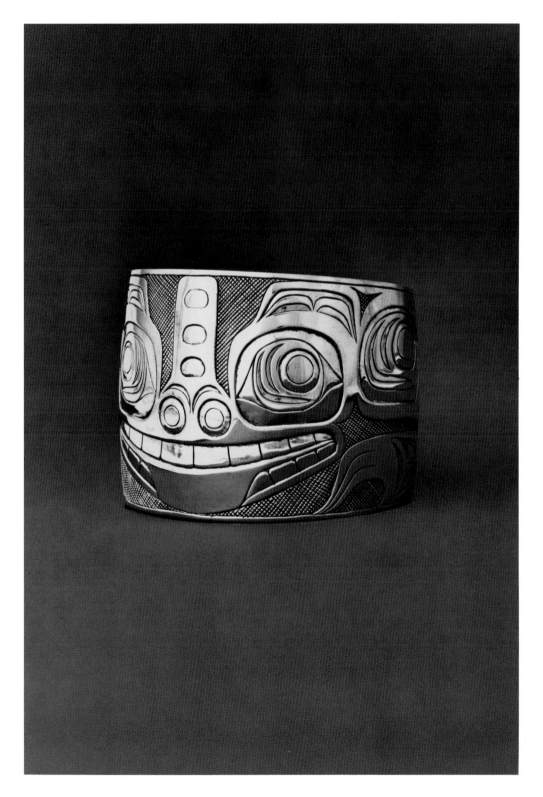

constantly threatening disorder and formlessness which his forebears had to control and which he has had to face in his own past. Inevitably, deep-carving/well-making lies at the heart of his aesthetic belief. It is the critique he applies rigorously to his own work. It locates the part of the creative process of which he is most aware, in which he is most comfortable and from which he derives most satisfaction. "Joy is a well-made object" is a statement he once read and frequently repeats, one whose truth he takes to be axiomatic and which is verified in his own deep pleasure in the making of things. Reid recognizes well-making as a central quality in the work of his ancestors, one he equates with their humanity and their historical achievement and which he has brought forward as part of his own continuity. (Ironically, while attaching obsessive importance to the well-made quality of objective things, he works out of a state of continuous and compulsive disarray. It is almost as though he is symbolizing in his own small sphere the larger chaos from which man has been compelled by his nature to create some kind of order.)

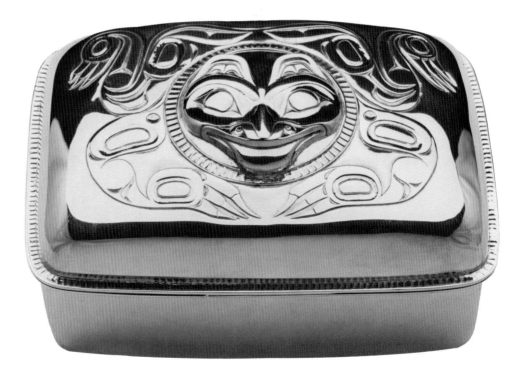

Silver Covered Dish

Silver Spoon
Wolf design 1970
15.2 cm long

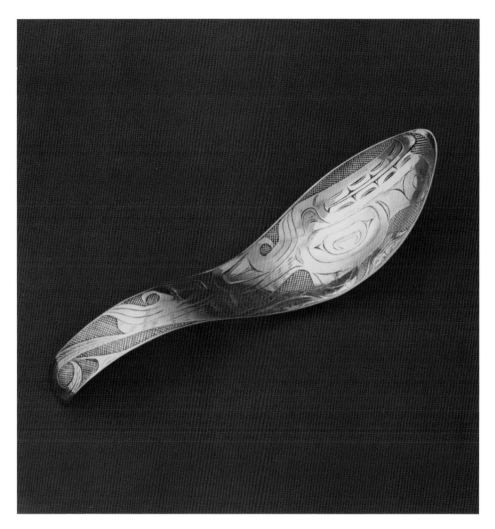

Reid's notion and practice of well-making, though neither starting nor
finishing there, attaches great importance to technical mastery, workmanship, or what we used to simply call craftsmanship. In recent times, when art
forms have emerged which place little value on the art object as such and
when artists have seen their role to be variously that of commentator,
interpreter or theorist, conspicuous craftsmanly involvement is sometimes
perceived to be irrelevant or, at the thoughtless end of the critical scale,
mindless busy work. (Of course, when art is unrelated to an animating
conception it is sometimes just that.) For Reid the committed maker of
things, the ability to use tools and equipment with assurance, skill and
finesse in the giving of form and shape to materials is an assertion of essential humanness that carries its message across the ages: "that sudden aching
sense of identity with the distant cousin who first lovingly made . . . the
elegant line, the subtle curve, the sure precise brush stroke."[3]

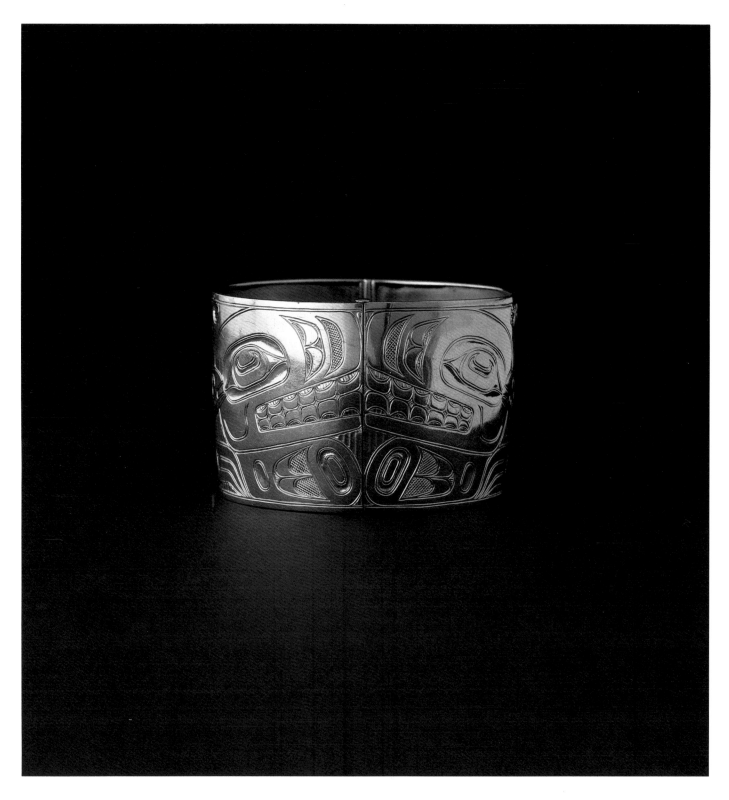

DEEP CARVING

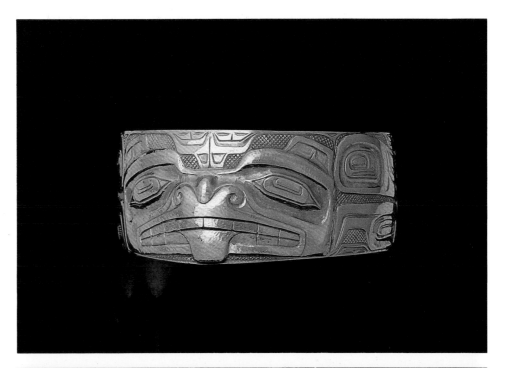

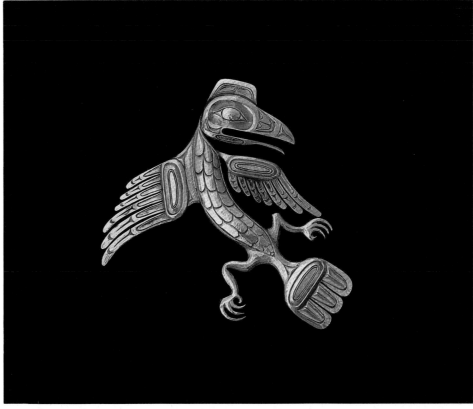

Hinged Gold Bracelet
Design adapted from two sides
of an argillite house model c. 1957.
4 cm wide

Gold Bracelet
Wolf design 1968
2.6 cm wide

Gold Brooch
Raven design after Edenshaw c. 1954
6.3 cm long, 5.4 cm wide

91

"I never intended to be *a artist*," he says with great mocking deliberation, "and it came as a shock when people started referring to me as such." The art versus craft distinction, which seems to be an issue for those concerned with categories or status, does not impinge on Reid, working as he does out of an art tradition that existed long before such a differentiation would have been possible or meaningful. "I try to make a well-made object," he says; "that is all anybody can do." If something beyond that "creeps into my work, if some message comes through, [that is] something over which I have no control." He is inclined to like the notion of "inadvertent art" — art that has come into being while bypassing the whole self-conscious structure of theory, promotion and presentation which has taken possession of it in our time and confirmed it as a special category in our life and experience. "Once you start thinking you are a philosopher or something like that," he says, "the appeal and richness of art are lost." This is one of the reasons why he has such admiration for Watts Towers, the loving lifework which Simon Rodia, an immigrant Italian tile-setter and humble folk sculptor, built in his spare time outside his home in a depressed area of Los Angeles.

Reid is fascinated with the tools and equipment of his art, human-sized objects which belong to the intimacy of the hand and the movements of one's body. His "distant cousins," after all, at least in the beginning, fashioned their tools with their own hands and out of their own ingenuity, though when new ones came their way they were quick to make use of them. He too is ingenious in making or adapting existing tools to his own special purposes, in adding to their meaning with hand-carved handles, in keeping blades or adzes sharp and ready. Technical invention comes to him as naturally as it did to his great-uncle Charlie who, having seen engraving but having no idea how it was done, adapted tools and devised his own system (an impossibly awkward one according to modern craftsmen) for engraving designs on gold and silver bracelets, and for bending them into their rounded shape. Reid in turn added to the European jewellery-making techniques he had learned any number of small technical procedures and innovations by which the bracelet could be given a sculptural richness and intricate strength beyond his ancestors' imagining. For instance, he invented his own "bracelet-bender" — as far as he knows, an original concept — which today is used by virtually all natives making bracelets. Everything for him must be pushed to the farthest reach of its possible technical perfection, and his demanding virtuosity is constantly being demonstrated in the sure handling of the engraving tool or repoussé hammer, in the working out of complex designs, and in the fashioning of intricate hinges and clasps on many of his jewellery pieces. He tells a story of a recent trip to Paris during which he undertook a fellow-Canadian's first introduction to the Louvre.

Somehow under his guidance they managed to bypass most of the standard masterpieces, but found themselves spending hours in a room containing a box, the work of the famed Russian virtuoso Fabergé, that boasted a miraculously crafted hinge which for them outshone all the other attractions. When asked what they had experienced at the Louvre, their response was, ''We saw a hinge.''

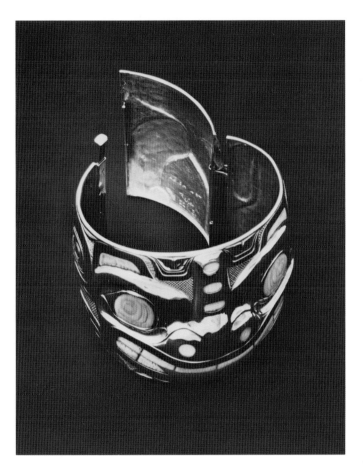 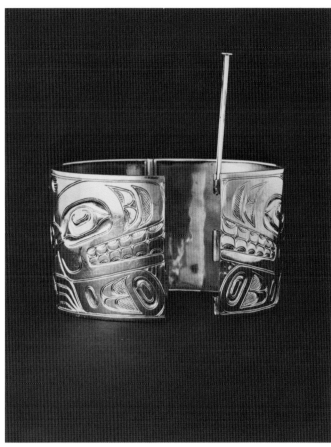

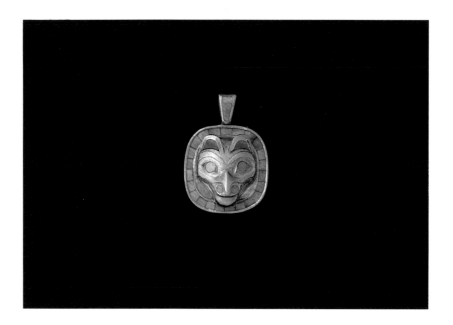

In a tour-guide spirit, he would direct a visitor to New York's museums who had only enough time to see one thing to the Flemish boxwood rosary bead carved in the early sixteenth century and now in the Metropolitan Museum's collection in the Cloisters. A wonder of conspicuous craftsmanship, its hinged sections open like the wings of a tiny altar-screen (or, as Joan Vastokas appropriately noted, "like a clam-shell")[4] to reveal its inner secrets: minutely carved scenes of the birth and death of Christ. Reid is acutely sensitive to the intense psychological presence granted to miniature objects which compress qualities and meanings, including that of craftsmanship, into a small scale. They possess an irresistible cunning and a privileged secrecy, and they may also harbour messages of great import. Haida carvers, in small ivory charms or horn spoon handles, showed that they knew about the magic of miniaturization, as does Reid in much of his finest work.

Like all fine craftsmen, he is not only sensitive to materials but also is in love with those with which he has a special affinity, seeing in them the magic it is his work to fully reveal. He has that love for cedar and he has it for gold. The wonder he feels for gold is enhanced by its history, which stretches back to the earliest annals of man. He considers it a serious omission in his life that his travels have never permitted him to see the Hermitage's unique collection of Scythian gold pieces, the miraculous work of those early nomads whose technical finesse he claims could not be duplicated today. And if he could exchange places with one person in the world's history, he would choose to be the Russian archaeologist who discovered that collection's great gold torque with its mythical figures and horses and other animals.

Gold Pendant with Abalone inlay
Wolf design 1982
2 cm long, 2 cm wide

Ivory Earrings
Raven design c. 1967
Oval, 2.4 cm long, 1.5 cm wide

Fossil Ivory Pendant
Eagle 1969
5 cm long

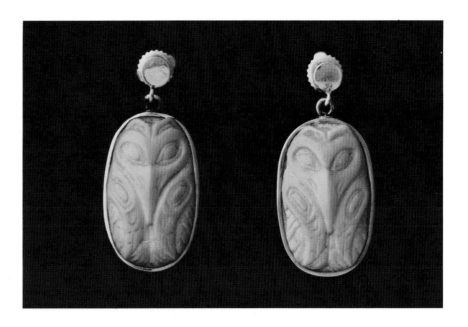

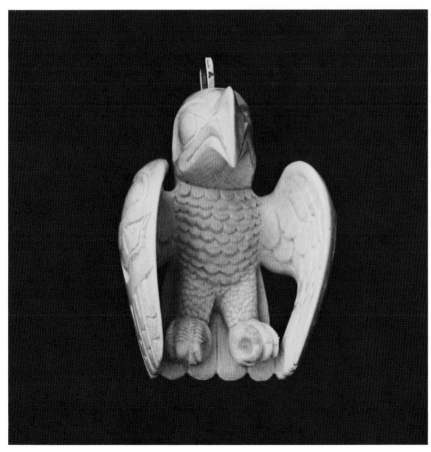

It was probably the sheer joy and satisfaction of *making,* with the attendant pleasure in tools and materials and all their possibilities of exploitation, coupled with his veneration for the traditional art, which led Reid to a comprehension of *form creating,* that other level of mastery which, if we are talking about art, must be included in any discussion of making-well.

He had technical training in jewellery-making, though no art training as such, and very little experience of it when he started on his journey to the past. By the time he had discovered a useful little government pamphlet on Indian art, *A Corner Stone of Canadian Culture* by Alice Ravenhill, and had begun to read Franz Boas's book *Primitive Art,* all the while continuing to study the old pieces in museums, he had already made some straight copies of pieces by Charles Edenshaw. When in 1965 the publication of Holm's book gave definitive analysis and a terminology to that complex and elegant "surface style" whose conventions had been repeated over no one knows how many years until they had settled into an apparent set of rules (and which are, in fact, today referred to as rules), Reid had already worked out those principles for himself. Indeed, Holm acknowledges Reid's part in the discussions leading up to their formulation.[5] The book was to become virtually a manual for young artists seeking to learn the deeply encoded formal system their elders had developed. But of course what Reid has done, as any artist of consequence must, is to transcend the rules with which he started and to grasp the vital life of the forms, an interiorizing process which analysis alone cannot accomplish.

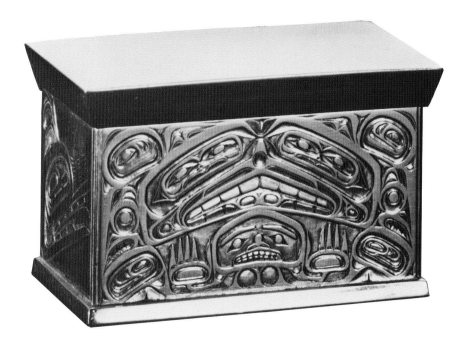

Hinged Gold Box
Bear, Wolf and Human design 1973
5.5 cm long, 2.8 cm wide, 3.5 cm high

Gold Pendant with chain and stand
Human Face design 1976
5.5 cm diameter, 1.3 cm deep

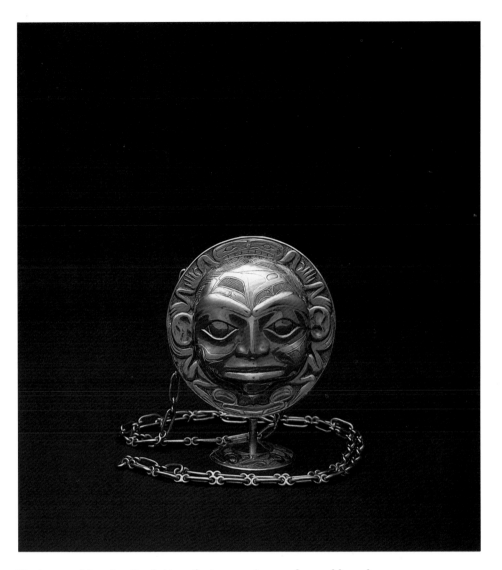

He is capable of articulating that grasp in words, and has done so on many
occasions, but nowhere more succinctly than in his statement in the 1967
Arts of the Raven exhibition catalogue: "The basic lines of a box design start
with a major image, rush to the limits of the field, turn back on themselves,
are pushed and squeezed towards the centre, and rippling over and around
the internal patterns, start the motion again. Where form touches form, the
line is compressed, and the tension almost reaches the breaking point before
it is released in another flowing curve."[6] The understanding revealed in
those words came not from a following of "rules" but from a prolonged
immersion in the *making of things,* which for him is always the critical path
to knowledge, though as an intellectual he must always have an articulate
grasp of the problems he deals with.

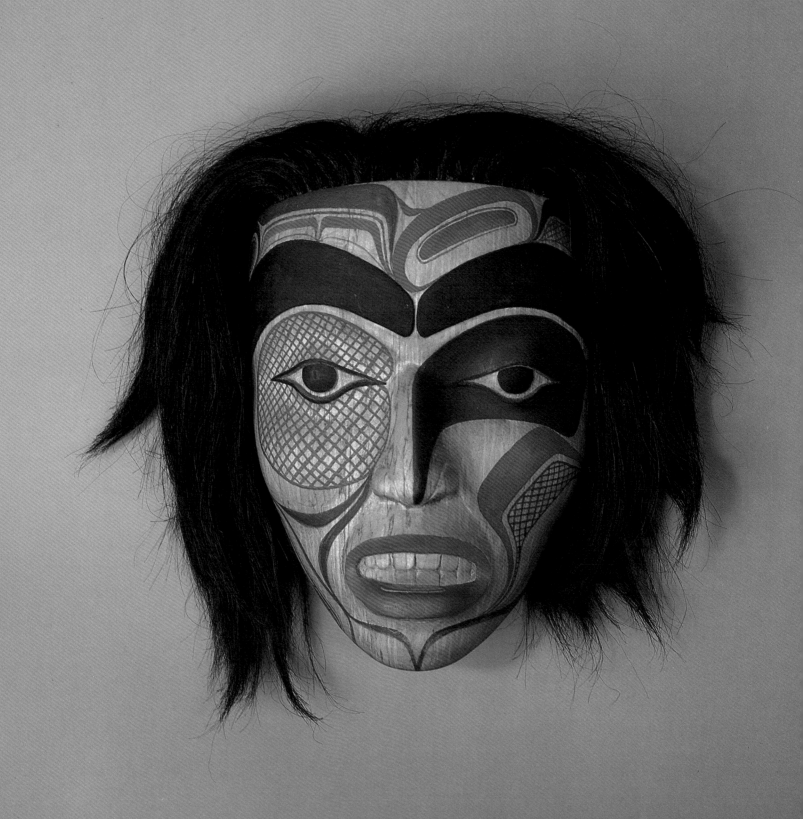

So there is a sense in which his art has taken him *into* the past. Slowly, patiently, knowingly working within the traditional form system until it was part of his vocabulary, as natural and eloquent as speech; releasing the images, the descendants of those awesome creatures his ancestors had brought into being, out of the resistant wood, silver or argillite, he has achieved that particular inner knowledge which comes only when body, eye and mind in all its dimensions are engaged. Although at first he was far removed from his culture, perhaps even reluctant to get as involved as he has, this patient process has drawn him into its spiritual core.

Those early years of willing submission to the great original models enabled him to touch the old centres of awareness where song and dance and art and the spirits and man and nature all merge. In so doing he has regenerated that sensibility and spirit for himself: in a manner of speaking, he himself has become deeply carved. There is today, as there was not when he first ventured into the old territory, a sense in which he *knows* what it was like to be Indian. "When I work I am trying my best to get inside a traditional artist's skin, an old-time artist, and do what he would have done with the benefit of modern technology."

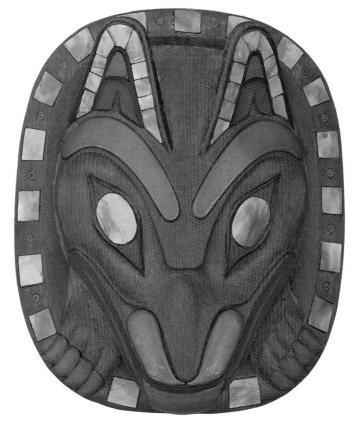

Cedar Female Mask
with paint and hair 1970
21 cm high
University of British Columbia,
Museum of Anthropology

Yew Pendant
painted, and inlaid with Copper
and Abalone
Wolf design 1978
8.3 cm long, 7.1 cm wide

The art that would give him this deeper understanding needed to have the solid, tactile, earth-oriented materiality that was the basis of his ancestors' art, and that would give well-making the fullest dimension of its expression. Reid did not initiate but was one of the many artists who participated in the production of silk-screen prints bearing native designs which had great popular success in the 1960s and seventies. The old tradition of painting on house fronts, interior house screens, canoes and wooden boxes provided a historic precedent for contemporary two-dimensional design. There had been earlier examples of Indian motifs being adapted to contemporary graphic purposes, often at a level of tourist items, and in fact, in the early fifties, with the encouragement of fine-art printer and typographer Robert Reid (no relation), a few exquisite small prints were pulled from designs that Bill had engraved on silver plates, and one or two even appeared on greeting cards. The silk-screen phenomenon which began in the mid-1960s, however, drew in many artists of serious potential, offering them a commercial outlet for their work and hence an incentive, as well as the opportunity to experiment in a medium less demanding than traditional carving or engraving. Between 1972 and 1979 Reid produced nine prints, and planned on doing at least one design a year, the return from which constituted his only sure income during that period. He spent much time and his usual meticulous care in working out the designs and doing the drawings, all of which read as single-creature images centred on the paper: the Haida Raven, Dogfish, Killer Whale, Salmon, Grizzly Bear, Eagle, Beaver and Wolf, and the Children of the Raven. Although lacking the substance of his other work, they are distinguished by the precision, elegance and refinement of form that characterize all he does. The silk-screen images are, of necessity, designs superimposed *on* paper, not imbedded in or drawn out of their medium; he did not cut stencils, pull the prints or became productively involved in the printing process. Nor did he get as much satisfaction from doing them as from his other work in which he manipulates material, like his beloved gold, where he has more complete control of the entire process, and where he can rely on the pressure of a tool against resistant material to slow down and control the curve and maximize its tension.

The several large public commissions he has undertaken in recent years have taken the work out of his hands — they have had to be cast, to be engineered, to be carried out with the help of others. With his customary sardonic twinkle he says that essentially he is a modest, retiring, quiet person; and adds that while of course he enjoys the kudos and other things that go with the commissions, part of him is deeply resentful of the big projects that take him away from his work bench. At that work bench, of course, he is in direct, intimate body contact with and master of his tools and his materials, asserting in his own way, while echoing that of his ancestors, his humanity in the act of deep-carving.

Haida Eagle
Silk screen 1974

Haida Dog Salmon
Silk screen 1974

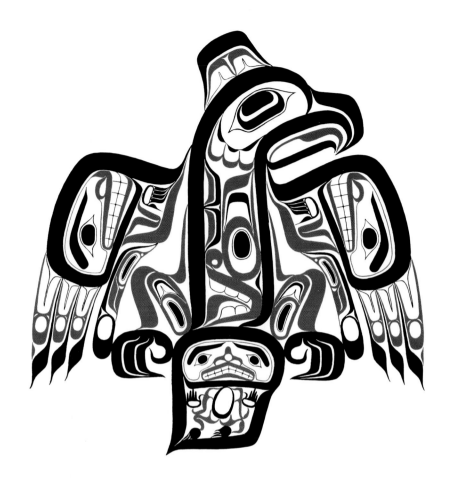

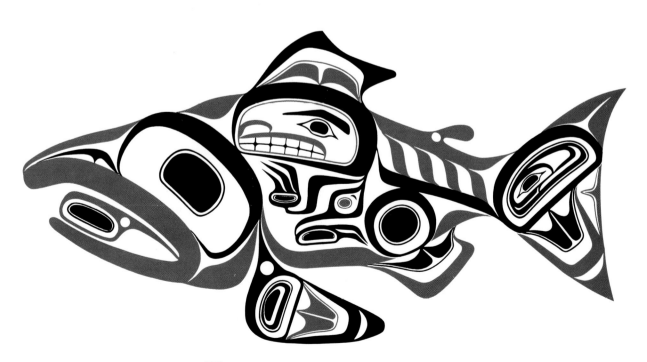

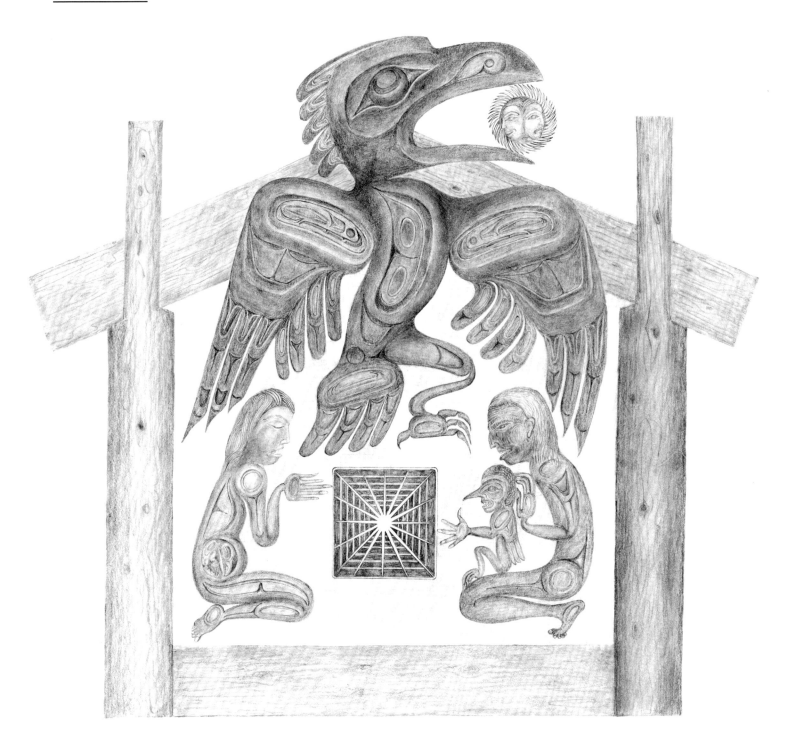

The Raven Steals the Light
Pencil drawing 1983
Reproduced in "The Raven
Steals the Light"

Nanasimget and His Wife
Pencil Drawing 1983
Reproduced in "The Raven
Steals the Light"

A series of pencil drawings Reid did in 1983–84 now appear as illustrations for his retelling of some of the ancient myths in the book *The Raven Steals the Light*.[7] They represent a departure from his previous graphic work and include some of his finest and most original pieces. His kind of drawing has nothing in common with the sort of free calligraphy of a Matisse or Picasso, in whose hand the pen can dance out its own linear shorthand. Reid goes at the image as something that must be whittled and coaxed out of the paper, sometimes with much erasure, stroke by little stroke of the pencil. He restores the "thingness" that the silk-screen images missed. Even on a flat surface, and even on a material that does not speak of substance and durability (as does a wooden chest front), he evokes a material world for transformation by his imagination. This is true even though the grey material out of which the particular creatures in these drawings are fashioned has a certain spectral quality, like branches that have smouldered to ash while retaining their form. This preference for an art that is rooted in substance, that is inseparable from its "thingness," is probably less a matter of choice than of natural disposition and orientation — and something he shares with the ancestors.

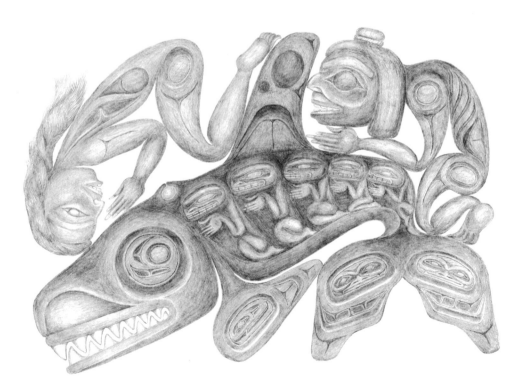

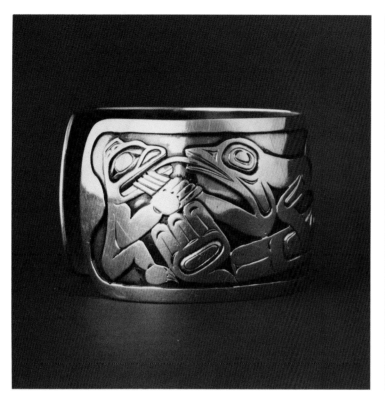
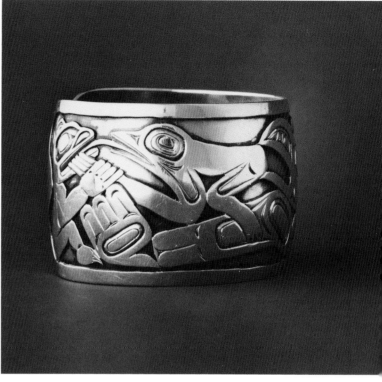

Silver Bracelet
Design includes Bear, Frog, Eagle,
Man, Killer Whale, Raven c. 1956.
3.8 cm wide

The notion of deep-carving gains richness and substance in the study of Reid's work, which in general is not single impact but requires a particular kind of scrutiny, one in which each detail is savoured and seen as part of the larger whole. The simplest bracelets, for instance, starting out as line drawings transferred to pieces of sheet metal, might be thought of as exercises in flat design — line engravings, often of great density and intricacy, on a curved band of silver or gold. They are virtually impossible to show adequately in photographs, and Reid is much intrigued by a photographing procedure that images the bracelet as a flat strip. He, of course, through long practice is able to bend the band in his imagination, but in fact such photographs are distorting, for the bracelet's curvature is essential to any appreciation of its design.

Other of his bracelets, as though missing the dimensions of colour or depth, add carving, or repoussé pushing the form out from behind, or inlays of abalone shell or ivory; or they apply cast forms when the demand for depth is beyond the range of the repoussé technique, thickening and enriching to the maximum the plane of exploitation permitted by that wrist-encircling band of metal.

104

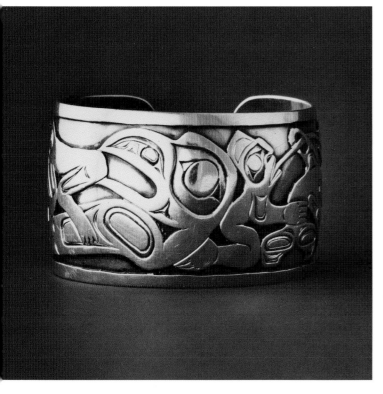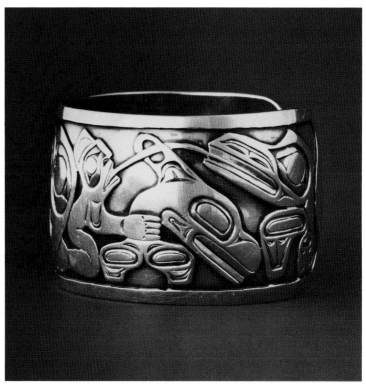

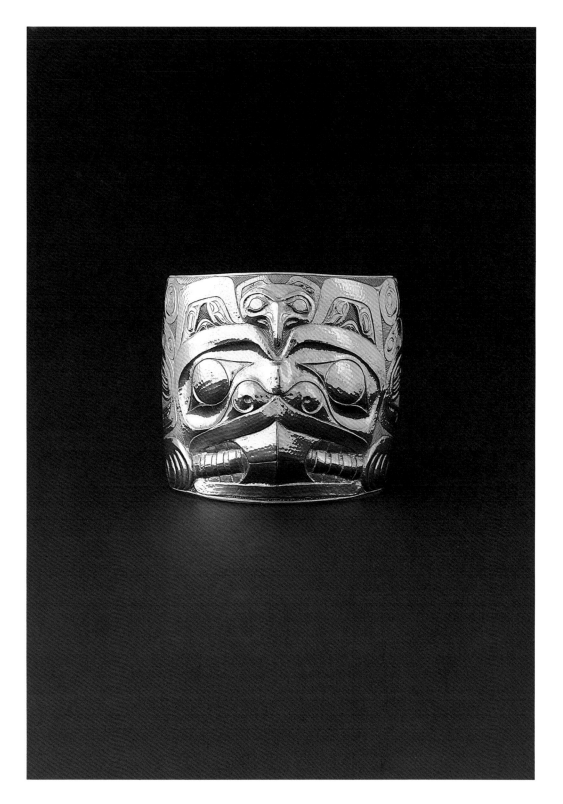

Gold Bracelet
Beaver and Eagle design 1970
6 cm wide

Hinged Silver Bracelet
Eagle design 1972
4 cm wide

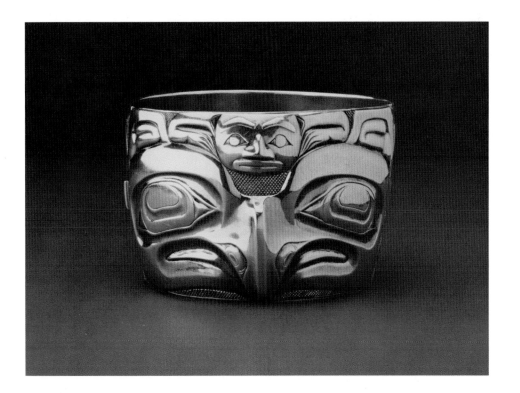

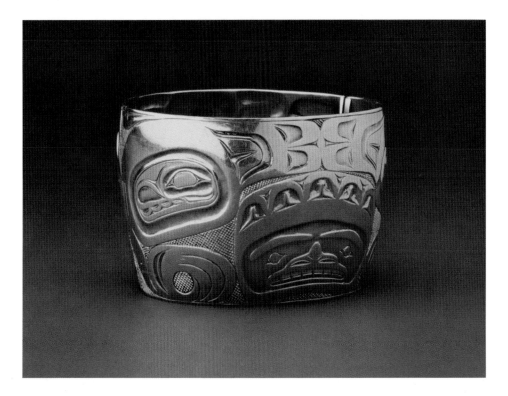

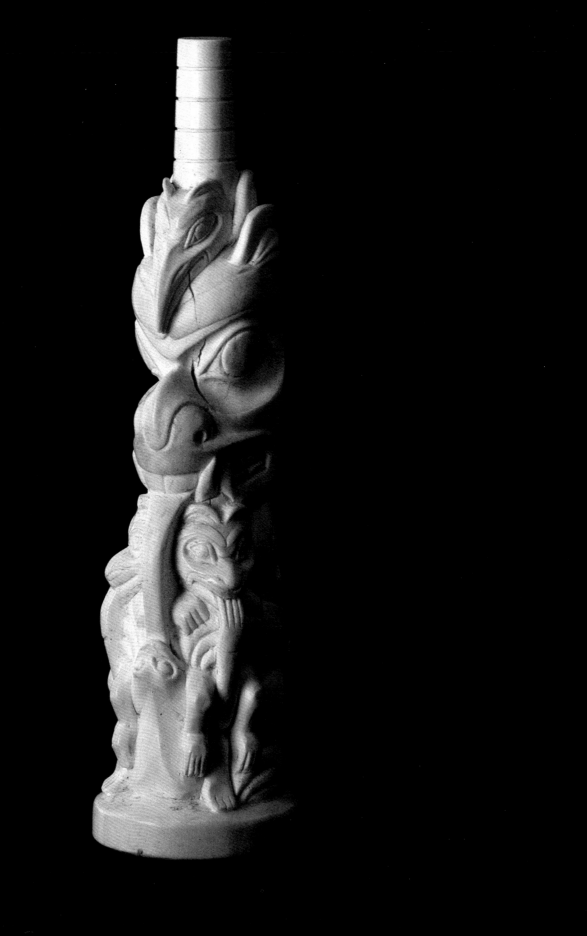

DEEP CARVING

As for traditional monumental work, Reid seems to have had an almost intuitive grasp of deep-carving. After those few days' carving with Mungo Martin, he had undertaken, with Doug Cranmer's help, the Haida village project in Totem Park on the UBC campus between the years 1958–62. Those mortuary and totem poles, while compositional adaptations mostly done from existing old poles or photographs, show his easy authority in fully realizing their interlocking density — their combination of technical virtuosity, formal complexity and compounded iconographic meanings. This trio of qualities is seen in his own small ivory pole carved in 1966. The Raven, Bear and twin cubs observe their proper rigid existential stance within the code of totem pole behaviour: beaks, chins, paws tucked in, eyes straight ahead; forms piled on top of one another in the additive manner of pole composition — but within that set of constraints, what straining to break out! Tongues, beaks, dangling legs and feet, overlapping, curling back in that continuous, complex interweaving, in and out, up and down, down and up, that countermands the vertical form's will to shoot off into space. The bear cubs' straining away from their frontal bind gives more vitality to the statement of tense creatural coexistence and shared power that welds them together. Of a very simple old helmet which elicited Reid's admiration he said, "This represents something . . . I can't do myself. If I can't make a thing work, I just add — put a bunch more junk into it — until finally the space is completely filled, and there's nothing more I can do about it. This guy did the most with the least . . . it almost makes one want to weep, or something."[8] Despite his deprecating self-reference, what he is talking about — the dense packing of forms within their given space — is surely the typical Haida mode which he handles so well. Certainly the packed richness of his little ivory pole does not, any more than the best Haida art, reflect a process of completion by uninspired addition; it projects rather those qualities of compressed power, tension and complexity — the achievement of "the impulse to push things as far as possible" — which he admires so greatly in the ancestors.

Ivory Totem Pole
Raven, Bear, Cubs and Frog 1966
11.4 cm high

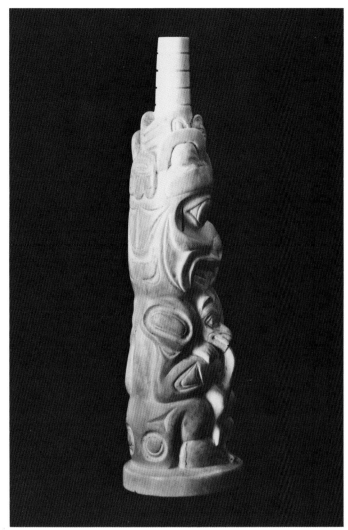
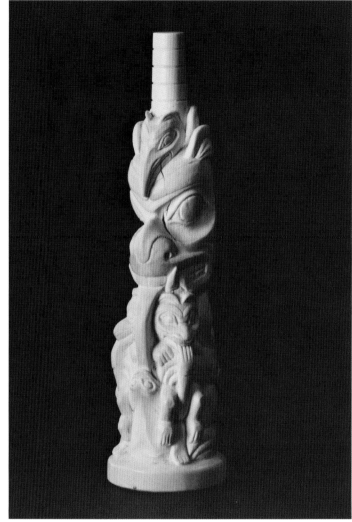

Detail of Reid's Skidegate pole

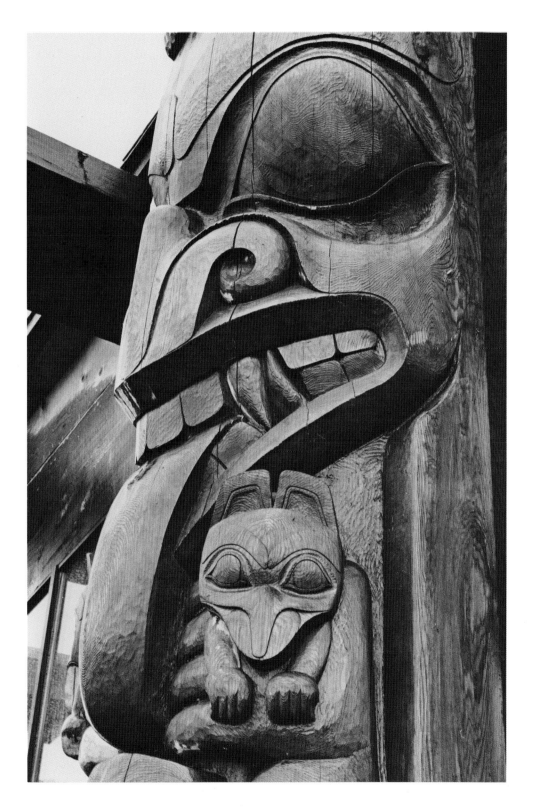

Then there is the 5.5-metre Haida canoe which in a technical sense has been his most ambitious enterprise in deep-carving. He has long felt what amounts almost to awe for the traditional Haida canoe and what it represents in terms of design and hand-facture: a functionally perfect, ceremoniously expressive and visually elegant vessel, at once technically ingenious and masterly. He says, "Think of the time it would take to fall a big cedar by burning through its base with a slow controlled fire, or felling it with a stone blade with your time divided equally between chopping and sharpening, to say nothing of the days it took to make the tool before you could begin. Then to shape the log into a canoe, and hollow it by more burning and scraping, and then to steam and shape it and fit it out."[9] He believes that "the dialogue between the material and the maker has never been closer than in the making of a canoe because the canoe retains its own independence, a control of its own shape, and there is a need to predict what will happen. . . . What you end up with is essentially a one-plank boat involving multi-curves that are achieved through seeking strength and dimension, and through the procedure of steaming. And you incorporate design elements which you couldn't have predetermined because of the will of the wood." He believes that the canoe played a generic role in the evolution of Indian art: "Western art starts with the figure — west coast Indian art starts with the boat."

Over the years he has devised various plots for repatriating to the west coast a magnificent 17.4-metre, ocean-going Haida canoe hidden away in the National Museum of Man's storage. "It was built at Masset by Robert Davidson's grandfather and great-uncle for the Alaska-Yukon-Pacific Exposition in Seattle in 1909, and the design on it was painted by Charles Edenshaw. It's a big canoe, high in the bow and stern, big enough to hold a crew of at least twenty rowers. It's one of only two left in the world; the other is in the Museum of Natural History in New York. The National Museum of Man in Ottawa hasn't displayed it in years. In Norway, longships are in palaces. We keep ours in warehouses."[10] The canoe is being shown in the Canadian Pavilion in Vancouver during the summer of 1986, an event which Reid's early efforts undoubtedly helped bring about.

There has been the deep joy and sense of accomplishment in "getting inside his ancestors' skin" and rediscovering the particular form of well-making involved in producing his own traditional canoe. He was tired, he says, of "seeing oversized banana skins [that is, poorly designed and made canoes] on the beach." The old skills and techniques were not handed down, but there is, as he knows, a fair amount of information in the literature and much to be learned directly from the old boats themselves. From Steve Brown, a Seattle disciple of Bill Holm who specializes in the canoe, Reid learned about the "flexible stick," a long piece of cedar about three-eighths of an inch square with which curves can be defined. Still, the long, slow process

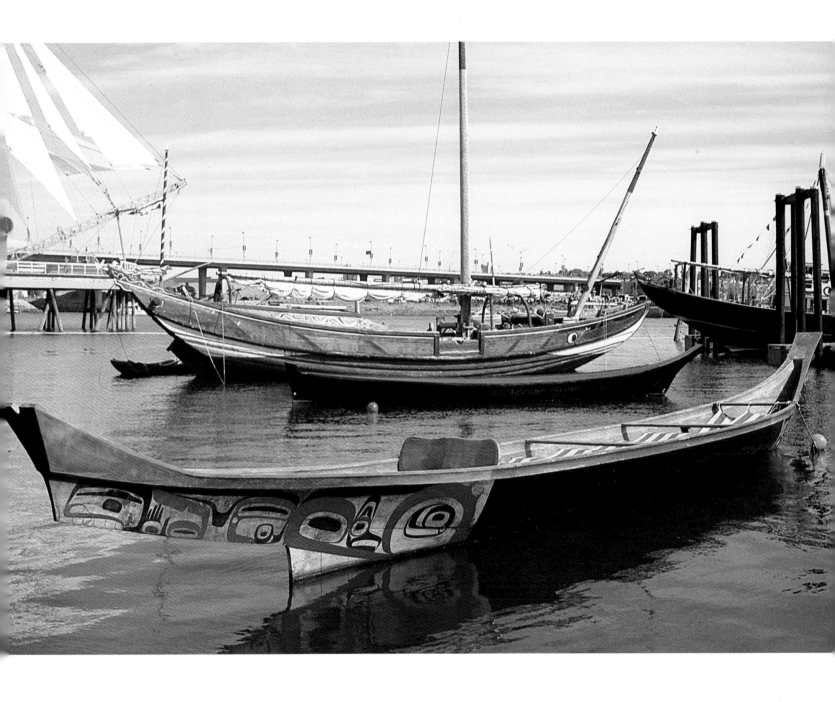

The 15.2-m canoe at Expo 86

of giving shape and form to the cedar — that "perfect substance for all material and aesthetic needs" — by employing cutting tools and by steaming from inside, with constant checking for even thickness and for the elegant accuracy of curves, could really only be learned in the doing. The obsession with which Reid carried out the project can only be understood as an indication of the sense of identity with his forebears — through the art of workmanship — that he derived from it. It was also, of course, a major undertaking, representing a large investment of time, energy and money, whose success finally had to be measured in demanding functional terms as well as aesthetic ones. Its 15.2-metre successor, which presented him with even greater challenges in engineering design and workmanship, has now been completed in Skidegate and made its triumphal appearance in the Waters of False Creek for the opening of Expo 86.

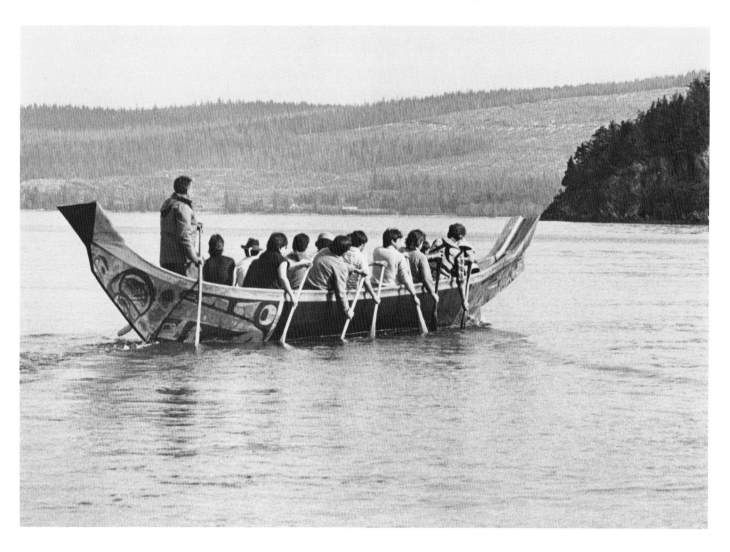

The big canoe on a trial run after completion at Skidegate, May 1986

The 15.2-m Haida canoe nearing completion in the work shed at Skidegate, spring 1986. Reid wearing hat and facing left in centre against the canoe. Canoe commissioned by the Bank of British Columbia

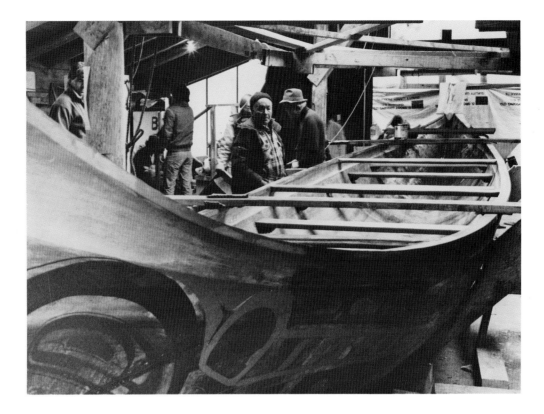

1 Foreword to *Bill Koochin* (Burnaby, B.C.: Burnaby Art Gallery, 1980), p. 2.

2 Haida word equivalent provided by John Enrico, Masset, Q.C.I.

3 *Bill Koochin*, p. 2.

4 "Bill Reid and the Native Renaissance," p. 162. (Illustration, p. 167.)

5 As the solid work of Holm's book has been absorbed into a changing critical sensibility, recent writers have sometimes seen his approach to northern northwest coast art as analytical and scholarly in a limiting sense, and in contrast with Reid's artistic and internalizing approach. In fact, as a rereading of the preface to Holm's book or of *Form and Freedom* would suggest, their approaches have not been that far apart.

6 See also Bill Holm, *Northwest Coast Indian Art: An Analysis of Form* (Seattle: University of Washington Press, 1965; Vancouver/Toronto: Douglas & McIntyre, 1965), pp. 83–84, for a clear statement on the subject of movement.

7 Drawings by Bill Reid with Stories by Bill Reid and Robert Bringhurst (Vancouver/Toronto: Douglas & McIntyre, 1984; Seattle: University of Washington Press, 1984).

8 *Form and Freedom* (Houston, Texas: Institute of the Arts, Rice University, 1975), p. 164.

9 "Haida Means Human Being," unpublished paper, 1979.

10 Quoted in Edith Iglauer, "The Myth Maker," *Saturday Night* (February 1982) 97:22. There is in fact a third comparably large canoe at the Smithsonian Institution in Washington, D.C.

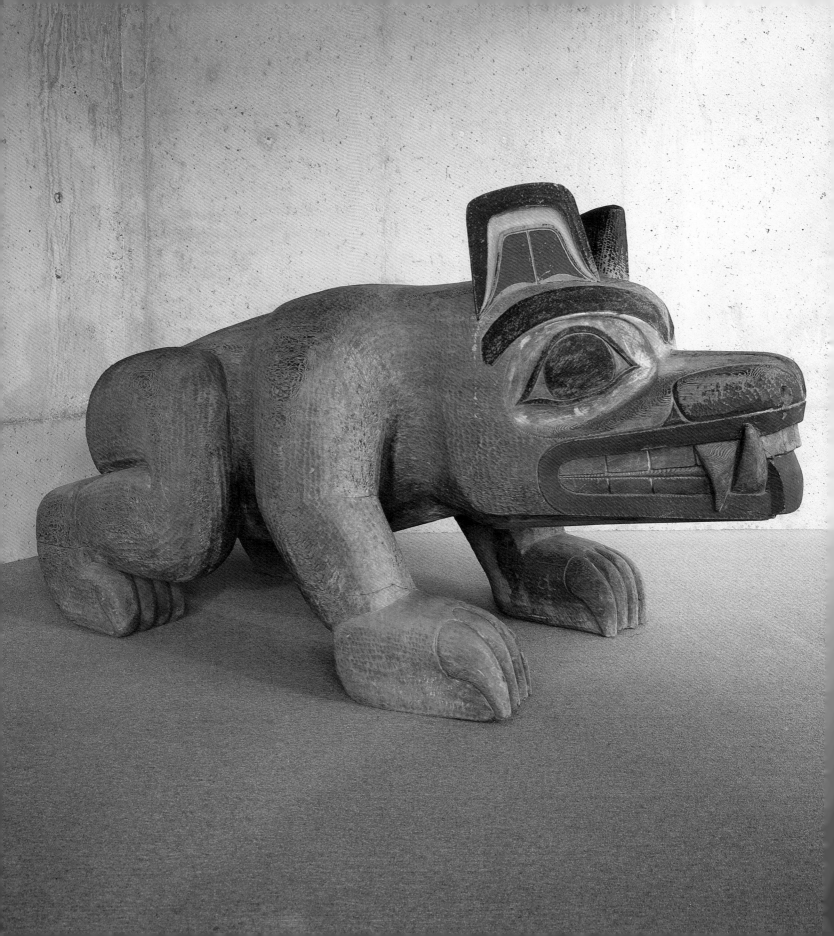

REID'S BESTIARY

The same creatures who lived in the old Haida myths and stories also dominated the visual art of the past. On the most obvious level they appear to be
what the art is about. The life they lived in the art however was quite unlike
that which they enjoyed in the myths, where they were creatures of action
and took part in extraordinary adventures. But when in the past they stepped
into the sculpture and designs, they became mute existential presences
behind and beyond action; they did not carry their actions or their particular
personalities with them. There is nothing in the depiction of a raven on a
housepost to tell us that he has the reputation of a trickster and a thief, or
that he was the inadvertent "creator of the universe"; that knowledge we
need to have brought with us. Such limited action as is represented — for
example, a human face swallowing a frog — is a symbolic rather than
specific dramatic action, one of compound cultural reference. Selected and
traditionally established features or attributes were sufficient to identify an
animal generically, leaving it free to take on whatever specific meaning or
meanings its cultural use assigned it, as, for instance, the bear used in one
place as a family crest and someplace else in reference to the Bear Mother
myth. There would have been no need for a narrative or explanatory art for
an audience who lived in an envelope of faith and understanding that gave
it all the necessary references. Its members would have recognized the
various creatures on a carved pole, have known how they figured in the
myth that was being referred to in the carving, how they related to the
owner's history and place in society; they would have been familiar with
other stories in which this or that animal played a part and what it stood for
in a general way and what its meaning was in the mythology.

That envelope of shared existence and unconscious assumptions in which
the mythological fauna had their vital meaning has long since evaporated.
Then when those creatures continue to be used by contemporary native
artists, how can they be made to have meaning for today's audience? There
is no question that the Indian art produced in recent times has had importance for the native people themselves — in contributing to a sense of
community, in rebuilding morale, and in stimulating a feeling of pride and
hope for a future as a people. For them, to whom the images belong, and for
the Indian artists who use them, the symbols and the art have a special significance and a reconstituting value denied the rest of us.

Carved Cedar Bear 1966
2.44 m long, 1.22 m wide, 1.4 m high
University of British Columbia,
Museum of Anthropology

But how are they to have meaning in the context of art as we understand it presently? Surely the answer is: in any of the ways that artists have used, presently use or may invent for future use, to release imagery from the culturally determined mould in which it was originally cast, and to find for it a new context. This does not mean divesting it of its associative values, an impossibility in any case, for association cannot be shaken off when it comes, bidden or unbidden, with a new or evolving meaning. Modern artists have not hesitated to use the forms and evocation of other cultures and other art when it suited their intention. Indeed some forms of recent art are entirely dependent on the spectator's familiarity with the past works which are being "appropriated" in toto and placed in a new viewing context characterized by ironic awareness. In a historically conscious museum-without-walls society, there are few people for whom native northwest coast imagery would not have some transferred meaning, more sophisticated and of more dimensions for some than for others.

Charles Edenshaw, whom Reid has spoken of as his "Rosetta stone," was in his time the outstanding representative of changes that were occurring in the circumstances and nature of the art. Not to be seen as separate from those changes is the fact that, coming from a past where artists were anonymous, he developed a discernible style of his own. Edenshaw lived through a time of highly accelerated acculturation, growing up in a traditional culture and commencing his work as a professional artist within a society that still had a vital need for his products; and then coming into full maturity as the beliefs and practices that gave purpose to his art were being challenged, undermined or prohibited by the encroaching foreign presence. And so, as an artist working within the Haida tradition, he carved poles and masks and made chests, boxes, frontlets and other items of traditional usage. But he also became a commercial artist, working for trade with white men, making silver bracelets, small totem poles and carved figures and elaborate walking sticks decorated with ivory and silver. Chiefly he was known for his prolific carvings in argillite. This work included many objects that parted with the culturally given form modality of frontality, symmetry and containment; and in a limited way, with their elements of contemporary if generalized iconography and their narrative or dramatic format, they took a significant step outside the time-locked, motionless world of the ancients. And even in those pieces such as the totem poles, which used a traditional (though miniaturized) format as well as traditional iconography, the creatures became detached from their social and cultural function as vital symbols affirming the continuity of a mythical and ordained past with a living present in constant need of shaping. That is to say, those little poles, now objects of commerce, by intention carried no crest and therefore no culturally sacred meanings, and the creatures who occupied them (though they also occupied the big old poles) were becoming culturally portable.

Edenshaw has been criticized by purist observers for straying from the traditional model, but for Reid, though in his opinion perhaps a little "too influenced by the *London Illustrated News,*" he was something of a heroic figure precisely because, in carrying on regardless of the changes he saw happening around him, he "did what he had to do." That included, says Reid, "becoming a very good tradesman. What he did he did very well, and he was very imaginative. He had something that made his work appealing and understandable to people." It is significant that both Reid's and Holm's concept of formline derives from Edenshaw who "got all that tension in his lines and kept an even, elegant and assured flow." It is that central matter of "making-well" that Reid most admired and studied in Edenshaw, but he also absorbed the implications of the culture-shift underlying Edenshaw's argillite style. Reid makes his entrance, so to speak, where Edenshaw leaves off, free to make use of his precedessor's innovations, or to stay close to the older traditional classic style at will.

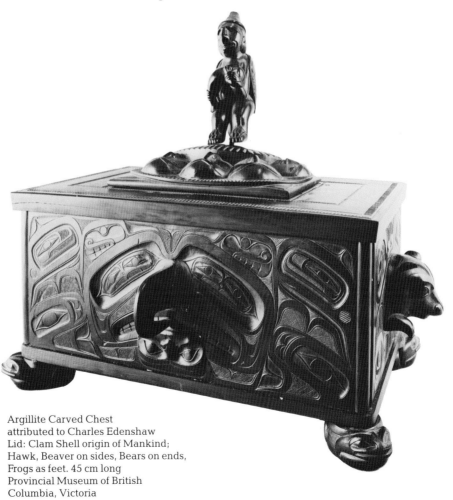

Argillite Carved Chest
attributed to Charles Edenshaw
Lid: Clam Shell origin of Mankind;
Hawk, Beaver on sides, Bears on ends,
Frogs as feet. 45 cm long
Provincial Museum of British
Columbia, Victoria

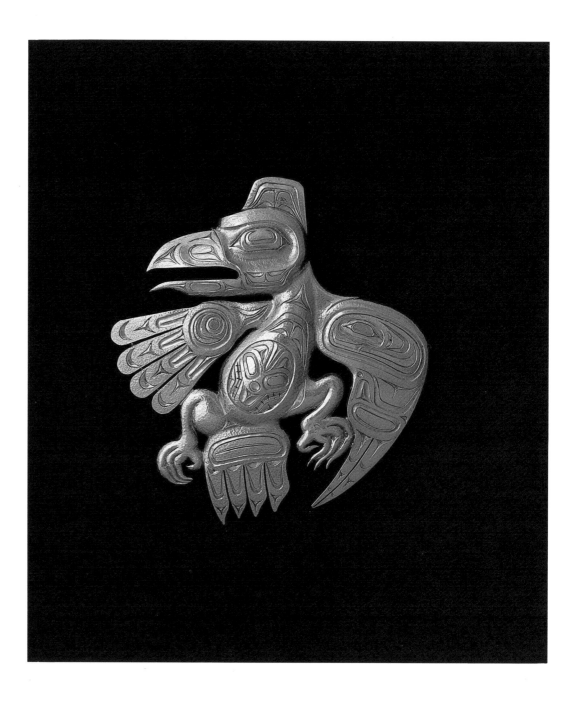

Gold Brooch
Raven design 1971
7 cm long, 6.5 cm wide

Reid's art, like that of the ancestors, finds its centre in creatures drawn from the northwest coast bestiary — animal, human, mythical — and just as particular ancestors had favoured casts of familiars based on inherited rights to crests and stories, Reid has also developed his own repertory, though the ground for his selection was of necessity different. As a contemporary person unbound by the old lineage patterns, and especially with the model before him of Edenshaw and *his* contemporaries, who had already used the creatures for commercial purposes, he presumably was free to choose from the extensive body of myths and all the characters in them recorded by Swanton and others. And yet we find him over the years claiming as his own a fairly small cast relating to comparatively few stories: the Raven, the Bear Mother and her entourage, Nanasimget's wife and her Killer Whale abductor, the Dogfish and mythical lady counterpart, the Wasgo or the Sea Wolf, the Frog, and a few others. What is the basis for Reid's choice? Some of the reasons are practical, for, as he points out, there are only so many of the stories that are reducible to simple terms for twentieth-century minds like his own to grasp. Then too, and hardly surprisingly, there is a marked correspondence between Reid's bestiary and that of his first artistic role-model, Charles Edenshaw. The Raven, for instance, had been Edenshaw's mythical hero whose escapades he celebrated in many carvings, and Reid was able to see photos of some of those carvings and read the myths to which they related, told in somewhat simplified versions in the books of Marius Barbeau. Nor can it be without significance that the Dogfish (or shark), a frequent theme of Bill's, was the dominant one in his grandfather's work.

To these creatures, taken on in the beginning because they were forms familiar in the standard repertory, as well as warmed by family association, Reid has over the years remained faithful. And slowly the relationship appears to have changed and deepened as the creatures have revealed themselves, illuminating the myths in which they find another form of being and at the same time becoming infused with Bill's own imaginative and symbolic projections for them. A reading of those myths which he chose to retell recently in *The Raven Steals the Light*, stories set in a time frame that binds the present into the mythical past and in which he is constanty tweaking our attention to their contemporary relevance, gives us the clue to the ideological framework of his bestiary: he is interested in those stories whose universal message he can receive and transmit, whose meaning can therefore be understood today. In the story of The Bear Mother and Her Husband, for instance, the bear husband/father allows himself to be killed, in a dignified and ritualized sacrifice, by his wife's hunter brothers in order that the Bear clan might be established.

121

This story, with its strong sense of destiny, was "written" in unknown myth-time, but its message was for the future, for it was retold by generations of Indians in real-time as part of the validation of their social patterns and belief structures: the symbolic past working constructively in the present. As the creatures charged with carrying such time-weighted responsibility became better known to Reid, it was perhaps inevitable that they would grow in dimension in the space of his imagination, asserting their own will, as it were, and as often happens in creative enterprise, to the surprise of their maker.

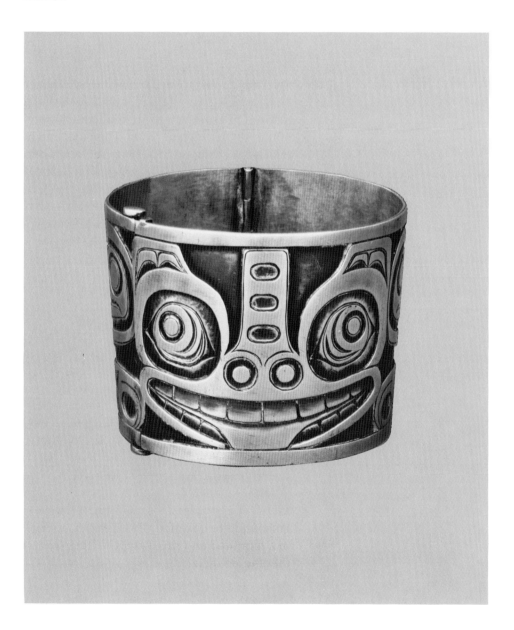

Hinged Silver Bracelet
Tschumos design c. 1958
4.4 cm wide

Silver Brooch
Tschumos design c. 1958
5.5 cm diameter

Silver Brooch
Raven, Bear and Frog 1957
2.6 cm wide, 7.9 cm long

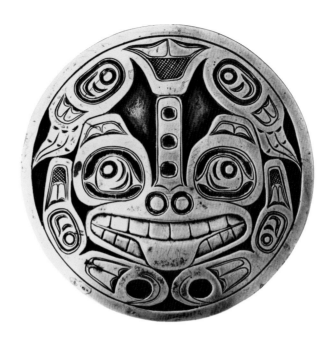

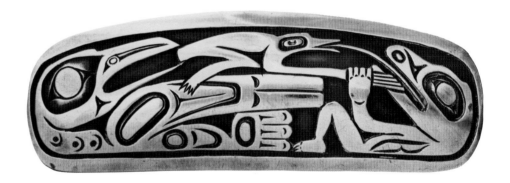

Reid's earliest work, as well as numerically constituting the major portion of his total oeuvre — and some would say his most characteristic and important — are his small pieces, the jewellery and boxes in gold and silver. At first he worked in silver, then later switched almost exclusively to gold, often enhancing pieces with inlays of ivory or abalone shell.[1] He has done many bracelets, a form which had its antecedents within the tradition. Made from melted-down silver and gold pieces the Haidas had received from white visitors, but for which they had little conventional use, bracelets were fairly commonly worn by women of rank, at least at the time of Charles Edenshaw who, Reid believes, reinvented the technique of metal engraving with which he decorated them.

123

But Reid also made brooches and pendants as well as smaller items like cufflinks and earrings in the early days when he had to think first of sales. Jewellery-making from the beginning offered him a way of holding on to the tradition while earning a living within the present consumer society, and it has given him the deep satisfactions that are connected with the intimacy of the workbench and with the practice of the formline system of surface design he loves and knows so well. It offers splendid opportunity for the display of design capability and technical virtuosity, and in both these areas Reid has set a standard which makes his work in this field distinguishable in any company. Only when he considers the possibility that he might have carried on in contemporary jewellery design without the connection of tradition do the possible limitations of the form occur to him. And jewellery-making might appear to offer limited opportunity for the expression of content — in fact, limited visibility for such content — for the ornamenting purpose of a piece and sometimes the aura of preciousness, even the dazzle of a precious material, can deflect the attention from the work itself.

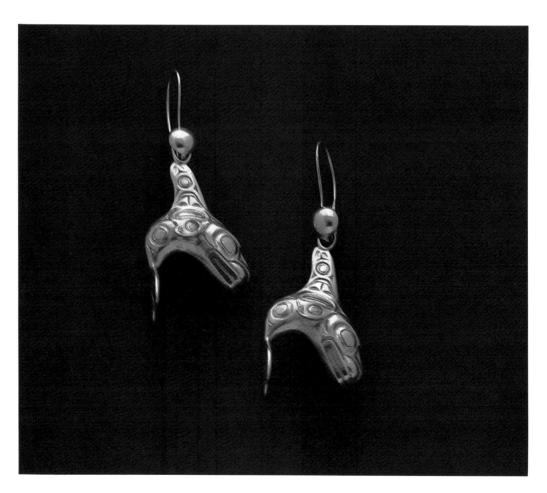

Gold Earrings
Killer Whale design 1974
2 cm long

Fossil Ivory Brooch
Eagle design 1965.
Oval, 4.3 cm long, 3.5 cm wide

Gold Earrings
with Fossil Ivory inlay
Thunderbird design
1964–65
4 cm long, 2.1 cm wide

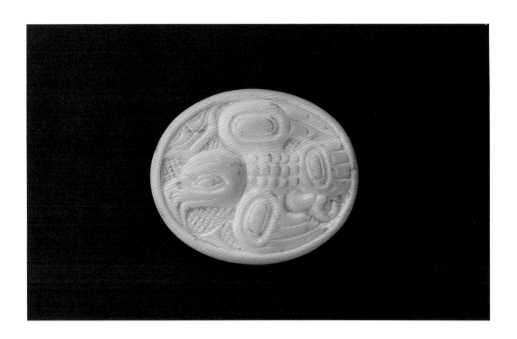

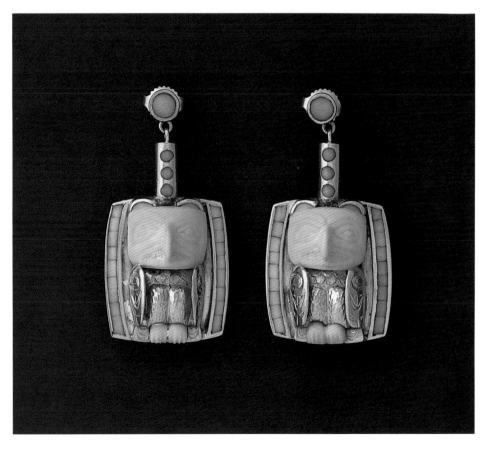

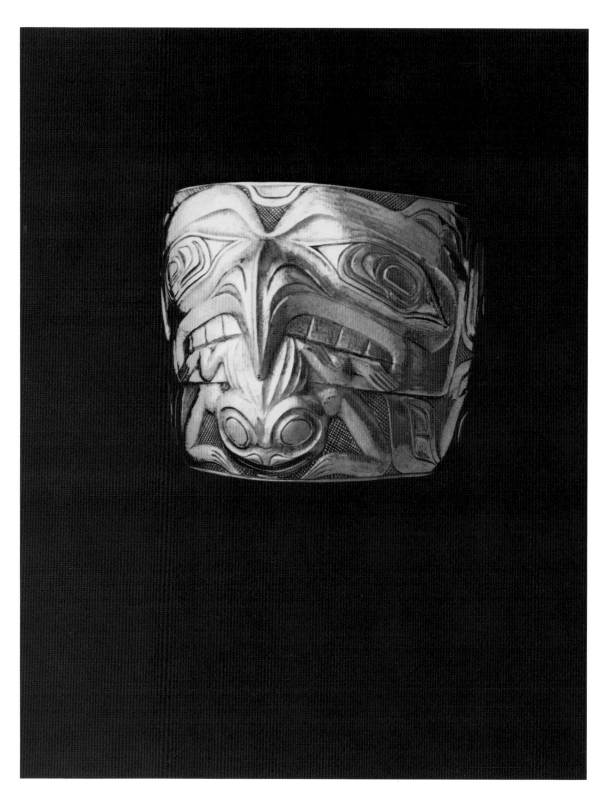

Gold Bracelet
Eagle and Frog design 1967
5.3 cm wide

Silver Brooch
The Woman in the Moon c. 1954
5.2 cm diameter

Man's Gold Bracelet
Wolf and Raven design 1969.
5 cm wide

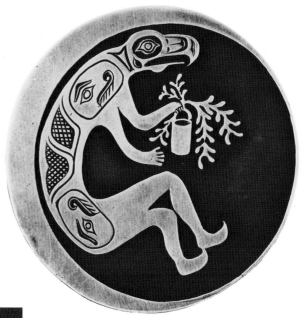

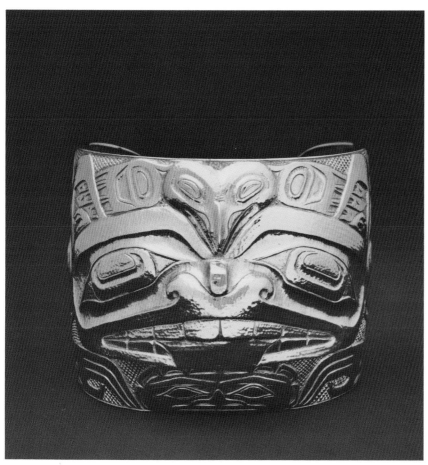

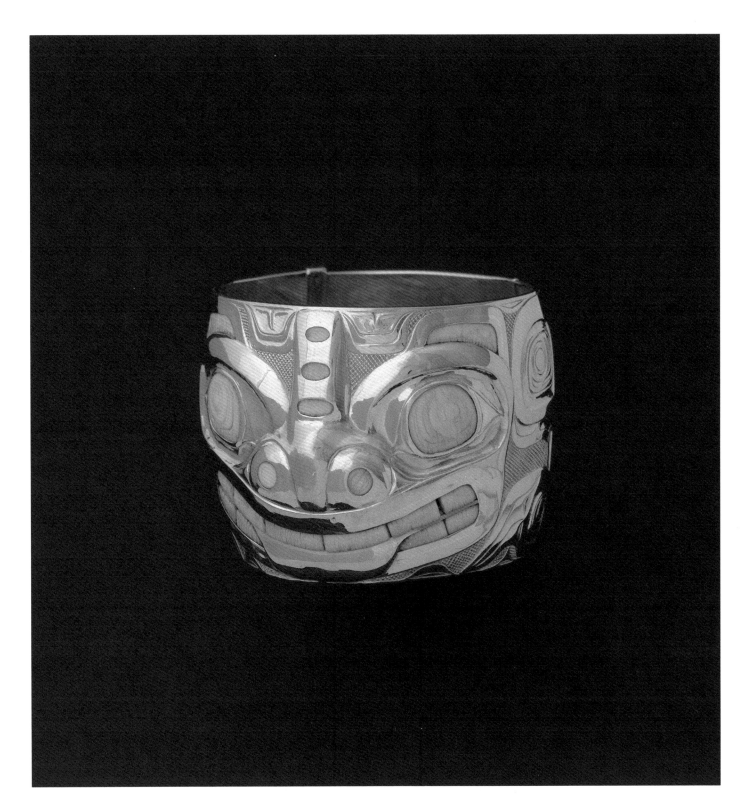

Yet Reid has succeeded in making jewellery a form of small sculpture, eminently wearable, exquisitely made, each piece presenting itself effectively as object and, when he wishes, as creature. The hinged gold Bear bracelet of 1964 with fossil ivory inlay has as much presence as an old carved chest despite its small size; in fact it is as though the spirit of the old containers had been transposed into a contemporary object of different size, material and function without loss of scale or import. The Tschumos, a mythological animal with the head of a bear, takes over the bracelet, its great head claiming the full front section, its thrust built into the bracelet's double curve, both its circumference and the outwardly swelling width of its band. The deeply carved image, its recessed eye sockets with raised edges and heavy eyelids, the elevated nose with extended nostrils, the wide-stretched row of teeth with protruding tongue, rather than adorning the gold absorbs it into its existence as formidable creature. In such a piece Reid has exploited the three-dimensional possibilities of the bracelet to express a strong creature presence within the bracelet function.

Other approaches lend themselves to a more decorative intention, as in the silver brooch bearing a design based on an illustration of the legendary Man in the Moon which he found in Alice Ravenhill's government pamphlet.[2] There is a copy of the same drawing by Bill's grandfather in the Archives of the Museum of Anthropology, so perhaps he made use of the design as well. Ravenhill also tells the story behind the drawing, that of the man who, while washing out his bucket preparatory to filling it with salal berries, was seized in the rays of Koong, the Moon, along with his bucket and salal bush, and carried up into the moon where they can still be seen when it is full. The tiny labret in the lower lip of the creature in both the drawing and Reid's version of it actually indicates a woman in the moon, rather than a man. Reid did a number of copies of the brooch which was very attractive and very salable. The technique is basically that of appliquéing shapes cut out from sheet silver to a background piece of the same metal. The whole piece is then chemically blackened and the dark oxidization removed from the raised surfaces by polishing. This technique produced a very clean-cut and elegant flat design based on clarity of contour and the contrast of bright clean silver shapes against the sooty oxidation. Once the object was in use, however, the effective tonal contrast was dissipated as the oxidization wore away, leaving the piece difficult to maintain, and so Reid soon abandoned it.

Hinged Gold Bracelet
with Fossil Ivory inlay
Tschumos design c. 1964
5.3 cm wide

The carved cedar Bear of 1966, which is now in the collection of the UBC Museum of Anthropology, is modelled on the large sculptures that served as catafalques in the traditional society — carved structures on which a body was laid "in state" while awaiting the making of a mortuary pole and the organization of all the necessary ceremonies. Reid's bear remains very close to the traditional sculptures — solid, rigidly frontal and four-square, shoulders bulky and massive, outthrust head held rigid by glaring eyes and menacing teeth; it is as though it had been conceived within a giant rectangular box which gave it its shape and its frightening compression. In the museum where it stands today it commands its own psychological space as compellingly as the older companions with whom it keeps company.

The 17.4-metre frontal pole, which was his gift to Skidegate in 1978, appears to be a traditional Haida pole in every way. The main characters — the Bear (of the Bear Mother myth), the Raven, the Killer Whale and the Dogfish — are all traditional crest animals of the Eagle and the Raven, the two main clan divisions of the area. They occupy the main terrain of the pole and determine the major strategy of the composition while secondary characters sprout from ears or mouths, straddle dorsal fins or squat between knees; there are human faces with bird-beak noses, bird tails that become little faces, and three little watchmen on top of the pole looking out in different directions, just as their antecedents did many years before from similar poles on the same beach. The pole, like those earlier ones, is dense with interlinked creature life and compacted formal energy. There are also Bill's touches of fun, whose apparently irrational counterparts he takes pleasure in noting in the old pieces, like the little men he spent two weeks carving into the Raven's ears.

There is, however, a significant way, not revealed in the pole itself, in which it differs from its antecedents. In traditional usage the pole had specific heraldic function, the main creatures at least having crest value for its owner, or relevance to stories important in the establishing of family lineage and rank. Here the four main creatures are selected as world symbols, signifying the elements of land (the Bear), air (the Raven) and sea (the Whale and Dogfish). Of course Reid had for some time been using animals long since detached from their home place in a belief structure, but this was the first time he had consciously asked them to take on a universal meaning that was prior to, though certainly not inconsistent with, their specific mythic meanings. In 1969 Robert Davidson had carved a pole for his native village, Masset, which like Reid's was not attached to family significance. In his pole he too was careful that all his people should be represented, and so had given prominence to the main crests of the two chief Haida clan divisions.

Perhaps these are the first poles in native villages not concerned with family status, but which instead, as the work of socially and historically aware

Reid's Pole of 1978 in front of
the Band Council building at Skidegate

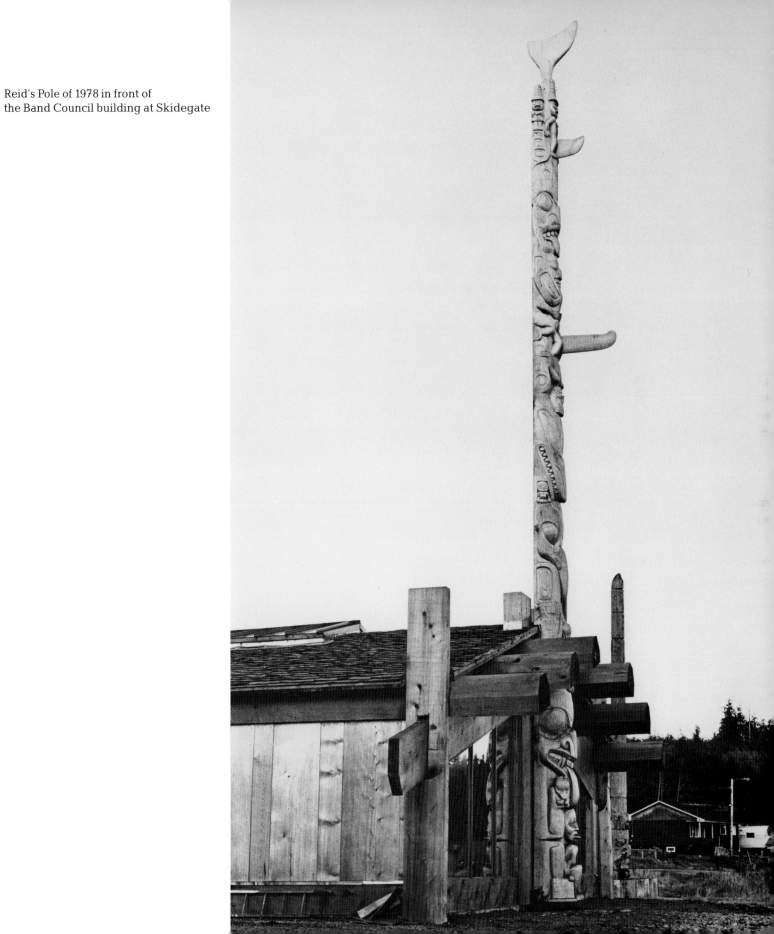

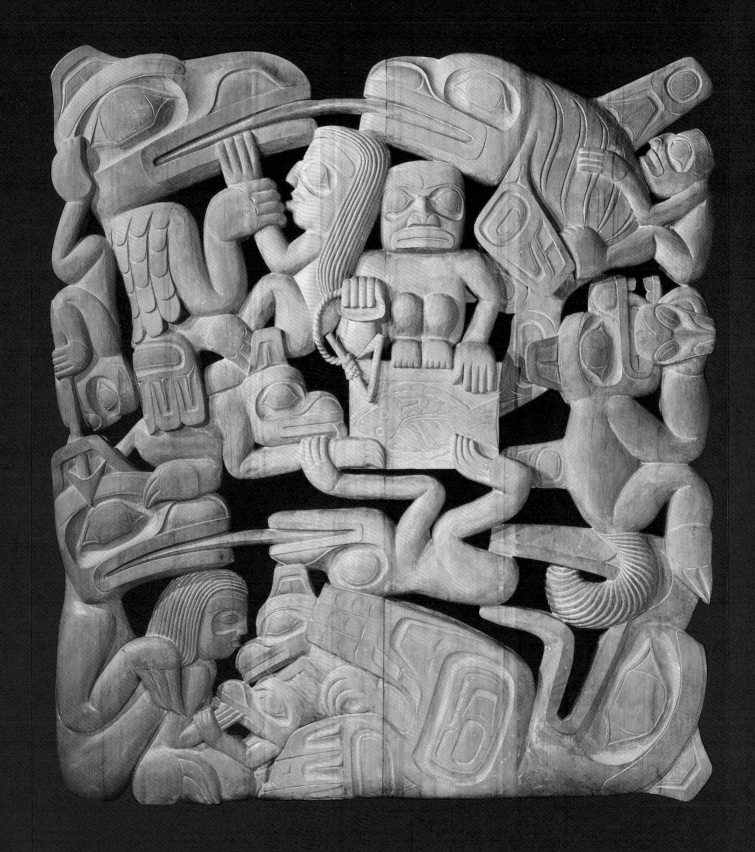

contemporary artists, aspire to a broader relevance. The irony is, as Reid points out, that the old ranking customs and modes of thought have retreated so far into the past that probably few if any villagers recognize the animals in his pole, or wonder what their meaning might be.

A more visible adaptation of the tradition to a contemporary use can be seen in the large laminated cedar screen Reid carved for the British Columbia Provincial Museum in 1968. The style and the concept are based on that of the nineteenth-century carvers of slate pipes who laid their figures out, usually sideways, in lateral compositions held together by the dense compacting and linking of creatures in acts of holding, confronting, clinging or other kinds of interrelation. The frequently grotesque postures of the figures in those pipes is felt both as the expression of a kind of spastic energy belonging to the creatures, and formally, as the result of compression by an implied, but unstated, enclosing outer perimeter, generally somewhat lozenge-shaped with a flat base. Reid's innovation lies in transposing the style to another material and onto a large scale, while working within a nearly square field which denied him the relative ease of a horizontal composition. "Seventy-five dollars worth of stories" is what he says of the five narratives referred to in the piece: starting clockwise lower left, the Bear Mother and Father and his dog; the Raven who changes himself into a fisherman; Nanasimget who rescues his wife captured by killer whales; the Seawolf with his spiralled tail; and the Eagle and Frog who are part of the Eagle Prince story. Shaped by their square container while crowding it to the full, like passengers in a subway car, the creatures are arranged in interlocking complexity, one form with the next and over or under, around the sides of the square, each creature transmitting its energy to one or more of the others while the frontal figure of the seated fisherman serves as the stable pivot. It is another statement of the archetypal Indian dialectic: the holding container and its seething contents. Most of these characters will appear again fifteen years later in Mythic Messengers, a bronze outdoor work in which Reid provides them with an even larger stage.

Laminated Cedar Screen
Several Haida stories are referred
to in representations of the
Bear Mother, Raven, Big Fisherman,
Nanasimget, a Sea Wolf, Eagle
and Frog 1968.
2.1 m high, 1.9 m wide, 14.6 cm deep
British Columbia Provincial
Museum, Victoria

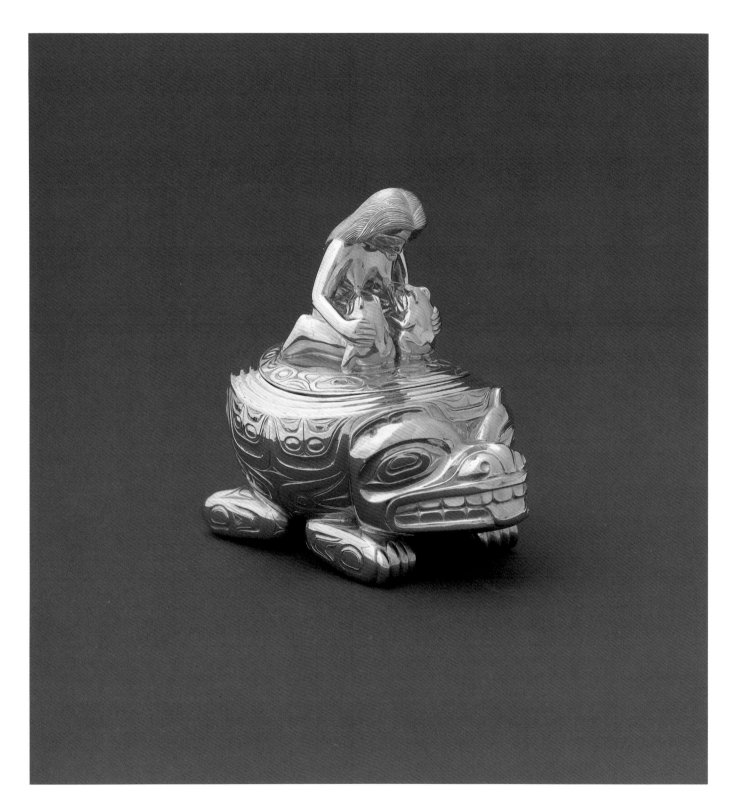

134

Drawing inspiration from traditional chests, boxes and bowls, the making of their contemporary versions in silver or gold required only the extension of his metal-working techniques, already well developed by 1967, the date of the first box. Of the dozen or so he has made, the covered gold bowl in the form of a bear with a lid bearing the cast forms of the Bear Mother suckling her two bear cubs is undoubtedly the most ambitious, conceptually and technically. Giving a vessel a multiple meaning, which includes that of its function, its significance as animal and the surprising new meaning arising from their synthesis, was standard practice in the old tradition. The synthesis would have been intuitively understood within the cultural context without any need to have it articulated. Reid, in this fresh and bold statement, tightens the synthesis without indulging in mimicry: the bowl as a valid form and the bear coexist, each in terms of the other. Unlike his straight-sided boxes formed by soldering panels of sheet metal at the edges, the swelling form and rounded lid of this bowl were "raised," that is, shaped by hammering against a steel form. The protruding and deeply modelled head and the large supporting feet were added to the squat couchant body, transforming the gold, enriching it as it were, with the new meaning, the new presence of Bear. The group of Bear Mother and cubs on the cover were hollow cast by the lost-wax method, a risk-filled procedure in those days when Bill used a silicone mould which was destroyed during the process, leaving no backup should anything go wrong in the first run. Apart from the labret worn in the mouth of the woman, and somewhat conventional eye-sockets and brows, the group is modelled in a style of simplified naturalism; there is no northwest coast Indian stylization to suggest her lineage. Theoretically this difference between the handling of the bowl and the figures on the lid might have been seen as a failure in stylistic unity, but in fact it works positively, serving to connect in our imagination a past which is known only at second hand and a possible living reality — the past, that is, given a present dimension. In this bridging of realms, the labret is like a small atavistic memory. Charles Edenshaw had also applied the Bear Mother theme to a covered vessel, in his case a round argillite comport; the bowl carries the image of a beaver, and a carved human mother with a single bear cub serves as the handle on the lid.[3] But Edenshaw's work reads as an assemblage of parts; there is neither the fusion of forms nor the integrity of meanings that Reid has achieved in his piece.

Gold Dish with cover
Dish formed in shape of a Bear,
raised cover surmounted by cast
three-dimensional Woman
suckling two Cubs 1972.
7.3 cm high, 7 cm long, 5.2 cm wide
National Museum of Man, Ottawa

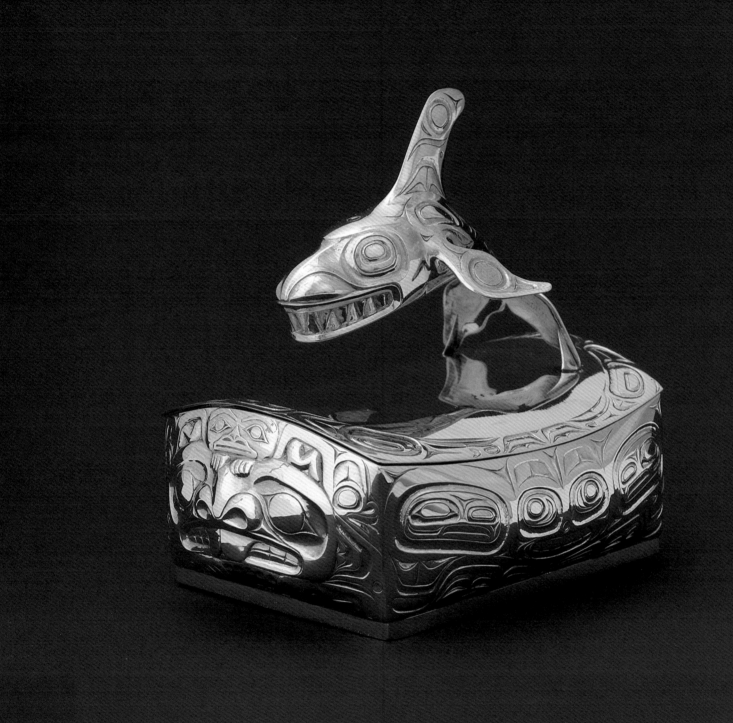

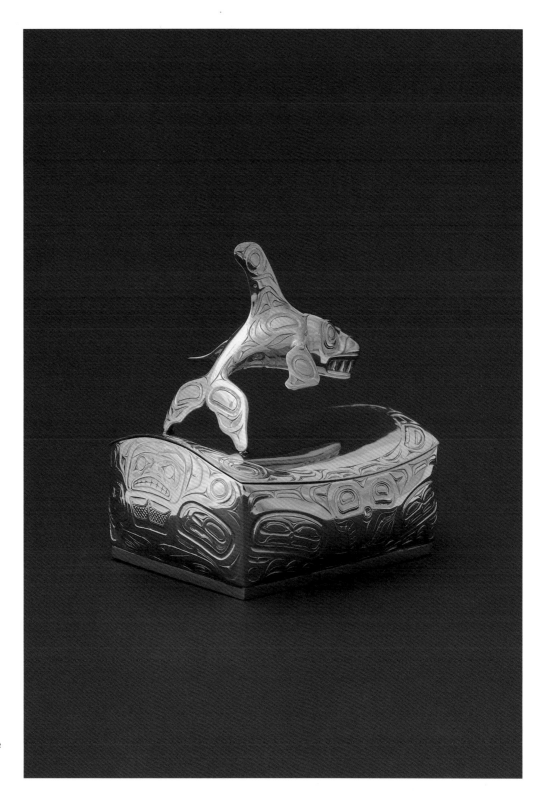

Gold Box
Beaver and Human design on box
and cast three-dimensional Killer
Whale on cover 1971.
9 cm high, 9.9 cm long, 7.9 cm wide
British Columbia Provincial
Museum, Victoria

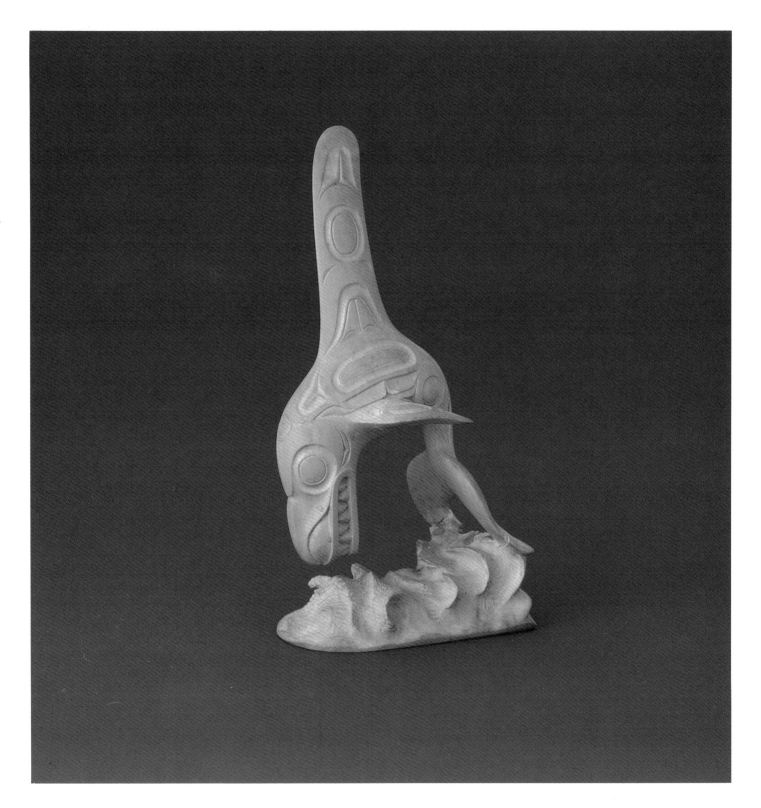

138

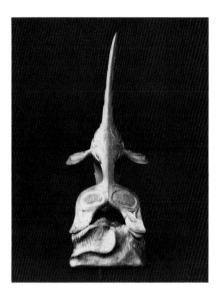

A similar juxtaposition of naturalism and stylization occurs in his small boxwood sculpture of the Killer Whale where the stylized whale rises from an intricately carved wild and tormented sea. A miniature piece still owned by Reid, it is known only through the large bronze version (for which it served as model) commissioned for a position outside the Aquarium in Vancouver's Stanley Park, where thousands of visitors have seen it. There are also cast versions in several sizes and materials. The progenitor for the entire family can be found in the whale that rises from the lid of a gold box done in 1971 (in the collection of the British Columbia Provincial Museum). In all the versions the whale is an assertively three-dimensional form to whose body and dorsal fin Haida design has been applied, making its ancestral connections very clear. And nearly all the versions, unlike the small original boxwood, have formalized bases; the Aquarium whale, for instance, rises from a small circular pool whose surface forms a glassy smooth disc. The tiny boxwood whale carries Reid's original idea that there should be a ''real'' sea as a base from which the whale might rise, rather than a formalized base on which to rest and to give it an abstract context. That original idea resulted in a strong piece, and one that carries its special poignant message: Reid's inescapable ache for the past and will for its meaning in the present. On one of his many cruises in the waters surrounding the Queen Charlotte Islands, Reid was observed showing a photo of this carving to the ship's captain, and demanding, after a night of wild storm, ''There, does *that* look like Hecate Strait?'' Reid today does feel, in the experiential sense, the past as a living continuity in the present. And the expression of that continuity, for which he failed to find an artistic solution in his illustrations for Harris's book, he achieves in both this little whale carving and the Bear Mother gold box: the problem of seamlessly welding two modes of vision, one relating to the

Boxwood Carving
Killer Whale 1983
11.5 cm high; Base: 5.9 cm wide

139

mythic past, the other to a present experience. Although he would deny any claim so apparently self-conscious, the effective marrying of myth with some felt experience of reality may, in fact, be seen by others as the central concern that he has taken on in recent years.

It was essentially the same problem that he tackled, though in a different way, in his first boxwood carving. Only three and a half inches high, and done in 1970, the Raven discovering humankind in a clamshell marks an important point in his career, not only because it is a fine work in itself and one which led some ten years later to the large version, The Raven and the First Men, but also because it indicated a significant break with the old tradition. Reid's verbal retelling of the story behind the carvings is marked by a sense of ridiculous and quixotic mystery which the boxwood carving captures and which seems precisely related to its size. There is humour in the huge and cocky raven squatting possessively on his prize, and in the humanoids outrageously oversized for their clamshell, while dwarfed by their unfeeling discoverer, squirming out of its murky interior or crawling back in presumed apprehension at the prospects outside. We are witnessing the precise moment marking the beginning, not only of biological existence for man but also of human consciousness and feeling. In his recounting of the story (see The Raven Steals the Light) he tells how those little men, once outside and on the beach and sexually overcome by the chitons which the Raven had hurled at them, "were astounded, embarrassed, confused by a rush of new emotions and sensations. They shuffled and squirmed, uncertain whether it was pleasure or pain they were experiencing." While sharing the same conceptual qualities, the large version, a big public statement requiring the participation of a number of carvers, as a sensory object inevitably loses some of the immediacy and magic. Areas in the small piece left for the imagination to complete, like the interior of the shell glimpsed between bodies, arms and legs, in the large version become substantial spaces that cannot avoid being made explicit; the vigour left as the trace of the carving tool, which could with one direct flick create shape, in the broad expanses of the larger work becomes mannered; the humanoids have lost some of the primal urgency they had in their more delicate articulation. This in no way diminishes its importance as a large-scale statement capable of touching a broad public with its strong and affecting message.

The old Haida myth from which the subject is drawn had been used by Charles Edenshaw in argillite carvings, and Reid, in his remarks at the official unveiling of the large version, acknowledged that the work was a direct outcome of Edenshaw's treatment of the theme. Reid had used it on a silver bracelet and earrings in the fifties, and it also became the subject of one of his silk-screen prints. However, despite its link with Edenshaw, the concept in an important way is entirely Reid's own. The typical surface

140

Boxwood Carving
*Raven Discovering Mankind
in the Clam Shell* 1970
7 cm high
University of British Columbia,
Museum of Anthropology

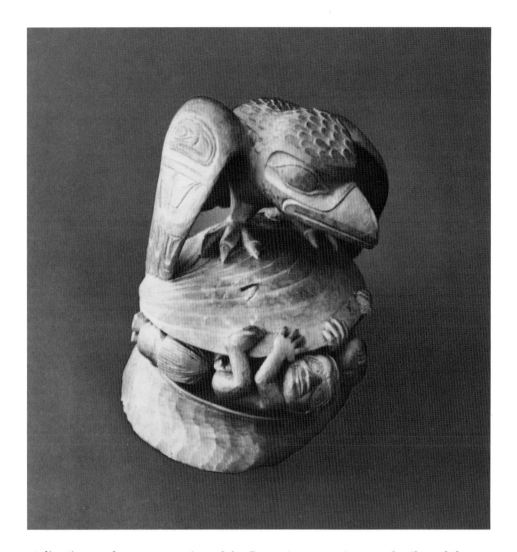

stylization and ornamentation of the Raven's eyes, wings and tail, and the
masklike faces of the little men with eyes sunk in ovoid sockets clearly claim
their origin in traditional Haida art. And there is again (in the boxwood)
the quality of exquisite miniaturization to relate it to so many of the small
ancient objects — the carved handle of a horn spoon, for instance — where
a large world, as though viewed through a magic lens, is by reduction made
immediately comprehensible in all its complexity and detail, and as in this
piece, where both the act of physical-making, reflected in the tool-marked
surface, and the overall concept of the piece are apprehended in the same
intimate recognition.

In addition, and more completely than any of his previous work until then, it
has stepped out of the ancestors' frame of arrested time into real time where
events take place and creatures move in dramatic interaction. The work is

141

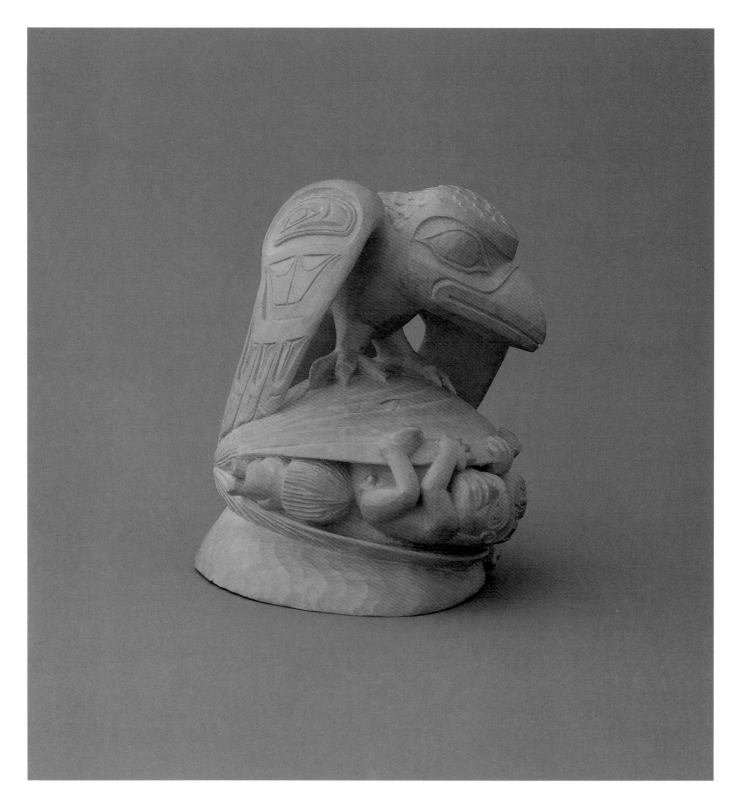

not dependent on the viewer's prior knowledge to grasp what it is about — it tells its own story. A fully three-dimensional piece, broken out of its outer skin or container, and no longer held immobile by a central frontal axis, the composition moves and twists from within, and the effective tensions no longer operate only on a surface plane of limited depth. It must be experienced, not from four sides like one of the old chests, because it has no "sides," but from all angles in continuing movement.

Such observations reflect western European-based assumptions about art and how we look at it, perhaps so securely lodged as to require no elaboration, yet their deep significance when seen in a context that includes the traditional art of the Indian past might be overlooked. Edenshaw, in his own time and way, considerably cracked "the container." But he did not break out as Reid did in this piece. Reid's ambition is not to free himself from the tradition. He is a conservative artist, as he admits, not given to sudden flashes or changes, and the old art, which he took such time and care to learn and absorb and which was so interwoven in its complexity as to defy easy dissection, so tied to his own roots, was not the material for casual plunder or experimentation. So the shift represented in this piece was for him a major one: moving beyond the formal dictate of a culture he could admire but not be part of to the position of personal artistic determination and choice permitted to artists in his own time. He had moved out of the past without losing his connection with it, retaining both the mythic reference and selected stylistic features, and in the process of change, freeing the creatures, who continue to be the centre of his work, to find new connections in a modern world. In this case the shift is primarily a dramatic one, off the icon into the theatre, with the Raven and the first humans acting out in the work itself that moment of startling discovery which the story tells. Reid would continue to return to the containing paradigm; but from now on it would be an option of personal choice, as it is for any other contemporary artist, to be used for its particular inherent expressive possibilities, or for whatever reasons might be suggested by external considerations. How appropriate that the Raven in the act of releasing mankind into the world by breaking his clamshell container should provide the image through which Reid secures his own release!

Reid recently wrote an article taking to task anthropologists and other writers dealing with northwest coast Indian mythology for their practice of dropping the article when referring to the creatures of legend, that is speaking of "Raven" or "Bear" rather than "*the* Raven," or "*a* Bear."[4] While delighting in the parody and fun of the old myths, he respects their serious poetic function and responds to their underlying symbolism, and he would not have that significance diminished by language that reduces them to the level of children's bedtime stories.[5]

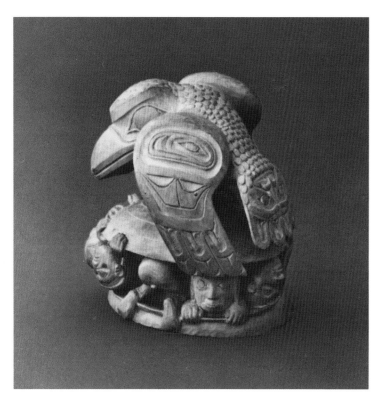

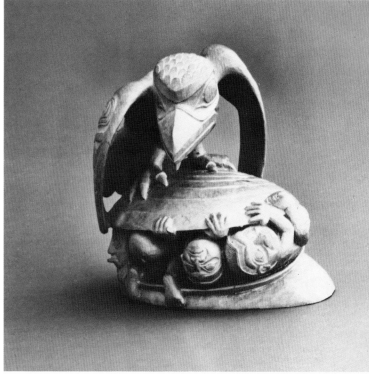

In this connection, a discussion of The Raven and the First Men offers an appropriate point of reference to that slowly changing evolution in Reid's inner relation to the creatures whom in the beginning he frankly "used" as design components, not having been concerned with their possible mythic aura or dramatic context. (He still does, of course, use them that way when the occasion calls for it.) As he has worked with them, and given them form, in the slow processes demanded by most of his art-making, they have taken on that aura and, if he so desired (as in the case of The Raven and the First Men), dramatic context; and in addition they have assumed psychological dimension and imaginative reality for him, becoming creatures wielding their own mythopoetic power in the present. Out of their number a special few have emerged — those in which he has found an archetypical meaning that he can personally relate to — and with these it appears he has come, in some sense, to identify. The Raven is chief among those already familiar ones whom he has interiorized. The fact of identifying the clan to which his grandmother belonged, and being the "hero" of Edenshaw celebrated in so many of his carvings, gave the Raven a privileged place in Reid's bestiary from the beginning. For Reid that place became consolidated with the Raven's emerging character as the original wunderkind whose world-

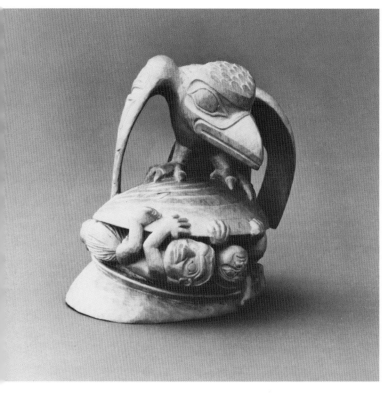
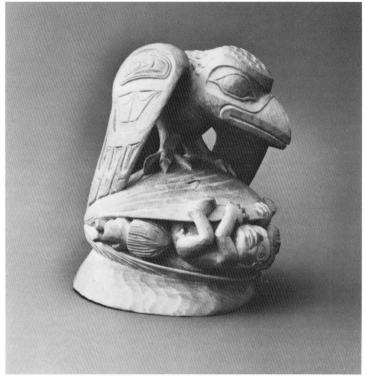

shaping, wonder-making transformations had nothing to do with pious good intentions but emerged from an improbable but fortuitous creative intuition coupled with a detached and open self-interest. A toughened survivor without illusions, able to cope with all the unpredictables life hurled at him, the Raven — perhaps the first existentialist — presents a world that cannot be reduced to a neat system since it is by nature illogical and unintelligible. Reid, in full ironic and delighted awareness, finds this trickster a creature capable of being his hero, just as he also was, though in relative cultural innocence, to his great-uncle Charlie. But for Reid something beyond admiration of qualities or actions for which a contemporary relevance can be found is involved here; there is an inner recognition, a willing granting of continuing immanence as a potent force or spirit, an involuntary "testament of faith" on his part — a testament which his pragmatic intellectual self would deny but the truth of which is to be found in his late work and witnessed in his involuntary and often poetic asides. The Dogfish with his/her female alter ego and, for Reid, her quintessentially female mystery and power is another deeply interiorized personal/universal symbol; and the Frog, it would appear, may well be in the process of becoming one.

145

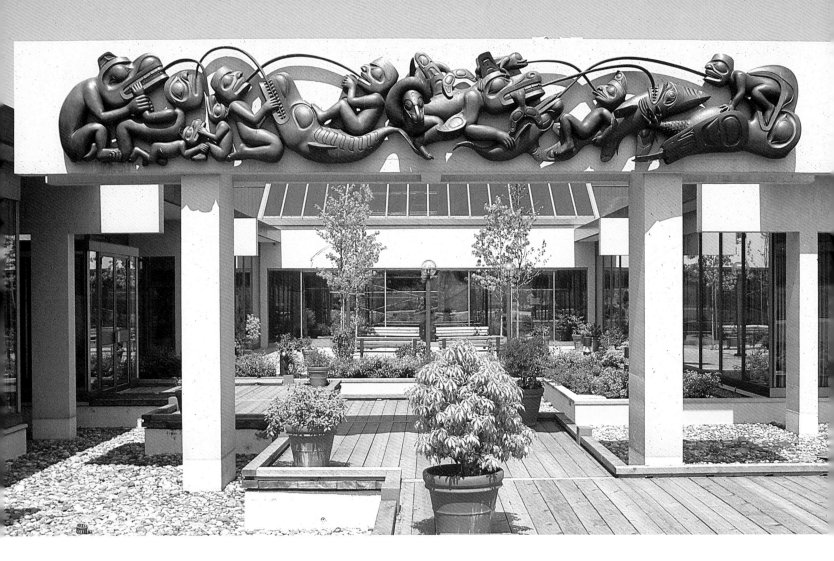

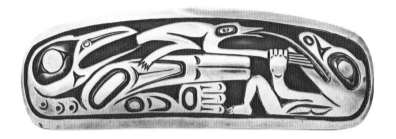

146

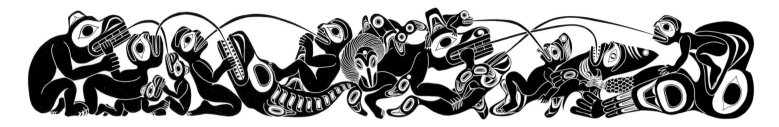

Bronze Relief Mural
Mythic Messengers
From the left,
the Bear Mother, Bear and Cubs;
Nanasimget, his Wife and her
Killer Whale abductor;
the Sea Wolf; the Dogfish Woman;
the Eagle Prince
8.5 m long, 1.2 m high, 45.7 cm deep
Teleglobe Canada, Burnaby 1984–85

Drawing: Jerry Grey

Vitalization of a different kind from that in The Raven and the First Men transforms the creatures in Mythic Messengers, a work commissioned by Teleglobe and completed in 1984. This is the second large outdoor work in bronze (the first being the Aquarium's Killer Whale of a year previous), and Reid is the first Indian artist to do substantial work in this medium. He would claim particular distinction for this no more than he would reject purist criticism for the innovation, pointing out again his ancestors' capacity for taking advantage of new materials or tools when opportunity arose. The responsibility in undertaking these large works is enormous, especially for someone with health problems. He was thoroughly familiar with the casting of small objects and had experimented with various types of moulds and casting processes, but the technical challenge of the big piece is of a different order and required his dependency on the special skills of others. The stylistic lineage of Mythic Messengers goes back once again to the argillite pipes of the nineteenth century, a form which we can see Reid accommodating to his own use in an early silver brooch of 1959. Its lozenge shape (really an elongated ovoid here) relates to the pipes, as does the running low-relief approach to composition, and the enforced interconnectedness of creatures which occurs in so many of them. His wooden screen, already discussed, is another link in the evolutionary chain. Argillite, he points out, is not an ideal substance aesthetically and so its nature "must be transcended"; besides, he says, with a mediating grin, it is nasty to work with, producing so much fine black dust in the process of carving that it should only be undertaken in a high wind. Nonetheless he overcame his reservations and in 1969 carved his own slate pipe (as well as other argillite pieces), demonstrating that he could produce a good intricate piece in the manner of the nineteenth-century Haida carvers. From left to right, spread in a lateral composition, sometimes piled on top of each other, clutching, hanging on with the mouth, kneeling, lying, squeezed into curious positions, are: the Bear Father and Mother with their twin cubs, a Raven and Frog, and the Seawolf with his daily ration of three whales.

147

This pipe presents an interesting comparison with the Mythic Messengers with which it shares, in addition to the basic horizontal low-relief concept, a large part of its subject matter. But while maintaining its connection with the tradition, and in addition to the change in scale and material, it represents a transformation in form and content that makes it accessible to twentieth-century sensibility. The implied frame or containing perimeter, which in the pipe appears to be the force that compresses the figures in a constricting proximity, opens up in the bronze, allowing the figures breathing space and the expression of their physical individuality. It gives clear visibility to the vast tongue exchange which is going on in great thin, stretching arcs of bronze, connecting all but three of the sixteen figures in the composition. Communication is the clear message conveyed by those linking tongues in their modern situation, but it is presented as an extension of the mysterious older messages, whatever they might have been, giving them special resonance. Apart from their identifying attributes, the figures are generalized as befits their shared mythical existence, their bodies serving for male or female, animal or human, as in the tradition. But there is a different vitality; they have moved out of the claustrophobic space and convulsive nightmare frequently projected by the early pipe and are now clothed in the gleaming sinuous flesh of bronze. A surreal note is still there, but it belongs to a dream which our imagination can inhabit.

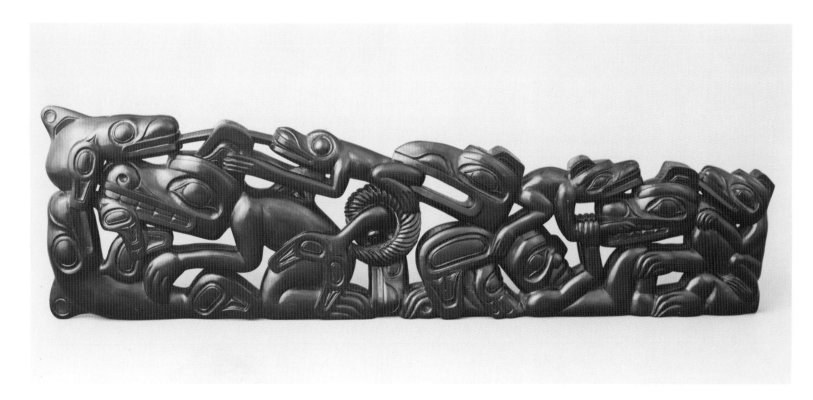

148

Argillite Pipe
Figures from the Bear Mother
legend, and Raven, Sea Wolf,
Killer Whales and Frog 1969.
27 cm long, 8 cm wide,
1.2 cm deep

Argillite Totem Pole
Beaver and Frog 1962
9.3 cm high
University of British Columbia
Museum of Anthropology

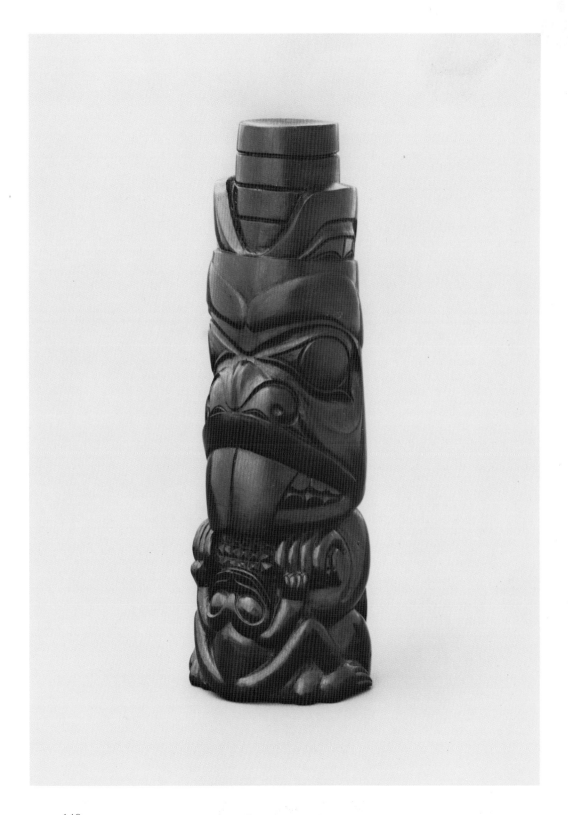

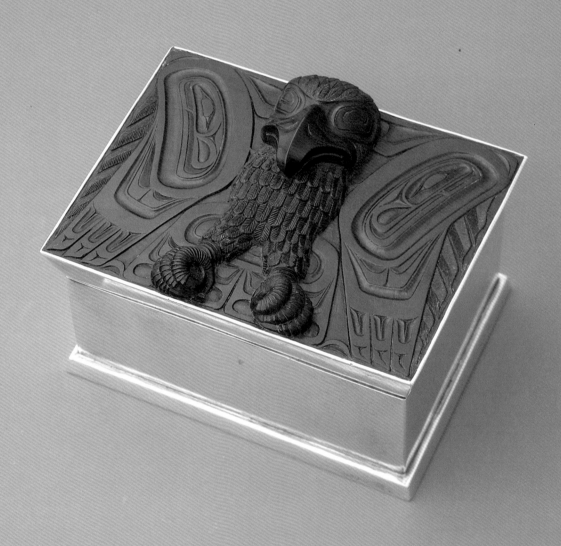

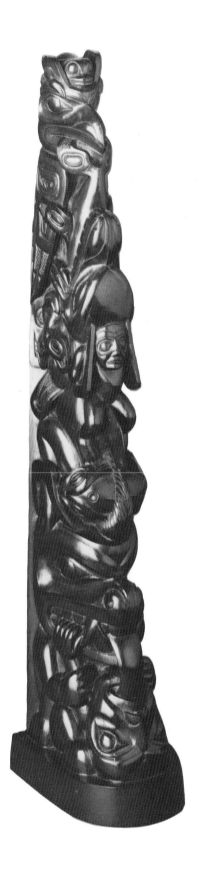

Silver Box
Hinged Lid inset with Argillite
Eagle design 1971
Box: 7 cm wide, 9.7 cm long, 3.9 cm high
Lid: 8 cm long, 10.5 cm wide, 1.5 cm high

Argillite Totem Pole
Base: Grizzly Bear and Human;
SeaWolf, Killer Whale, Human on
dorsal fin, Eagle and Frog 1966
32.4 cm high

The progressive freshening and revitalizing of Reid's mythic creatures was probably stimulated by a literary immersion in some of the myths to which a sequence of events led him early in the 1980s. George MacDonald had asked him to do a series of drawings as chapter headings for his *Haida Monumental Art.* To introduce the various sections of that book, which deals with the houses and poles of the vanished Haida villages, Reid did a set of small black-and-white pencil drawings. They would be more accurately referred to as grey, for the figures, softly shaded, emerge out of darker grey pencilled backgrounds. He referred to these later as "monochrome ghosts," and it was a development of their style that he was to use in *The Raven Steals the Light.*

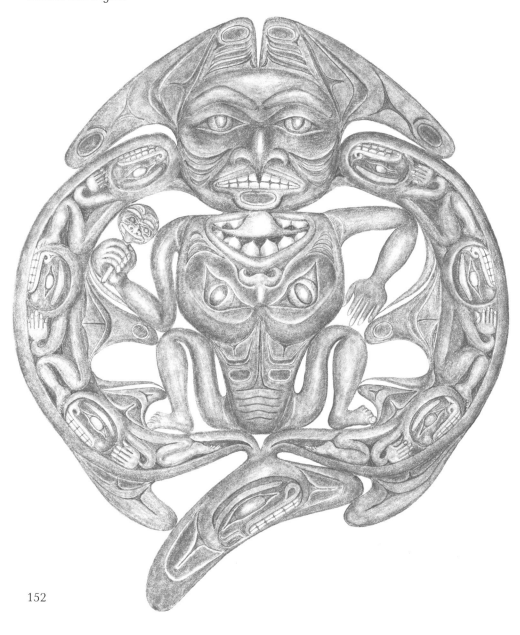

The Dogfish Woman, the last drawing in the latter book, may be, he says, "the strangest and most powerful" of the ten, and interestingly, it is the one for which there is no accompanying story, a situation freeing him from any narrative requirement and compelling him to incorporate all its power into the drawing. In fact, it may well be the strangest and most powerful, the most innovative single work of his career. It draws its theme, its symbolism, its form motifs from the past and yet manages to be entirely its own creation. More than anything it emanates that sense of presence, of spirit-creatures watching and waiting, that so many of the old pieces have, but it does it in its own spirit of ferocity and unnerving intensity. Charles Edenshaw never achieved that dimension of psychological expression. Wilson Duff, an Edenshaw scholar and great enthusiast, pointed out that his little figures "often portrayed emotions." What Edenshaw's figures do is put on the configuration of emotion: they simulate emotion like persons playacting, but they do not become it. He was unable, given his time, to push through his sophisticated if somewhat bland formalism to really penetrate, or reveal, the dark and shadowy realm behind his ancestors' imaging.

The dogfish, a small species of shark noted for its voracity, appeared frequently as a crest animal in Haida art though it was rarely so used among other northwest coast people. It had another form of mythical existence in the Dogfish Woman, a female shaman of reputedly prodigious powers, though the stories that would support her reputation seem to have been unrecorded. Reid's early attraction to the dogfish was probably an admiration for its "classical representation" which, he says, "may well be the most ingenious exercise in abstraction in the whole Haida bestiary." The shark was his grandfather's favourite theme, and a fine drawing by Edenshaw of a labretted woman inside a dogfish was translated by Reid in the late fifties into a gold brooch. In the interval between that brooch and his drawing for the book, it is clear that the subject had become for Reid something quite other than an exercise in abstraction, however ingenious. The Dogfish Woman can be seen in fact, in her persona within Reid's increasingly interiorized bestiary, as foil to the Raven — the female counterpresence in magic and mystery. There had to be a place for such a presence in Reid's own developing mythopoetic bestiary, a metaphor capable of enduring, and holding for possible future expression (as the old forms did in their mute repose) all the personal yearnings and dreams and premonitions that a male image could not represent.

153

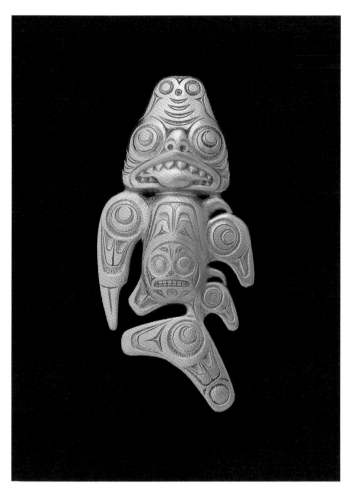

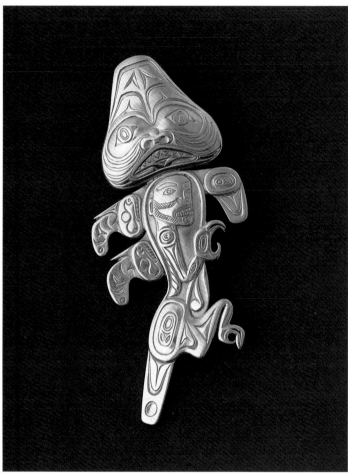

Gold Brooch
Dogfish design 1972
3.8 cm wide, 8 cm long

Gold Brooch
Dogfish design after
Edenshaw c. 1959.
8 cm long

Gold Pendant and Chain
Grizzly Bear design 1972
5 cm diameter

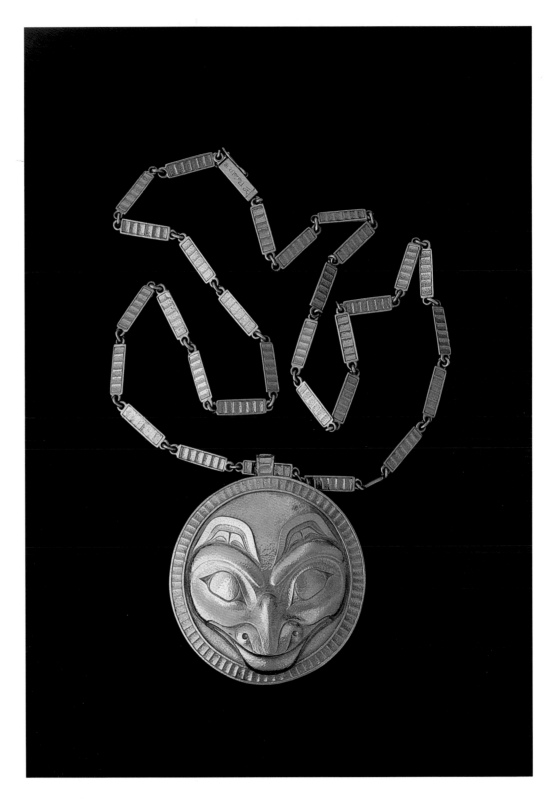

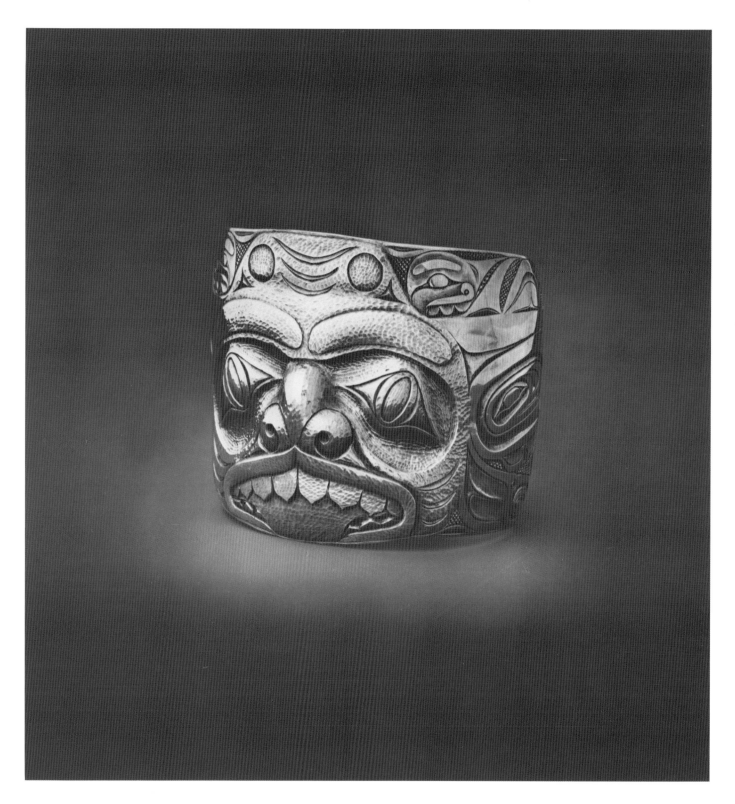

The female presence was given prominence in Haida society for many reasons, and Reid has always been enormously susceptible to feminine beauty and charm, both as biology veiled as grace and as symbolizing an essential part of the structure of poetic truth. In his amalgam of the feminine, beauty, breeding, refinement, elegance, sensitivity, toughness of fibre all are important; it is not a sentimental image, and he does not, when he represents it in his art, reject the labret, that grotesque intrusion into the lip of high-ranking women, for it simply demands a greater beauty to transcend it. His ancestry, his upbringing, his own temperament — the little boy who was fond of nature and did not take to macho behaviour, the man who will fight for the preservation of Lyell Island because it is a "temple, a place of [spiritual] renewal," his distrust of technology and the notion of progress — all his likes and dislikes and inclinations demand a familiar spirit, a "totem" of feminine being to relate to. The Bear Mother, a theme of which Reid is also fond, is woman too, mother and lover, but to those attributes the Dogfish Woman adds that of shaman/magician. That she has lost the legends that would give narrative form to her magical powers only makes her more mysterious and potentially more powerful, and we cannot help but notice that in the book, it is she who is most potent and "has the last word."

What would the ancestors have made of this Dogfish Woman in which nothing, in a way, is new, except the whole new entity? This drawing is no exercise in abstraction. It is, on the contrary, a fleshing-out, the concretization of a metaphysical notion, the coexistence of dual beings, animal and human, spirit and flesh in one body, one form. Reid has observed the conventional identifying features: the gill slits on the cheeks of the woman, a beaklike nose that curves back to the mouth, which wears a labret, the mark of a high-born lady; the Dogfish with its downturned mouth full of sharp teeth and extended tongue, high-domed forehead, two dorsal fins and spines. The ancestors would have read such signals without difficulty, and surely they, in whose art Reid finds so many instances of visual wit, would have delighted in his major stratagem: the woman's torso upside down becomes the shark's head. This is an original statement of transformation with Reid, but it finds an equivalence in the famous transformation masks of the Kwakiutl with their mechanical switch from one identity to another. The circular shape created by splitting and giving bilateral spread to the woman's crown and the shark's body (turned underside out to avoid the crenellation of the dorsal fins) has clear expressive intent; it encloses and gives oneness to the dual existence it contains.

Although carried out on a two-dimensional surface, it does not employ the flat two-dimensional surface style of Haida art, but seems to have been modelled after a new form of low-relief sculpture which exists only in Reid's imagination. It belongs to a spectral world where all has become greyed and

Silver Bracelet
Dogfish design with carved texture 1967
6 cm wide

157

tenuous; where the customary energy of ovoid and formline are felt to be too robust and exuberant and therefore have been superseded by elongated and tapering lozenges; a world where arms and legs of sinuous curve and tapering terminals carve slivers of space that echo almond eyes forever open and seeing all while seeing nothing. The strange little creatures with large teeth and eyes and small humanoid bodies who crouch inside the shark's interior are, Reid tells us, "the vertebrae in the fish's spinal column." This surprising information, along with the fact that the shark does not have a spinal column, is communicated with the straight face and smiling eyes he assumes for matters of serious fun, and they indicate the degree to which Reid is able imaginatively to enter the dicta of the old artists while looking on with detached amusement. A new life has been breathed into new creatures, a strange demonic life that is enriched by its reference to the past but projects its own power. If the boxwood carving of The Raven and the First Men broke through the traditional container in its dynamic formal aspects, then the drawing of the Dogfish Woman breaks its psychological shell.

Among some of the native artists working within the extending tradition, there is a certain sensitivity concerning personal style. After all, the notion of individual style — that an artist should leave his personal imprint on his work — is very ingrained in the modern concept of what art is. The more closely an artist accepts the confines of the formalized style within which he agrees to work, the more his "imprint" becomes a matter of manner or inflection — a particular habit of curvature, the shape of an eyelid or the flare of a nostril; it is comparable to an individual accent in speech, or perhaps a scribe's "hand" in writing, though the language used is common to all. Even Reid sometimes wonders if he has his own style. Of course he has; anyone who has put as much of himself into his art as he has over the years is bound to leave his mark, in that sense, on everything he does. What is more significant is that he is also altering the language in his own way; he is leaving his mark in the content of his art.

The technical processes of Reid's work are long drawn out, requiring discipline and patience — wood carving which allows the gradual emergence of its buried image, metalwork with its many steps, even drawing as he practises it with its erasures and slow-building. This means that the images are carried in his head over long periods of time until they become familiars, interacting with and contributing to his own states of being. There are some contemporary artists for whom the mythical creatures are simply forms to be manipulated plastically. Reid is not one of these, nor ever really was, even though his earlier work gave the creatures less space in which to move and develop their imaginative potential while recent pieces like the Dogfish Woman drawing suggest the deep psychological reality such imagined creatures have for him personally.

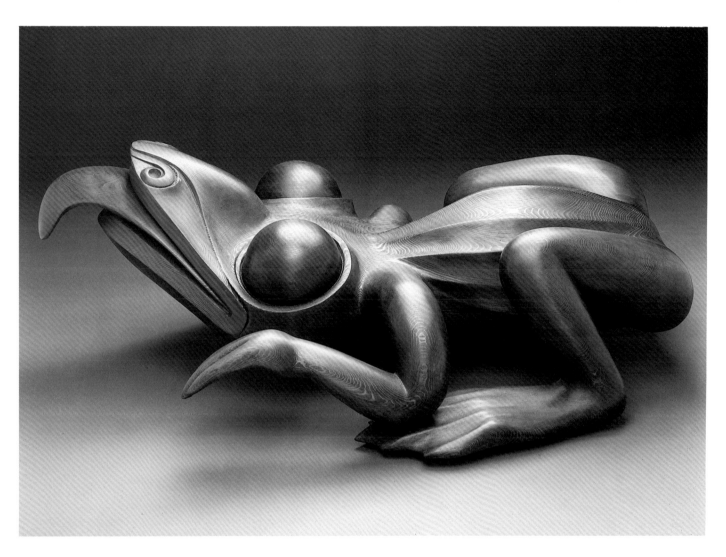

Cedar Frog
Phyllidula,
the Shape of Frogs to Come, 1984–85.
45 cm high, 97 cm wide, 126 cm long
Stain finish

That drawing has a spiritual successor in a 1.2-metre cedar Frog which shares something of its dark satanic vitality. In an earlier free-standing animal carving, the catafalque Bear of 1966, the creature's great unmoving bulk holds the inner energy in check. In this clawed and emaciated Frog, tongue thrusts and eyes push grotesquely out of sockets in an upward-straining head, and the body in all its parts is twisted out of a stable symmetry by the creature's own neurotic energy. Freed of its formal container and ready to spring, the Frog is an image of such frightening psychic intensity that Reid was starting to have disturbing dreams while working on it. Even the highly polished and colour-stained skin — no longer the adzed surface that retains the marks of the tool and speaks of the materiality of wood — befits a creature of the dark and slippery realm of nightmare.

159

While there are no true frogs on the Queen Charlotte Islands, toads are abundant, and the Indians do not distinguish between the two, using the English word "frog" for both. The creature appears frequently in Haida art and mythology, a realm where transformation is the norm and where it is a conspicuous example. The Frog often turns up in Reid's bestiary, but this one is clearly no Haida Frog, as its title emphasizes: "Phyllidula" — and he adds the significant postscript — "the Shape of Frogs to Come." Phyllidula is the lady from Ezra Pound's poem of that name; she is "scrawny but amorous, / Thus have the gods awarded her, / That in pleasure she receives more than she can give; / If she does not count this blessed, let her change her religion." Reid has freed this frog completely from its cultural as well as its formal container and has given it his own meaning. He has always liked the notion of the sculptural image as something buried in the block which it is the carver's task to reveal, a notion literally true in this case, for he started work without drawing or plan or clear idea of the kind of frog he wanted, permitting it to shape itself in, for him, an exceptional act of extended spontaneity.

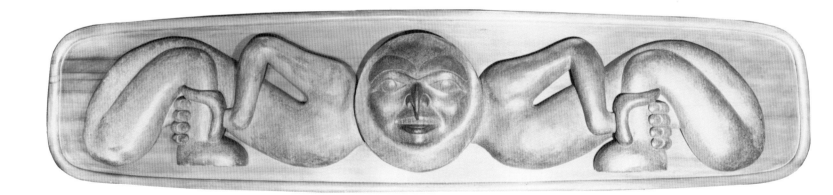

The New Moon Woman
Cast Ceramic Panel mounted on wood
No. 1 of edition of 5 1984–85
193 cm long, 44.5 cm high, 15 cm deep
Westcoast Transmission, Vancouver

Gold Brooch
Frog 1971
3.8 cm long, 3 cm wide
University of British Columbia,
Museum of Anthropology

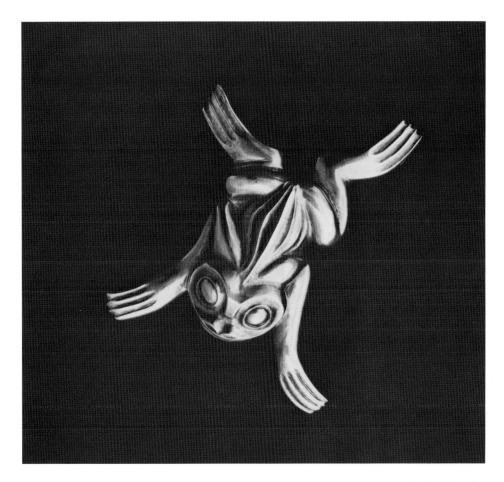

Another recent culturally liberated creation is his cast ceramic relief of 1984, the New Moon Woman. Certain of its characteristics can be seen in relation to the old tradition: its symmetrical composition with a centred head and a centrally split body whose identical but reversed halves are spread laterally, resulting here in an image that could also be seen as a double-bodied creature (like the Kwakiutl's mythical Sisiutl); the moon face with its recurving beak or nose, its labretted mouth, its flattened brows are all to be found in northern Indian art representations of the Moon; there are even precedents for the extraordinary double-jointed anatomy displayed by this creature such as seen on the 1.8-metre Heina box front in the Field Museum, Chicago. But all these connections with the traditional art are only subdued echoes in Reid's work, which creates a whole new presence bearing little relation to any known creature. Clay was used because he wanted a casting material less expensive than bronze, and the serene and beaming "moon face" was one of the designs he had considered (and already cast) for the circular blowhole of the bronze whale at Vancouver's Aquarium. From those two practical starting points his imagination simply took off.

REID'S BESTIARY

Gold Transformation Pendant
and Necklace
Dogfish Woman design 1983
Detachable female ''mask''
8 cm diameter;
mask head: 5.5 cm long

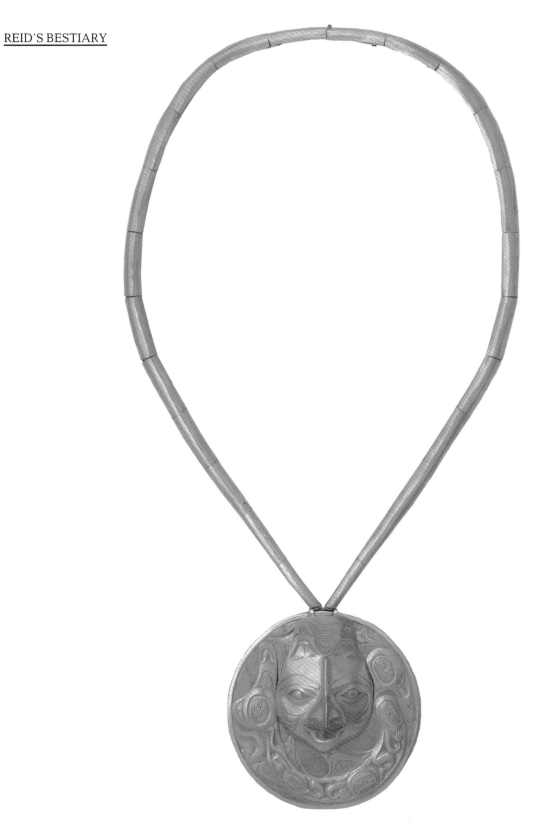

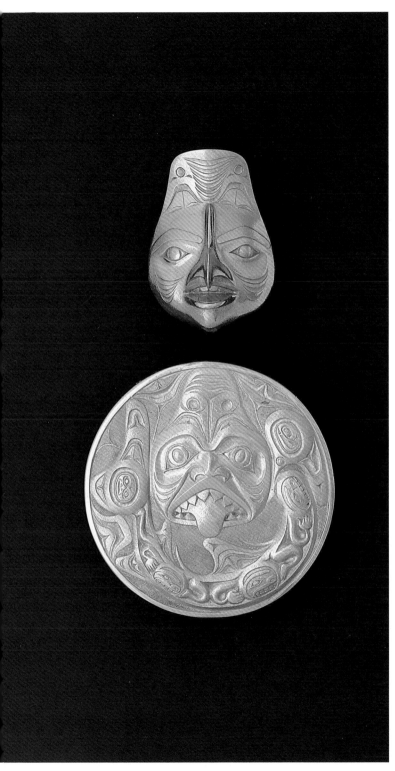

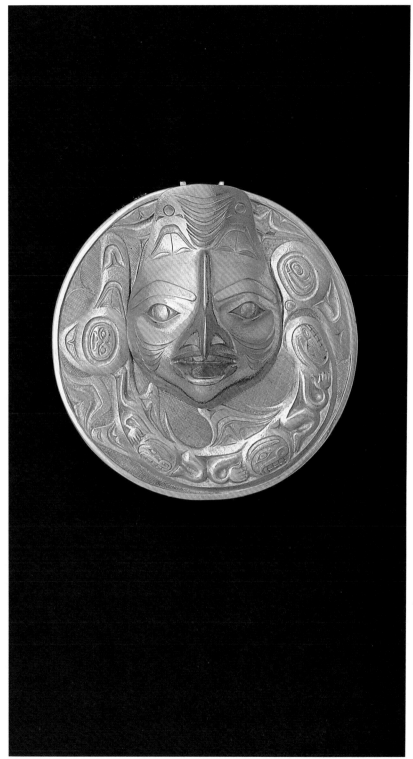

Reid's beginning in the art field started in an apparently straightforward and practical way. Jewellery-making, which demands the standards of craftsmanship he learned from and shared with his mother, seemed to offer the possiblity of a livelihood, and fortuitously it already had been adapted to the art tradition in the form of bracelets with Indian designs with which he had been familiar in his childhood. What he could not have foreseen was that the central message, so deeply encoded and consistently expressed in the aesthetic structure of the old art that it reverberated however faintly even in the humblest bracelet, provided an exact fit for his own emerging personal needs: an aesthetic which supplied a stable and ordering framework strong enough to contain and shape the potentially chaotic energy within. Because he felt the truth of that aesthetic statement as part of his own experience, a metaphor for a certain state of being which set his own echoes ringing, he came to understand the art, not just admire it, and so was able to recreate it in his own imagination. It is that personal empathy, underlying his artistic understanding like an underground spring, that gives his work its authenticity, even though it has stayed close to an artistic model from the past.

The concurrence of a collective expression belonging to an old culture and the personal expression of a younger devotee advanced in time and removed in place, even though connected by genes, is not automatic. In Reid's case, it was something given — a matter of temperamental equivalence — something intuitively seized, and something in addition to his form-making capabilities. This has to be the deep meaning of his remark: "There is a sense in which I feel really strongly identified with my ancestors"; that is to say, through their art he found a truly elemental and sustaining connection. The fit was to remain comfortable for a long time, giving him space to move, to introduce new techniques and materials, to produce an impressive body of authentic work. The long-entrenched style matrix he was late in approaching was complex and slow to yield its secrets, and during the period that he was learning to understand and master it, he was very respectful of its rules. "Then one day I did something different, something that didn't relate to the old design, and I realized that I could do different interpretations of the old forms." Today he questions the importance of the rules, while his late work clearly shows the degree to which it has become a vehicle of freer expression. Indeed, in one or two very late pieces he is projecting a lingering darkness, a psychic shadow of his own that layers powerfully with the residual content of his forebears. This has been not a willed but an involuntary shift, and therefore its authenticity cannot be denied. For him the old art, while in the early days a support to lean on, has become a bridge to walk over into his own present future.

1 Haida metal jewellery before Reid's time consisted almost entirely of bracelets made by melting coins and hammering the resulting ingots into strips of metal which were then formed into bracelet shapes and engraved and carved with crest designs. Reid's earliest work followed this pattern of procedure except that he used manufactured sheet gold and silver. See example page 87. His training in traditional European goldsmithing techniques, which involved building up a complete unit from preformed segments by means of soldering, led him towards greater technical complexity and design of more sculptural quality. See examples pages 82 and 85.

In the 1950s he made his so-called "black-and-white" pieces, using a technique of silver overlaid on silver. The entire piece was then blackened chemically following which only the highest surfaces were polished to remove the oxidization. See pages 104, 122 and 123. His use of the traditional native decorative material abalone shell, set in the manner of gem stones in the customary European manner, is to be seen on pages 46 and 47, and of ivory on pages 125 and 128.

In the late fifties he first used the technique of repoussé, i.e., forming and shaping a negative image by hammering a piece of sheet metal imbedded in pitch for support. The negative image is confirmed and finished by reversing the piece and hammering from the front. See examples pages 39 bottom and 161. The natural tendency of the repoussé technique to produce a hammered texture led to the use of a deliberate added textural effect by a final fine-hammering of the surface. The adzed surface of much wood carving probably inspired this development. See pages 46 and 47. The first casting was done from handmade models in metal made for subsequent repetition. In 1970 he made the first carving in wax for casting by the lost-wax method. Since that time he has used the process with increasing frequency to produce both complete objects and elements of more complex pieces. See pages 134, 136, 137 and 155.

2 The original drawing was done for John Swanton by John Wika.

3 Referred to in Marius Barbeau, "Haida Myths Illustrated in Argillite" (Ottawa: National Museums of Canada, no. 127, Anthropological Series no. 32, 1953), pp. 118, 151.

4 "The Anthropologist and the Article," *Culture* (Journal of the Canadian Ethnology Society) (1984) 4: 63–65.

5 Bill Holm is among those, including the author, who would disagree with Reid on this position, saying that *Raven*, when referring to the culture hero/trickster, is a proper name, not a generic term for a particular kind of bird.

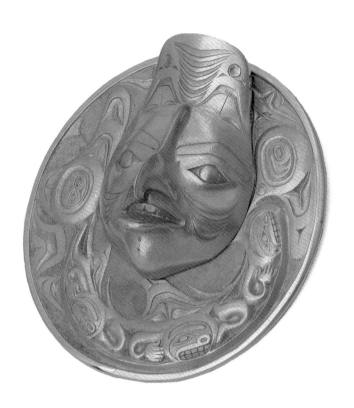

BEYOND ART

It was personal need, not cultural determinism, that urged Reid to look backward as the time approached for his entrance into the world of responsible thought and action, and the looking and the reaching were, and still essentially are, to the art of the past. Various projects he has involved himself in beyond his own art — exhibitions, the great book of west coast Indian "masterworks" he has dreamed of for years and which has yet to be compiled — focus on the tangible part of his ancestors' cultural accomplishment: treasures he says are equal in concept, intellect, emotional content and technique to any of those of European or Asian origin which we regard with such justifiable pride and affection. But it was inevitable that his interest should be taken beyond those treasures, tied as they were to the culture that produced them.

Many of the turns in his life seem to have followed practical directions; talking about his past he will say, "I returned to the coast from . . . for economic reasons" or "I needed a place to live" or "I had to get out of broadcasting." But it is clear that the deeper tug of "the Indian thing" was at work even in the gold and silver bracelets worn and made by relatives of his great-uncle and grandfathers' generations, his first magnetic links with an ancestral past — the "Indian thing" that would pull him in ways not anticipated or wished for, and push him to his own fulfilment both artistically and humanly. It was a search for identity which led him to gravitate towards his Haida ancestry, the "need for some cultural roots and those were the only ones I had." The art was not separable from the culture and the bracelets and the jewellery-making, and the attendant reading and looking grew into a profound respect and feeling for their makers' larger accomplishment as human beings, something anthropologists in their required detachment tend to shut out. He has become the silver-tongued spokesman for his "fabled Haida" ancestors and not only of their great artistry; part of him is exerting constant effort to compel the world to recognize his forebears' essential humanity, as individuals and as a people, through his eloquent writing, frequent interviews, and, though he does not seek a public platform, in appearances as guest speaker at conferences, openings and other occasions where he can deliver his message.

While in hospital in 1979 he decided to get his thoughts in order in preparation for a proposed Institute for Northwest Coast Indian Studies (which to his disappointment has never materialized), and he wrote a long paper entitled "Haida Means Human Being." In it he speaks of the early people, claiming no special status for their humanity among that of other early cultures, but giving it a focus too often neglected: "A small population which over the centuries has learned to live in the same harmony with its environment as other living creatures who shared it, developing skills and techniques sufficient to cope adequately, but little more. [They created] a number of complex social systems with their attendant supporting myths and rituals. These in turn [were] supported by varying degrees of artistic expression — graphic, sculptural, musical, theatrical, poetic. Each intricate cultural structure [was] firmly held in place by a completely formed dense framework of language." He does not present a romantic picture of that past, recognizing its physical harshness and precariousness, its rigidly hierarchical society with its slavery component, its constant intertribal conflicts, but still he proposes that "tribal societies in general, and the Northwest Coast version in particular, probably accommodated the individual better than any system that has succeeded it." As he articulates it:

No one except slaves, and there is some evidence to show that even they participated to some extent, was excluded from the diverse physical activities of the community. . . . Everyone had a hand in the harvesting and preserving of food, while the best hunters and fishermen, and probably the most skilled observers and preparers of food, had added status in the communities. And after these seasonal subsistence activities which seemed to have been considered easy, almost holiday time for the people, like a prolonged picnic, came the serious activities. It meant everyone was not only encouraged to display his abilities, but required to do so. It would seem that all men practised all the men's trades and arts — boatbuilding, carpentry, tool-, weapon-, utensil-, vessel-making, and so on, as well as painting and carving ceremonial objects, as all the women were preparers of food, weavers, basket-makers and so on, and all were singers and dancers, actors in the ritual dramas which were such a part of the winter ceremonies. Of course, all were not equally skilled. But those who excelled were apparently recognized and rewarded and everyone with a special talent — the great painters, sculptors, weavers, bards — was cherished by the group. Access to these skills was denied no one — every child from his first conscious moment was in intimate contact with the most highly skilled adults in the community, if for no other reason than that he or she was in intimate contact with every individual in the community. With no forced training, the young effortlessly learned all the wisdom of the group, the natural environment, how to exploit and live with it, the nature of the material available from it, the complexities of the social environment, the genealogies of the great families, the myths of their origins, the use of tools needed to give visible and oral reality to this wealthy symbolism including the greatest tools of all — the rich complex languages of the coast. . . . So every child grew up with as complete a knowledge of his universe and how to cope with it as he was capable of absorbing. He had the highly developed powers of observation which gave him a better than average chance to find his way in this world and wrest from it an abundant livelihood. He learned all the complexities of his society and what his place was in it. He had a body of myths and history embodied in the genealogies of his people, which provided him with guideposts and reference points to help determine the course of his life. And he had a language of sufficient vocabulary and structure to communicate to the rest of his group and to himself all the information necessary to survive culturally, to think his way through his problems and so solve them and to exercise his imagination creatively to enrich his life and his community. In other words, he was a human being, a well-realized product of the unique and marvellous process going back thousands of years by which man invented himself, learned to use and make tools, to live together in social groups, to divide labour, to develop unprecedented uses or parts of his amazing unspecialized body, to communicate in various ways, culminating in the greatest result of his genius — his amazing unbelievable, magical, triumphant creation — his language.

Reid, in ways consistent with the customs of his ancestors, never ceases to acknowledge his personal debt to them with gifts for relatives and friends — jewellery, fine tools with hand-carved handles, the pole he made for his mother's village. Acknowledging his debt and honouring the ancestors has brought him satisfaction and the pleasure of giving; but the bracelets, those humble connections with an artistic past, were a cultural lure in which was concealed an extra hook, waiting to draw him into the uncertain and disturbing present.

His vision of an earlier society in which the shared assumptions of the higher and lower ranking members were bound together in a mutual, workable, productive interdependence is in glaring contrast with the present picture of village life as a moral, spiritual and material wasteland in which popular western culture at its most vacuous has taken over. So many times had he reviewed the long, erosive and inhumane course of the white man's takeover of the natives' life and lands, sharpening the comparison of the way things used to be with the way they now are, that he became fixed in an attitude of loss and pessimism. He brings the account up to date:

The integrated school system, far from encouraging equality between the two societies, pointed out the complete lack of preschool preparation of the native children to compete adequately in the arcane obstacle course society has designed for the education of its young. Almost without exception, children found themselves considered failures from the first day they were surrendered to the school system. . . . The excessive use of alcohol and more exotic drugs continues to be a much more dominant part of "Indian culture" than any of the older ways. A disproportionate percentage of the jail population is still drawn from the native sector. Attempts to leave the reserve life and move to a more urban setting too often led to the dreary life and early death on the skid road. The increasing technical sophistication of the fishing industry with the resulting need for bigger, faster, and more expensive boats resulted in the exclusion of most of the native fishermen from its more lucrative aspects, and effectively brought to an end the native boatbuilding and maintenance activities. Most of the canneries on the coast were closed and although they have not perhaps offered ideal conditions of employment, the lack of such a market for their labour was a blow to the economies of many communities. And the decline in morale among native male populations affected their reliability as workers, undermining the confidence of the employers. The Department of Indian Affairs introduced many programmes ostensibly to help alleviate the situation, but far too often they were ill thought out and poorly administered. An intensive rehousing programme was initiated, but the houses were poorly designed and of second-rate construction, and most telling, were for the most part assembled by outside contractors instead of being used to help retrain the village people in skills which would make them more self-sufficient. Government funding for reserve projects was often lavish but poorly researched and inadequately followed up with the result that many, if not most, were never completed and the money wasted, either dissipated on unproductive labour or chanelled into the pockets of shrewder and less scrupulous members of the community. Agencies were set up with the intention of improving aspects of native life with inexperienced or all too often self-seeking personnel appointed, so that most of the sometimes excessive funding was wasted on administrative costs or used by the administrators themselves to further their own ends. In fact it seems that the only solution the authorities have for dealing with native problems is to dump a load of money into the problem area and pretend that in some magical way that's going to solve it.

He speaks of the young: [the records of] failure, apathy, lives lived at the minimum level of achievement and interest, . . . wandering confused and undirected from meaningless episode to meaningless episode. And always the consuming, dominating, corrosive anger often repressed with the aid of booze and drugs, and a lifestyle precariously designed so that yesterday exists only in fantasy, and there is nothing beyond tomorrow. Or to remember is to realize how it used to be or at least how one imagines it used to be. And to think is to know that tomorrow holds no promise of that fabulous education that was going to make one a doctor or a lawyer or a professional of some kind. It holds no promise even of a job or an adequate home in a stable community, of a family to continue a tradition going back to myth time. It just holds more of the dreary same.

He has, he says, no solutions to the problems which plague the native society, *but I do know that if there are such things as aboriginal rights, which the first inhabitants of this land have a right to insist on having restored, and that we all have an obligation to see are restored, they are not primarily land or resources or traplines or fishing rights or any material possessions, but the right of the people to have put back into their existences what the intruding power took from them in the last two centuries — their basic humanity.*

"I never wanted a weighty role," Reid says in conversation. "I never wanted to revive the culture, to be involved in all these social problems." And yet in his own ways he has become involved. Those ways are always those of the humanitarian outsider, one who has privileged information and experience of that minority society as well as racial ties to it, but who lives his life as a sophisticated and, because of his personal stature, privileged member of a larger one which embraces his "Indian-ness." By legal definition (in effect until the summer of 1985) Reid, the son of a woman who married a non-Indian, was himself a non-status Indian; but in any case, in any political, social or experiential sense, he never has been "an Indian." His hope for the future would be that "we may all move a little bit along the way to becoming at last, or again, true North Americans — neither displaced aborigines, nor immigrant settlers" — the route his background, his intellectual bent and his experience have permitted him to take himself. He is however very aware that he has benefitted from his Indian connection, and not only in the material success his "leaning on the ancestors" has brought him. He reveals his own perspective in a letter to his young grandson, a boy of mixed parentage like himself, whom he advises to come to an understanding of the appalling disasters which decimated the people, debased their culture and took away their pride.

But he says: *You must [also] understand and forgive the people who caused these disasters and destruction, and their descendants. Because the irony of it all is that you're also one of them, as much as you're a descendant of the conquered. It won't be easy but it has its rewards. . . . It gives you a position a little apart from the mainstream of North American life, and considering the direction in which that stream seems to be flowing these days, that isn't a bad place to be. The main thing to remember is that being an Indian isn't an excuse for anything, unless it's accompanied by the cultural disadvantages which afflict most native people these days.*

Despite this detachment, his concern for the future of the people is real and passionate. Knowing that one person can do very little, he does what he can. When he began to carve the pole in Skidegate in 1978, he put out a notice calling for assistant workers, hoping to use the occasion to introduce at least a few young people to the traditional skills and techniques of carving. A few came, but they stayed for a half-hour or so, wondering why he was spending time on plans and drawings instead of getting on with the job — and they never came back. However, he still has hopes that plans for a carvers' workshop there, perhaps with himself in charge, will materialize. The Haida canoe, whose building in time for the opening of EXPO 86 was in his charge, took place in the Queen Charlottes, where the enterprise, from start to finish, could spread its excitement and its note of regeneration throughout the village, actively involving a number of people in its various stages: the finding of a suitable log, its felling and towing to the chosen location, the making of a special set of tools and the challenge of actual construction. In Vancouver he draws young natives into his work projects whenever he can, offers interest and encouragement, welcomes the opportunity to participate in native celebrations as he welcomes natives to his, and always keeps up his concerned commentary from the sidelines.

There are today natives of a younger generation who approach the problem differently, the dual problem of their own personal resolution and that of community decay. A few assume overt political stances; others are making objects intended for village use — masks, blankets, staffs — and they are relearning (in many cases out of necessity reinventing) the songs, dances and ceremonies that go with them, and creating the community occasions that require them: potlatches, naming ceremonies, feasts. They have had first to learn how to accommodate to the outside urban world but are spending more of their time and effort in the causes of their own people. These are artists who are working within the changing Indian consciousness, whatever that may turn out to be; people whose background and temperaments permit them to do so as Reid's do not. He is respectfully skeptical of their approach, believing they are trying to recreate the old cultures as they are recreating the old designs that came from them. Too many of them, he believes, while having learned "the rules, are feeding too much on themselves, losing touch with the old forms, and on a deeper level, losing touch with the animals and monsters who inspired those old forms." And in a harsh judgement he says, "Hopping around with your face painted is not dancing. Scratching on a piece of silver is not art. Invented ritual is church basement entertainment."[1] The pole he carved for Skidegate and the new band council house built in the traditional form became the occasion for a large-scale celebration requiring the making of regalia — blankets, head wear — and the relearning of songs and dances. Looking back on this example of pagaentry and ceremony of which he was the occasion, Reid today is almost apologetic, emphasizing the purpose of his pole as a "memorial to the Haida of the past, not a drive to turn the clock back." He does not wish to be seen as having slipped into "potlatching" and revivalism. Following the celebrations there were those who credited him with having given them back their culture and the possibility of being proud to be Haida again. Reid remembers the young man who said, "If I weren't a Haida, I wouldn't be anything," and Reid comments, "the sad truth was that being a Haida didn't make him any more than he was before he realized he was one — he was still unemployed, unskilled, uneducated in any culture, and alcoholic."[2]

But surely it is too soon to dismiss all that activity as irrelevant or misguided. There are people today deeply committed to the view that the Indian culture, while clearly in a difficult state of transition in which virtually all the outward patterns of life and social structure have had to give way, still retains its will and its identity, and something of its spirit and its sensibility. And among the younger generation of cultural activists are at least some whose motivations are as seriously humanitarian as Reid's and whose art has benefitted and to some extent modelled itself after his example of thoroughness and depth in the tradition. It is with the sincerest intentions that some of them are relearning the songs and dances, practising ritual cleansing and reintroducing ceremonies like the potlatch. They are probably not naive enough, as he fears, to imagine that they can recreate the old culture, but they believe in the regeneration of their communities and they know, whether they wish to articulate it or not, that the bond of ritual, that close cousin of art, can be strong enough to keep a people together. In any case, they are approaching the problem in all earnestness, and often with much desperate courage, by the route that seems appropriate to them and which they will have to learn as they go along, as he had to learn his before them.

Reid sees the native art activity of recent years as something quite apart from the cultural problems of the reserves, and he believes that references to it as a "renaissance" or "revival" have been inappropriate. It has been produced for and stimulated by southern urban markets (which largely he and, a little later, Robert Davidson, created) and supported by museological and anthropological interest and encouragement. To a large extent contemporary native art has not entered the critical institutional or commercial mainstream of the art establishment. Whereas the old Indian art had long been accepted as a cultural expression more appropriately belonging in an anthropological environment, art by contemporary natives tends to have been seen as commodity items, part of a separate and determined commercialism in which products were marketable because they were Indian, without regard for quality. So the new art has not received much objective scrutiny or questioning in the art world though that situation is beginning to change. And it must also be observed that so far, at least, the new art, drawing on a tradition that was so tightly in-wound, even that which sees itself as having social or political purpose, does not often reflect within itself the content of a new social and political reality. A case in point is Joe David's large carved work which has become associated with his people's protest against logging on Meares Island — a "welcome man" who, despite the conspicuously restrained welcoming gesture of the arms, reads as a traditional figure.

173

Still, Reid knows that his own art, and his position and his success, cannot be divorced from the current native art situation. He was effectively the first to take up the challenge put before him by his ancestors, to produce work in his own time that took its measure from theirs. He not only provided a model of practical success for a younger generation but also one of serious-ness of attitude and exacting standards of production for those capable of responding. He cannot be held responsible for encouraging those younger "artifakers" (a term which he gives Bill Holm credit for inventing and which he used to frequently apply to himself in a wry amused gesture of apology) who do not take the trouble to learn and understand the tradition; nor those who, he laments, ply their wares while being cynical about both the white and the Indian communities, and so debase their heritage.

Perhaps he should be reminded that their proportion is certainly no greater than the "art-fakers" in any other segment of society. And, of course, some younger native artists have been capable of responding and are producing good work, and it is on the basis of confidence gained in the larger Canadian society that they now direct some of their efforts back to their native commu-nities. Reid himself is inevitably part of the renewal of native spirit that is taking place. Through his work and his personal stature he has won a firm and distinguished place for himself in the dominant society whose approval is always needed, a society which, whatever the subtleties of the situation, has always labelled him a Haida artist; in so doing he has helped to open up for the native people a channel to the respect for their heritage and therefore themselves that they were in danger of losing. There are many routes to the self-respect without which no meaningful change in their condition is possible, but even such a circuitous one can help reverse the flow of energy.

And happily it can be said that Reid's dark recall of past events and gloomy appraisal of life in the reserve villages are increasingly relieved by flashes of hopefulness and acts that do not speak of despair. The interest and activity generated among native people who came to Vancouver for the launching of his first canoe prompted an admission that he found a lot of residual vitality among villagers in comparison with the other segments of society — "responsible adults and kids who are self-contained and able to carry on lives of involvement with each other."

And beyond the level of direct action, he clings to a vision of future possi-bility. Out of his intense empathy with the historical and mythical past of the Indian people, both the somewhat known and the only imagined, comes his will to believe that a future is there, unknown but possible. The old myths with their element of time folding back on itself while it loops into the present and rolls into the future (an element Henry Young had first pointed out to him) presents a case for such optimism, and he gives voice to it when he speaks in the language of the mythmaker which takes him into poetic distance. At the time he wrote the legend for The Raven and the First Men (1980), his expression of that possibility was a mere whisper. "It's almost all over now. Most of the villages are abandoned, and those which have not entirely vanished lie in ruins. The people who remain are changed. The sea has lost much of its richness, and great areas of land itself lie in waste. Perhaps it's time the Raven started looking for another clamshell." In his text for the Dogfish Woman, written four years later, the expression of promise is more positive and the gloom has lifted. Out of greater acceptance has come hope. He now writes: "The light the Raven stole has grown a little dimmer for all of us, but it still flickers faintly in the houses of the people of Haida Gwai. And the old magic of the Islands, which were there even before myth-time, is still strong. The old ghosts will continue to haunt the land until new spirits can be born. This may be another time before anything was. But on the banks of some river somewhere, you may be sure, someone or some-thing, even if it isn't us, is living, and the Raven and the Mouse Woman are wily enough to keep their stories going."[3] What Reid is saying is that as long as the primal truth of the myths can continue to be felt, the cycle may continue. In this understanding myth time *is* the real time. That is the meaning of his remark that "the totem pole I carved for Skidegate may have put the village back into time."

Just as Reid has achieved a personal perspective in which he sees himself as a member of a larger North American society which includes his Indian kinship, so his frustration, anger and sadness with the present problems of Haida society does not cut him off from a larger concern with the insensitive depredation of the natural world, and the consequent dark implications for the human spirit, by the conscienceless advances of technology, industry and "progress." He sees the short-sighted indiscriminate logging being practised in the islands of the Pacific west coast as symbolic of a progressive loss of those qualities essential in any definition of humanity, and he has said that he would like to contribute whatever fighting energy he has left to the current effort to have the South Moresby area designated as park. He wrote an impassioned plea for a halt to the depredation of Windy Bay on Lyell Island, part of the area under discussion, which appeared in the *Vancouver Sun* of 24 October 1980 under the title "The Enchanted Forest," commencing with a quotation from F. Scott Fitzgerald's *Great Gatsby:* "gradually I became aware of the old island here that flowered once for Dutch sailors' eyes — a fresh, green breast of the new world. Its vanished trees . . . had once pandered in whispers to the last and greatest of all human dreams; for a transitory enchanted moment man must have held his breath in the presence of this continent, compelled into an aesthetic contemplation he neither understood nor desired, face to face for the last time in history with some-thing commensurate to his capacity for wonder."

There are stands of ancient forest at Windy Bay, and one or two other locations in that area (but not many more) that have never been burned or suffered other destruction and that contain trees — spruce, cedar and hemlock — at all stages of growth and of all ages up to eight or nine hundred years. These forests are living organisms whose life stretches back some four thousand years. To walk or to sit quietly in their moss-covered interiors is to become absorbed into their still energy, to apprehend oneself as a part of the infinitely long and slow process of time, to be reminded of, even to experience for a moment, our deep bond with larger nature which we seem bent on breaking. It is for the deeply nurturing experience they offer and their symbolic meaning as living talismans of man's small place in the universe that Reid values these old stands. He says: "It may be argued that few will ever set eyes on such a remote spot, but those who still hold to what is left of the 'last and greatest of human dreams' will find their way there, or find solace in the knowledge it still exists unspoiled." He makes it clear that he is not mounting an attack on logging, loggers, or the lumber industry, but pleading for the institution of "true multi-use of the forest with due regard for its own regeneration, the wildlife it nurtures and, most neglected, its aesthetic values — that is the nurture it affords human life. . . . To my way of thinking, sustained yield in tree-farming, as in other farming, should mean bringing at least some of the crop to maturity. We should have fifty-year-old trees, one-hundred-year-old trees, five-hundred-year-old trees. After all, our great-great-grandchildren may enjoy seeing some big trees in mature forests, and may also find some use for beautiful clear lumber. They may not feel overjoyed that their ancestors got a little richer by using it all up at once."

And in the chapter he contributed to *Islands at the Edge*, a volume compiled to state the case for the creation of a South Moresby park, he sums it up: "Perhaps saving [the islands] is a promise and a hope, a being conscious of their continued existence, whether we as individuals ever actually see them or not, so that we may return to a more peaceable kingdom with a full knowledge of its wonders. Without South Moresby and the other places like it, we may forget what we once were and what we can be again, and lose our humanity in a world devoid of the amazing non-humans with whom we have shared it."[4]

Reid wrote that article and that chapter some five and three years ago respectively, articles which presented aesthetic and ecological arguments for the Islands' preservation and which put his concern for human rights on a universal level beyond those of native issues. Looking back today on the work of the Islands Protection Society, which he supported by statements such as those as well as in other ways, he sees that its efforts, however useful and educational, were "directed by the knowledge, sentiment and sensibility of the good, middle-class Caucasian, immigrant liberal." Today he

176

argues for the same cause but from an altered position, for there has been a significant shift in his viewing of the situation and his relation to it, one in which he not only locates persuasive humanist reasons for supporting native land claims but also finds the clear hard signs of moral regeneration among Haidas he had earlier despaired of ever seeing. And it is a shift that acknowledges a point of arrival in a process of inner conversion that had been going on for years though never outwardly acknowledged: "I've spent most of my life with a feeling of identity with the Haida people, always of course, at a safe distance in some urban location. Recently, however, I've finally had to face up to what it really means to be Haida in the latter part of the twentieth century and at last, in fact, may have to become a Haida."[5]

The trigger for this shift has been the confrontation that took place in the fall of 1985 on Lyell Island and which has become a focus for the debate concerning the future of the South Moresby area. There he witnessed the Haidas in a heartening display of unity, for forty days successfully standing up against representatives of authority and paper legality; that is, he saw "the Haida [coming] alive again after a century or more." He attended meetings, made two lithographic prints with the proceeds from their sale going to support the struggle, and in an eloquent statement made in January 1986 before the Wilderness Advisory Committee set up by the provincial government, he presented his interpretation of the underlying meaning of native land claims, which by this time had become a central issue in the debate. Although his language and images reflect his European-conditioned perceptions, he is now speaking as someone who wishes to give witness to his human condition of being Haida.

[The Indians' pressing of land claims] does not mean that the native people want to drive all non-Indians into the sea. As far as I know there is no sentiment in favour of de-industrializing the society. Some people may see the land claims as a way to get rich. But in regard to South Moresby, why should the Haidas — we Haidas — want this particular morsel of wilderness left untouched? Certainly not for the reasons I gave previously. . . . No, there is, I think, and I can almost begin to feel it myself, a much more direct response — a closer identification with these areas than anything which is filtered through the veil of conditioning that most people carry with them. Those descended from European stock, and probably from Asiatic as well, still feel a slight unease, the tiny remnant of the old looking-over-the-shoulder anxiety of the strangers in a strange land. And in the back of most immigrant minds is the ghost of a thought that they'll return to their real homes some day.

The Haidas have also been in exile, ironically more so than those who displaced them. Once all of Haida Gwai was theirs. We all know of the plagues that decimated their numbers and caused them to gather together

177

in the two centres of population that endure today [Skidegate and Masset]. These in effect became tiny islands within the large island mass of the Charlottes, and the people lived within these narrow confines, emerging to go fishing, to visit the cities of the mainland, but hardly ever venturing back to their ancestral sites.

Well, that's all changed now, and the first tentative probes are now reaching out to re-establish ties with the old territories, and in places like South Moresby to find links with the past. For it is only in places like South Moresby that the past can be found intact and unchanged. Every other aspect of Haida culture has been eroded away — the language is almost gone, the songs, stories, the very genealogies that were the threads that made up the fabric of Haida life are almost forgotten. Even the people's names have been erased from the consciousness of those who should own them, to be replaced by the monosyllables of common English. So we have left only the sea, and a few sacred groves unchanged since the great change that began two centuries ago. . . .

The Haidas never really left South Moresby, or the other areas they once controlled. They only went away for a while. And now they are coming back. As for the people who claim control of these areas, well, they remind me of a tourist who turned up in Victoria with a couple of fine West Coast masks. When asked where he had got them, he said proudly that he had stumbled on an abandoned cabin, and rummaging around, found the masks under the bed. Of course, the cabin wasn't abandoned; the occupant had only left for a while, and the tourist, no matter how ignorant and insensitive, was guilty of theft.

The Haida must have their ancient lands back unviolated to re-establish the links with their distinguished past and build a new future. If those remnants of those former riches are not returned, it will make the act of theft a conscious one, perpetuated by the people of today. . . . And in killing the forests, the only authentic voice of the Haida past is stilled forever — and their symbolic ancestors are murdered once more.

And from his new-found centre as a Haida he moves out again to the universal perspective: *So that is what I think the land claims are all about. As for what constitutes a Haida — well, Haida only means human being, and as far as I'm concerned, a human being is anyone who respects the needs of his fellow man, and the earth which nurtures and shelters us all. I think we could find room in South Moresby for quite a few Haida no matter what their ethnic background.*

For Reid, many things have finally come together. His art, through which he first began to discover the personal meaning that his Haida kinship had for him, and his conviction of his ancestors' and their descendants' essential

178

humanity — these have been the channels, sensitized by his feeling as a youth of his own failure, and his later chronic illness, through which he has worked his way to his present outlook: embracing compassion for fellow sufferers, and a sense of loss at the spectacle of wasted human potential. But now also he glimpses a future for the Haida people where once he saw only darkness ahead.

1 Bill Reid, "A New Northwest Coast Art: A Dream of the Past or a New Awakening," unpublished paper, c. 1983.

2 "Haida Means Human Being," unpublished paper, 1979.

3 *The Raven Steals the Light* (Vancouver/Toronto: Douglas & McIntyre, 1984), pp. 90–91.

4 In Islands Protection Society, *Islands at the Edge, Pt. I: The Legacy of change*, "These Shining Islands" (Vancouver/Toronto: Douglas & McIntyre, 1984; Seattle: University of Washington Press, 1984), p. 30.

5 From Reid's verbal statement to the Wilderness Advisory Committee, Vancouver, B.C., January 1986.

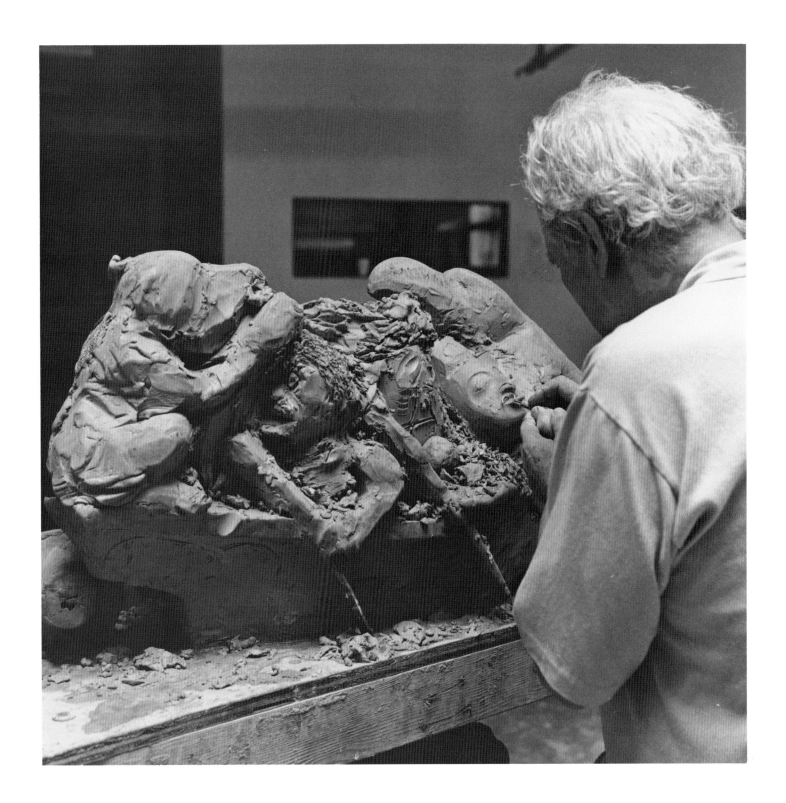

EPILOGUE

Until recently Reid has been more discussed in anthropological than artistic circles. It was anthropologists who first found him relevant to their field, and who provided opportunities and gave him encouragement and a context for the creation and presentation of his work. The northern Indians of the west coast, with whom he had a genealogical connection, were strongly revealed in and identified by the distinctive and developed art which was so prominent a part of their cultural expression, and it had long been the subject of extended study. Reid could be seen from the anthropological viewpoint, through his personal efforts of reclamation of its art by means of his own, as a living repository of much of the old culture's knowledge, and, though not politically inclined, as a representative of the emerging new Indian consciousness. At the same time, he was a privileged outsider with objective interests like their own. He was living and working within the white urban culture at a time when the separability of art from society was a demonstrated fact, and yet he was emulating the art of his ancestors which had, in another time, so clearly spoken of their indivisibility. Of his own volition he was producing Haida art so seriously as to make it, for the first time in this century, a component that must be reckoned with in any monitoring of the changing cultural situation.

181

Anthropologists have not hesitated to place Reid against the large screen on which he must be viewed. Lévi-Strauss locates him with erudite sensitivity and precision within the context of the several northern traditional styles:

The art and imagination of Bill Reid has been progressively enriched by all that the arts of his neighbouring peoples could bring to him. His primary inspiration, that of the Haida tradition, unites with primary sources of the Kwakiutl freedom of invention, the deeply human sensibility of the Tsimshian and, perhaps above all, with the dreaming lyricism of the Tlingit. Within his art these diverse but related traditions blend: synthesis is achieved. . . . Faithful to his home tradition, Bill Reid has fully assimilated its laws but his own genius has allowed him to continue and diversify it without ever repeating the message of his ancestors. Sensitive to the universal import of this message he has released it from the special conditions in which it was conveyed for generations. He continues to draw from this irreplaceable heritage without feeling bound to conceive of his works in relation to the demands of practical life, or social or religious rites which cruel history has ravaged. Hereafter, thanks to Bill Reid, the art of the Indians of the Pacific coast enters into the world scene: into a dialogue with the whole of mankind.[1]

Let us ask how it is that Reid has put that Indian art into a dialogue with the whole of mankind. Is it simply the fact that he is producing today for a modern market, "releasing it from the special conditions in which it was conveyed . . . the demands of practical life, of social or religious rites"? That and following the rules — does that of itself reveal the universal quality of the ancestors' art?

The truth of Lévi-Strauss's claim lies in the hard-won authenticity of Reid's work. Reid recently made a small line drawing diagramming his view of the course the art has taken. It shows the traditional past art on a high plateau, then taking a fairly steep downward incline from which Charles Edenshaw protrudes as a large bump. The incline levels off into a low stretch of "tourist production," and from that bottom level a few lines begin to stretch upward again; one represents Reid, one Robert Davidson, one or two are unnamed. Edenshaw was Reid's necessary bridge to past and future. Not only was his work of distinguished design and technical quality but it also possessed a suave elegance that made it appealing to form-trained eyes. Equally important was the fact that he was connected with an identifiable body of work out of the anonymity of the larger past, an individual, and one so close in time that Reid, especially with the connection through his grandfather, could practically reach out his hand to him (indeed, he was able to handle his tools). Edenshaw already in his day had to make some changes to the old art in response to changed external circumstances and his own altered being.

Reid would be carrying on that necessary process of evolution, but now on the difficult basis of full historical awareness and conscious choice, the only way in which some kind of continuity could happen; for the old skills and the knowledge of the forms were nearly gone, as was the belief system in which they acquired their meaning. Reid's entry to all that was first through craft and technique, and then through an analysis of the forms, and gradually to a deeper and deeper understanding of and empathy with what they were expressing. Only in his own personal interiorization of what had once been culturally assumed could that which was universal in the old art be kept alive.

All his ambitious pieces in which he uses the ancestral mould, so to speak, show that personal assimilation, that authenticity. It is revealed with conspicuous clarity perhaps for the first time in the carved poles on the UBC campus. It does not matter that the compositions of most of them are based either on old photographs or poles salvaged from their sites; they all reveal that understanding of the principles of form-making inherent in the old pieces, and that imaginative grasp of their meaning which could be called a form of belief. Nothing that was carried within the objective reality of the old poles that we in our present could respond to has been lost. Bill in this sense, through an act of intense personal imaginative identification, has transported an art out of its time warp in the past, alive and undamaged, into a historically aware present. His work is there, as Edenshaw's was for him, for anyone to find himself in, to learn from, to build on, to transform into the unknowable future. He has already been that solid bridge for a generation of younger artists and would-be artists, and for the enlightenment of us all.

So he has recreated the past, in the true sense of that word, in works that apart from an absent patina of age, the new social and functional contexts in which they find themselves, and the modern materials and techniques they employ could not be distinguished conceptually and qualitatively from the best of their ancient prototypes. He has, in his own words, done "what his ancestors would have done, had they had the benefit of modern technology."

Wilson Duff — like all of us caught in our modern propensity to analyze, define, evaluate, locate — wanted to give Bill his contemporary position, and to see it with a present rather than backward-looking connection. Duff kept in mind the truth, which he had heard as Reid's own lament that the life had gone out of the Haida shell and he had not been able to put it all back in. He noted that the dates of Charles Edenshaw and Pablo Picasso overlapped; they were contemporaries in real time but separated by centuries in cultural time. "I think," said Duff, "that Bill has been using his eye and his intuition to jump the seeming chasm between Picasso and Edenshaw, his voice to urge the building of a bridge, and his hand to trace out its very foundations. To me, that is being the bridge."[2]

Duff's summation was good. Reid has been and is being a bridge, linking the past and present and leading to an open future, though the terms of the metaphor were not the most appropriate. Reid's bridge does not lead to Picasso. The name Picasso evokes the whole heritage of the twentieth-century modern movement in art, with its fierce independence, its visionary and rigorous search for its own truth, its intellectualism, its inventiveness, its daring. The art of the northern west coast Indians, given its guarded and inbred kind of creativity, does not invite comparison with that modern current in any meaningful way, even in Reid's increasingly outward-expanding versions of it. One could speculate that had he inherited the artistic temperament of the Kwakiutl with its stronger dynamic and its impulse to break out, he might have been in a better position to fulfill Duff's image of him and to enter the western intellectual art stream. Certainly he has the mental capacities to be an intellectual artist of the first order.

In any case, such discussion is beside the point, for what he has done is perhaps more important. Leaping is not his style, but slowly and surely, like Edenshaw before him, he has brought about those changes and innovations that make him his own man artistically, and relate him to his own time at a more intuitive and hence more significant level than that of materials and techniques. Working his way with respect and care bordering on reverence through a style that, by long following of precedence, had become hermetically involuted was in itself an extraordinary achievement; the golden reward at the end of that journey, from a personal point of view, was the rootedness he might never have found otherwise, and which meant his liberation. Pieces like The Raven and the First Men, the gold and ivory Tschumos bracelet, The Killer Whale, Mythic Messengers, and the late drawing of The Dogfish Woman and the carved cedar Frog Phyllidula show him weaving freely in and out of the tradition. Essentially, while retaining the old subject material of the mythical creatures — whether animal, supernatural or something in between — he has transported them, trailing their mythical auras with them and branded with the mark of their origins, into his own bestiary. There he isolates his favourites and frees them into light and space, so that they may be the bearers of messages phrased for modern ears. The traditional container in its restrictive aspect is no longer an imperative, but the energy and vitality it once served to accentuate continue.

So his personal achievement, considering his possible bondage to a noble but run-out tradition, that of a dynamic flowering of his own individual spirit expressed through a truly magnificent command of craft, which ultimately enabled him to transcend his origins and become an idiosyncratic artist of suberb accomplishment, is phenomenal. And this achievement is also one of the great western modes: the individuality of the artist as a whole, involved, compassionate human being whose struggle for personal identity is his heroic record and one which, in the final analysis, lifts his work beyond idiom.

For a while there were people aware of Reid's exceptional potential — his artistic gifts, his radiant intelligence, a certain grandeur — who thought of him as a tragic figure of legendary proportions, someone caught between two cultural worlds one of which was in a sad state of moral limbo, unsure of his cultural identity, tied to an old art form that might strangle him. That was a long time ago. It is a long time, too, since Bill has been heard to refer to himself laughingly as one of the "artifakers." Reid knows that he has made contact with the current at a level of its universality; as long as he can feel its force in his hands and in his heart, he is also the channel through which, in its continuing course, it flows.

1 *Bill Reid: A Retrospective Exhibition* (Vancouver, B.C.: Vancouver Art Gallery, 1974), n.p.

2 Ibid.

SELECT BIBLIOGRAPHY

Abbott, Donald N., ed.
The World Is as Sharp as a Knife: An Anthology in Honour of Wilson Duff.
Victoria: British Columbia Provincial Museum, 1981.

Barbeau, Marius.
"Haida Carvers in Argillite." Bulletin 139.
Ottawa: National Museums of Canada, 1957.

Barbeau, Marius.
"Haida Myths Illustrated in Argillite Carvings." Bulletin 127.
Ottawa: National Museums of Canada, 1953.

Barbeau, Marius.
"Totem Poles." Bulletin 119, vols. 1 and 2.
Ottawa: National Museums of Canada, 1950.

Boas, Franz.
Primitive Art.
New York: Dover Publications, 1955.

Carlson, Roy L., ed.
Indian Art Traditions of the Northwest Coast.
Based on papers of a 1976 symposium at Simon Fraser University:
"The Prehistory of Northwest Coast Indian Art."
Burnaby, B.C.: Simon Fraser University Press, n.d.

Downey, Roger.
"Apprentice to a Lost Art,"
Pacific North West 17, no. 8 (October 1982).

Duff, Wilson.
Images, Stone B.C.
Saanichton, B.C.: Hancock House, 1975.

Duff, Wilson.
"The Indian History of British Columbia:
vol. 1, The Impact of the White Man."
Victoria, Anthropology in British Columbia Memoirs, no. 5, 1964.

Duff, Wilson, ed.
Arts of the Raven: Masterworks by the Northwest Coast Indian.
Vancouver: Vancouver, Art Gallery, 1967.

Eliade, Mircea.
The Sacred and the Profane: The Nature of Religion.
New York: Harcourt, Brace & Co., 1959.

Geertz, Clifford.
Local Knowledge: Further Essays in Interpretive Anthropology.
New York: Basic Books, 1983.

Goldman, Irving.
The Mouth of Heaven: An Introduction to Kwakiutl Religious Thought.
Huntington, N.Y.: Robert E. Krieger, 1981.

Gunther, Erna.
Art in the Life of the Northwest Coast Indians.
Seattle: Superior Publishing, 1966.

Halpin, Marjorie.
"Totem Poles, An Illustrated Guide." Museum Note no. 3.
Vancouver: University of British Columbia Press,
in Association with the U.B.C. Museum of Anthropology, 1981.

Holm, Bill.
"Form in Northwest Coast Art."
In *Indian Art Traditions of the Northwest Coast*, edited by Roy Carlson.
Burnaby, B.C.: Simon Fraser University Press, n.d.

Holm, Bill.
Northwest Coast Indian Art: An Analysis of Form.
Seattle: University of Washington Press, 1965.
Vancouver/Toronto: Douglas & McIntyre, 1965.

Holm, Bill and Bill Reid.
Form and Freedom: A Dialogue on Northwest Coast Indian Art.
Houston, Texas: Institute of the Arts, Rice University, 1975.
Also published as *Indian Art of the Northwest Coast:
A Dialogue on Craftsmanship and Aesthetics.*

Iglauer, Edith.
"The Myth Maker,"
Saturday Night 97, no. 2 (February 1982).

Inverarity, Robert Bruce.
Art of the Northwest Coast Indians.
Berkeley: University of California Press, 1950.

Islands Protection Society.
Islands at the Edge: Preserving the Queen Charlotte Islands Wilderness.
Vancouver/Toronto: Douglas & McIntyre, 1984.
Seattle: University of Washington Press, 1984.

Lash, Mary Ann.
"New Life Is Given to the Craft of Haida Jewelry,"
Canadian Art 24, no. 3 (Spring 1957).

Lévi-Strauss, Claude.
The Way of the Masks.
Translated from the French by Sylvia Modelski.
Seattle: University of Washington Press, 1982.
Vancouver/Toronto: Douglas & McIntyre, 1982.

Lowndes, Joan.
"Bill Reid, Drawings at the Equinox Gallery,"
Artmagazine vol. nos. 63-64 (Summer 1983).

Lowndes, Joan.
"Child of the Raven,"
Vanguard 11, no. 1 (February 1982).

MacDonald, George F.
Haida Monumental Art: Villages of the Queen Charlotte Islands.
Vancouver: University of British Columbia Press, 1983.

Macnair, Peter, and Alan L. Hoover.
The Magic Leaves: A History of Haida Argillite Carving.
Victoria: British Columbia Provincial Museum, 1984.

SELECT BIBLIOGRAPHY

Macnair, Peter, Alan L. Hoover and Kevin Neary.
The Legacy: Tradition and Innovation in Northwest Coast Indian Art.
Vancouver/Toronto: Douglas & McIntyre, 1984.
Seattle: University of Washington Press, 1984.

Ravenhill, Alice.
''A Corner Stone of Canadian Culture: An Outline of The Arts and
Crafts of the Indian Tribes of British Columbia.'' Occasional Paper no. 5.
Victoria: British Columbia Provincial Museum, 1944.

Stearns, Mary Lee.
Haida Culture in Custody: The Masset Band.
Seattle: University of Washington Press, 1981.
Vancouver/Toronto: Douglas & McIntyre, 1981.

Sturtevant, William C., ed.
*Boxes and Bowls: Decorated Containers by Nineteenth Century Haida,
Tlingit, Bella Bella and Tsimshian Indian Artists.*
Washington, D.C.: Smithsonian Institution Press, 1974.

Vastokas, Joan M.
''Bill Reid and the Native Renaissance,''
Artscanada, nos. 198/99 (June 1975).

Wardell, A.
Objects of Bright Pride.
New York: The American Federation of Arts and the Centre for
Inter-American Relations, 1978.

PUBLICATIONS AND
FILMS BY REID

''People of the Potlatch.'' CBC film.
Script and narration by Bill Reid. Produced by Gene Lawrence, 1956.

''Totems.'' CBC film. Script and narration by Bill Reid, 1963.

''The Art — An Appreciation.'' In *Arts of the Raven.*
Vancouver: Vancouver Art Gallery, 1967.

Out of the Silence. Text to accompany Adelaide de Menil's
photographs. Fort Worth, Texas: Amon Carter Museum, 1971.

Form and Freedom: A Dialogue on Northwest Coast Indian Art.
With Bill Holm. Houston, Texas: Institute for the Arts, Rice University, 1975.

''Eulogy to Wilson Duff,'' *Vanguard* 5, no. 8 (October), 1976.

Foreword and graphics for *Haida Monumental Art: Villages of
the Queen Charlotte Islands* by George F. MacDonald.
Vancouver: University of British Columbia Press, 1983.

''These Shining Islands.'' In *Islands at the Edge.* Pt. I: The Legacy of Change.
A publication of the Islands Protection Society.
Vancouver/Toronto: Douglas & McIntyre, 1984.
Seattle: University of Washington Press, 1984.

''The Anthropologist and the Article,'' *Culture* 4, no. 2, pp. 63–65.

The Raven Steals the Light. Stories by Bill Reid and Robert Bringhurst.
Drawings by Bill Reid. Vancouver/Toronto: Douglas & McIntyre, 1984.
Seattle: University of Washington Press, 1984.

Gold Bracelet
Beaver and Eagle design
6 cm wide
p. 106

Gold Brooch with Abalone inlay
Eagle design
6.5 cm long, 4.7 cm wide
p. 46

Silver Spoon
Wolf design
15.2 cm long
p. 89

1971

Gold Box
Beaver and Human design on box and cast
three-dimensional Killer Whale on cover
9 cm high, 9.9 cm long, 7.9 cm wide
British Columbia Provincial
Museum, Victoria.
pp. 136, 137

Gold Brooch with Abalone inlay
Hawk design
Oval, 5.8 cm long, 5.4 cm wide
p. 47

Gold Brooch
Frog
3.8 cm long, 3 cm wide
University of British Columbia,
Museum of Anthropology
p. 161

Gold Brooch
Raven design
7 cm long, 6.5 cm wide
p. 120

Silver Box
Hinged Lid inset with Argillite
Eagle design
Box: 7 cm wide, 9.7 cm long, 3.9 cm high
Lid: 8 cm long, 10.5 cm wide, 1.5 cm high
p. 150

1972

Gold Bracelet
Thunderbird design
4.1 cm wide
p. 39

Gold Brooch
Dogfish design
3.8 cm wide, 8 cm long
p. 154

Gold Dish with cover
Dish formed in shape of a Bear,
raised cover surmounted by cast
three-dimensional Woman
suckling two Cubs
7.3 cm high, 7 cm long, 5.2 cm wide
National Museum of Man, Ottawa
p. 134

Gold Earrings with Abalone inlay
Killer Whale design
2.8 cm long
p. 47

Gold Pendant and Chain
Grizzly Bear design
5 cm diameter
p. 155

Hinged Silver Bracelet
Eagle design
4 cm wide
p. 107

Silver and White Gold Necklace
13 cm diameter
p. 45

1973

Hinged Gold Box
Bear, Wolf and Human design
5.5 cm long, 2.8 cm wide, 3.5 cm high
p. 96

1974

Gold Bracelet
Design refers to the Nanasimget story
4.2 cm wide
p. 48

Gold Earrings
Killer Whale design
2 cm long
p. 125

1976

Gold Pendant with chain and stand
Human Face design
5.5 cm diameter, 1.3 cm deep
p. 97

191